Son
OF A
RELUCTANT
IMMIGRANT

AN AUTOBIOGRAPHY
BY LEON ZAWADZKI

First published in 2019 by
FARAXA
www.faraxapublishing.com
info@faraxapublishing.com

Son of a Reluctant Immigrant

© 2019 Leon Zawadzki
© 2019 Faraxa Publishing

Interior design / pagesetting by Faraxa Publishing

Cover photo by Leon Zawadzki

Editing & Proofreading by Ramona Vassallo

ISBN 978-99957-96-02-0

FOREWORD

As a son, a brother, a husband, a father and a grandfather entering the world of retirement with time on my hand, I have taken up the suggestion of writing my life story.

Yes, I have a story to tell, as I have led a life of ups and downs, great experiences and bad.

I have travelled the world and seen life in all its glory and sadness.

Have I made a difference to the world that I have lived in? I believe I have, but I leave that for you to judge.

Leon Zawadzki
LORD OF BLACKWOOD

CONTENTS

ABBREVIATIONS & ACRONYMS

S hortly after sending this autobiography to my publishers for approval prior to publishing, I was informed that I had used numerous abbreviations and acronyms which may not be understood by many of my readers. After careful thought, I thoroughly agreed with the comment and concluded that the best way to rectify this was to write an additional chapter.

Since my days of going to school in the late forties and fifties, the educational system has completely changed along with today's modern technologies; a change that many of my generation could only dream about. As a youngster, I was taught the King's English, later to be called the Queen's English which to a certain extent has changed over the years, more so over the past decade with the introduction of mobile phones, computers, Twitter and instant messaging. This has also led to a big change in the written language with spoken and written word changing to just letters.

Prior to joining the British Army, abbreviations and acronyms did not really exist in normal everyday life although I did know what an abbreviation was, like the 'Ltd Co' normally seen on a shop or factory sign after its name, which referred to it being a 'Limited Company' or the 'P.O.' which meant Post Office. At a guess, the most common abbreviation known to all the youngsters and the elderly generations at the time was, USA or the United States of America.

With the technology that is now available, even to the youngsters of these present generations in everyday communications, it would appear that speed has become a driving factor in communicating, leading to an ever-increasing use of abbreviations and acronyms, whilst the elderly are finding it increasingly difficult and hard to understand what the youngsters are actually talking about. Most people understand ASAP (as soon as possible) or ETA (estimated time of arrival) but do they understand BYOB (bring your own bottle) or LGBTQ (lesbian, gay, bisexual, transgender, and queer/questioning)? And how about AKA (also known as)?

My first real encounter with abbreviations and acronyms started on the day I joined the British Army and they have stayed with me ever since and become part of my everyday life. In most cases when writing an article dealing with the military, you never really think that the person who is reading your article would have no understanding of military terms and abbreviations. So taking this into consideration, I have wrote this chapter in the hope that I can better explain some of the abbreviations and acronyms that I have used in my autobiography along with a description of British Military Units and their makeup.

My background is basically the British Army, but I have also had dealings with both the Royal Navy and the Royal Air Force which included meeting many high ranking officers and men from all three services. It is for this reason that I will highlight all the military ranks of all three services along with their abbreviations, where known. The military rank structure is broken into two classes, the first being the Officers (Offrs) and the second being the Other Ranks (ORs) or the Non-Commissioned Ranks (NCR).

ROYAL NAVY

OFFICERS		OTHER RANKS	
Admiral of the Fleet	**AdmF**	Warrant Officer	**WO**
Admiral	**Adm**	Chief Petty Officer	**CPO**
Vice Admiral	**Vice Adm**	Petty Officer	**PO**
Rear Admiral	**Rear Adm**	Leading Hand	**LH**
Commodore	**Com**	Rating	**AB**
Captain	**Capt**		
Commander	**Comd**		
Lieutenant Commander	**Lt Comd**		
Lieutenant	**Lt**		
Sublieutenant	**Sub Lt**		
Acting Sublieutenant	**Act Sub Lt**		

BRITISH ARMY

OFFICERS		OTHER RANKS	
Field Marshal	**FM**	Warrant Officer Class 1	**WO1**
General	**Gen**	Warrant Officer Class 2	**WO2**
Lieutenant General	**Lt Gen**	Staff Sergeant	**SSgt**
Major General	**Maj Gen**	Sergeant	**Sgt**
Brigadier	**Brig**	Corporal	**Cpl**
Colonel	**Col**	Lance Corporal	**LCpl**
Lieutenant Colonel	**Lt Col**	Private	**Pte**
Major	**Maj**		
Captain	**Capt**		
Lieutenant	**Lt**		
Second Lieutenant	**2Lt**		

ROYAL AIR FORCE

OFFICERS		OTHER RANKS	
Marshal of the Royal Air Force	**MRAF**	Warrant Officer	**WO**
Air Chief Marshal	**ACM**	Flight Sergeant	**FSgt**
Air Marshal	**AM**	Chief Technician	**CTech**
Air Vice Marshal	**AVM**	Sergeant	**Sgt**
Air Commodore	**Com**	Corporal	**Cpl**
Group Captain	**Gp Capt**	Junior Technician	**JTech**
Wing Commander	**Wg Comd**	Senior Aircraftman	**SAC**
Squadron Leader	**Sqn Ldr**	Leading Aircraftman	**LAC**
Flight Lieutenant	**Flt Lt**	Aircraftman	**AC**
Flying Officer	**FO**		
Pilot Officer	**PO**		

Apart from referring to a person by his or her rank and name, they can also be referred to by their actual appointments within their service environment. If I were to list all these various titles and appointments within the armed services, I would have to write and compile another book. As I am British Army trained, I will concentrate on the Army, but again as I was trained as an infantryman, most of my abbreviations and acronyms will relate to my Regimental environment.

Many will have heard the expression 'Squaddie' which is a definition of the lowest ranks within the services such as Private (Pte), Riflemen (Rfn), Trooper (Tpr) and Gunner (Gnr) depending on the actual branch of the army that they are serving in. They are also called Guardsman (Gdm) Guards Regiment, Paras of the Parachute Regiments, Signallers of the Royal Signal Regiment or even Red Caps of the Royal Military Police. While mentioning Red Caps, I may as well mention the Snow Drops of the Royal Air Force Police. Both Red Caps and the Snow Drops refer to the colour of their Military Hats.

The military rank structure within the army is the same throughout all units/branches but not necessarily being called by the same name. For instance a Corporal (Cpl) in the Guards Regiment is referred to as a Lance Sergeant (LSgt), while in the Royal Artillery he is referred to as a Bombardier (Bdr).

Within the Infantry Regiments, Staff Sergeants (SSgt) are referred to as Colour Sergeants (CSgt). This arose from the time when 'Regimental Colours' were taken and carried into battle by Sergeants.

All units and branches of the British Army have different setups depending on their military roles and it is only right that I concentrate on the Infantries' roles. I know that the setup of the various roles changes depending on the present day situations and the tasks that a unit may be assigned to.

An Infantry Regiment is a unit that is built up of a group of companies which, in my days, consisted of a Battalion Headquarters (BHQ), a Headquarters Company (HQ Coy),

3 Rifle Companies, normally A, B and C Company, as well as a Support Company (Sp Coy) and an Administration Company (Admin Coy).

The Regiment/Battalion is normally commanded by a Lieutenant Colonel (LtCol) while the Companies are commanded by a Major (Maj). As in any organisation, the various parts of the unit are responsible in bringing the unit together. Battalion Head Quarters (BHQ) is overall in control of the unit and where you would find the Commanding Officer (CO) along with his controlling staff, which would include his Second in Command (Bn 2i/c) normally a Major (Maj), the Adjutant (Adjt) which I can only describe as the CO's personal secretary, and the most powerful person in the regiment apart from the CO himself, the Regimental Sergeant Major (RSM), who is responsible to the CO for the enforcement of discipline within the unit among other duties.

Normally the largest Company within the Battalion is Headquarter Company (HQ Coy) which is commanded by a Major. This Company is divided into many different Platoons (Pls) Sections (Sec) and Departments (Dept) that control the togetherness of the Regiment. For instance, the Signal Platoon (Sig Pl) is responsible for all the communications within the battalion at many different levels. The Reconnaissance Platoon, (Recce Pl) is responsible, as the name implies, for carrying out recces (surveillance) and the Mechanical Transport Platoon (MT Pl) is responsible for all the transport problems within the unit. The Intelligence Section (Int Sec) is responsible for gathering and dispensing intelligence within the unit. These are all part of the front line troops. There are also the background troops that are not normally talked about but without which your unit could easily fall apart. This is normally called the Administration Company (Admin Coy) which is commanded by the Regimental Quarter Master (QM) who is basically responsible for all the supplies and distribution of goods to keep the unit fighting fit. Apart from everyday food rations, clothing and equipment, he also commands members of various units that are attached to the unit such as members of the Army Catering Corporation (ACC), the Royal Electrical Mechanical Engineers (REME), the Royal Army Medical Corporation (RAMC) plus many others, depending on the present day role. There are many others that I have not really mentioned such as the Drum Platoon and the Regimental Band.

The Rifle Companies were mainly commanded by a Major (Coy Comd) with a Captain (Capt) as his 2nd in Command (Coy 2i/c) and split into four platoons; one as the Company Headquarter Platoon (Coy HQ) and the remaining platoons each numbered as rifle platoon. For example the first rifle platoon in A Company would become 1 Platoon (1Pl) and the second would become 2 Platoon (2Pl) and so on.

Each Platoon was commanded by a Platoon Commander who was normally a commissioned officer with the rank of either Lieutenant (Lt) or 2nd Lieutenant (2Lt), with a Platoon Sergeant (Pl Sgt) as the 2 i/c. Each Platoon was further split up into four sections, the Platoon HQ Sec plus three Rifle Sections, with each alphabetically labelled. As an example,

1st Section of the Second Platoon of A Company would become (12a), which also became its call sign in radio communications. Each Sec was commanded by a Corporal (Cpl) with a Lance Corporal (LCpl) as his 2i/c.

Within each Coy HQ, apart from the Coy Comd and Coy 2i/c, you also had a Company Sergeant Major with the rank of (WO) commonly known as the (CSM), who was basically responsible for discipline and administration within the Coy, along with the Company Quartermaster Sergeant (CQMS) with the rank of Colour Sergeant (CSgt) responsible for clothing and equipment supplies along with other administration chores. Again you also had additional members within the Coy HQ including Coy Clerks, Signallers, Storemen and medical staff depending on the situation.

The last company within a Regiment is normally referred to as the Support Company (Sp Coy) and normally consisted of Platoons with heavier weapons such as mortars and anti-tank weapons.

As can be seen, the use of abbreviations and acronyms are a big part of my military life along with the phonetic alphabet and the morse code, all in aid of faster communication. This, as always, is a very important part of life that can make a big difference between life and death and it's very hard to get away from it in normal everyday life.

Many years have passed since I left the army and I know many changes have taken place both in structure and organisation within the services, but I am still in touch with many old friends of over fifty odd years standing along with many of the younger generations. If you need to know more on the above, all you need to do is Google it on your computer or smartphone. All the information is out there, somewhere!

Chapter 1
IN THE BEGINNING

Where do you start when taking up the challenge of writing a book on the 'Life and Times of Leon Zawadzki'? Truth is paramount, I think to myself, although at seventy-three years of age, it is at times hard to differentiate between the truth and a lie, or an impression. I am relying upon memories spanning my entire past. Thankfully in today's age of the Internet and communications, a lot of my input into this book will not only rely on my memory but on actual research where required.

I was born on 29 May 1944 in Nethermains Cottages in the small village of Chirnside, in the County of Berwick, Scotland. My mother was Isla Zawadzka born Wilson, and my father was Jozef Zawadzki.

I am now on the map and a living person, but before I go into the ups and downs of my life, it's only right that I introduce you, the reader, to the people and the world situation that I was born into.

At the time of my birth, the world was going through very hard times, having suffered the ravages of World War II (WWII) since 1939. It's a fact that I was born just one week before D Day, on 6 June 1944 when the Allied Armies invaded Normandy, and which resulted in the eventual overthrow and conquest of the Axis Armies in September 1945. Many years later, my father told me that just prior to the 1st Polish Armoured Division taking part in this invasion, I was held aloft in the outstretched hands of the Polish General Stanislaw Maczek, in front of the massed Polish Army, where he declared, "Ten jest to, co my walcza o," or in English, "This is what we are fighting for." From this, we can all conclude that my father was Polish and served in the Polish Army. So who was my father? That is a question that even I can't honestly answer but I will try.

My father, Jozef Zawadzki, was born on 18 March 1913 in Dzwinacz in the County of Tarnopol in Poland (now Ukraine) to his parents Leon and Karolina. His father owned and ran a small farm. One of my father's greatest joys in life was when he used to tell us stories of his younger days on the farm. Piglets, geese, goats and chickens used to run around the kitchen and where he used to sleep. All the animals had names and he used to reel them all off and attempt to translate the names into English. As a young lad, I was always interested in his time in the war as a soldier.

His experience as a soldier was something he was very reluctant to talk about. He did mention that he was a Russian prisoner of war on two occasions and that he escaped twice. He also told me that he was in the cavalry and that he had two horses shot from under him. He often talked about his horses; the brown one he called 'Czekolada' which means chocolate in English, and the other was pure white and named 'Cukier' or Sugar in English. He was always sad when he talked about his horses.

It was not until the year 2007 that I managed to catch up with my father's military service when I received his military records from the Ministry of Defence APA Polish Enquiries at RAF Northolt. Reading his service records instilled in me a great sense of pride in my father's achievements along with some great eye openers. It is only right that I write more about my father as he was an influence for my being who I am.

From the detail that I gathered, he was fairly well educated and spent four years at a grammar school before taking up a civilian occupation as a private official. At the age of fifteen, he joined the Polish Army (Malopolska Unit) on 20 May 1928 and stayed there until 9 October 1931, before starting full military service with the same unit on 11 October 1931 until 1934. Within this period he attended Officer School from 1 February to 1 August 1932. At the time, military conscription was in force throughout Poland.

My father took part in the 1939 September Campaign, serving with Squadron No 14 of an Infantry Division called Zoleszcyki. This was the prelude to WWII when the Russians, in collaboration with Germany, attacked Poland. It was, I believe, during this campaign that my father had the two horses shot from under him. On 27 September 1939, my father was taken prisoner by the Russian Red Army, from whom he later escaped on 18 December 1939 and made his way to France. I recall my father telling me that when he escaped from the Russians' POW camp, he had to walk across a frozen river. He made his way to France where he met up with and joined the Polish forces under the command of the French on 15 May 1940.

On the capitulation of the French Force, my father managed to get evacuated to the United Kingdom from the small French village of St Jean de Luz on the Polish liner, MV Sobieski, which arrived and anchored in Plymouth on 23 June 1940. After having been debriefed, he was posted to Motor Squadron, No 1 Reconnaissance Unit, 1 Polish Rifle Brigade, 1 Polish Corps. Scotland.

Sometime between July 1940 and July 1941, he met my future mother who was between 14 and 15 years old at the time in the St Andrew/Dundee area of Scotland and started a relationship with her. A relationship that was to end in disaster when she found out, many years later, that he had a wife in Poland.

From July 1940 to July 1944 my father attended many military courses while at the same time courting my mother and even marrying her. My eldest sister Sandra was born on 29 April 1942 in Dundee and I came along two years later. My mother was 17 years old when I was born, while my father was now 31 years old. It was only years later that I realised the complexities of my mother's ordeals in my early childhood. Two months after my birth, my father was sent on operations to France on 1 August 1944, and my mother would not see him again until August/September 1946 when he was on leave from his unit.

It must have been during this time that my father gave me a present of an electric train set which I recall seeing for the first time some eight years later. He also gave my sister a doll that was reputed to have belonged to a member of the Dutch Royal Family. I also learned sometime later that he gave my mother a German Luger pistol that he had taken from a German Officer during one of the conflicts he was involved in, for safe keeping. I always wanted to get my hands on that pistol but I was informed many years later that my mother threw it out of the train window as the train crossed the Forth Bridge over the Firth of Forth when she was returning home to England from a visit to Scotland. I think she did it as she never wanted the pistol in my possession.

From 1 Aug 1944 to 8 Aug 1945 my father served and was involved in many military engagements including action at Caen, Falaise, and Abbeville in France, as well as Ypres, Roulers, Thielt, Ghent, St Nicolas and Stekene in Belgium. These were followed by stints in Koewacht, Axel-Hulst in Holland then back to Belgium for action in Merxplas and Baarle-Heide, before returning to Holland, to Baarle-Nassau, Glize, Breda and Moerdijk. He also saw action on the river Maas. From there he went to Germany and again witnessed action on the Kusten Canal, Aschendorf, Papenburg, Ihrhove, and Leer. At some time during his military service, he was shot and wounded by a bullet that just missed his heart and exited under his left armpit. He never mentioned this injury or where he got it from, but the scar was clearly visible when he took his shirt off. From 9 May 1945 to his discharge from the army, he was under the command of the Allied Occupation Forces in Germany.

On his discharge from the Polish Army on 16 December 1946, he immigrated to Holland. It is at this stage that I have to speculate as to what must have been going through his mind, as at no time in later life was the following ever discussed or brought up as far as I am aware.

As I have mentioned, my father was already married before he met my mother. He was married to Olga nee Pachucka who would have been 29 years old on the 27 November 1946. She was still alive in Poland and had no children. He was also married to my mother who was 20 years old with two kids. I believe I can understand his dilemma to a certain extent. The war had ended; he was now redundant. He had no work and could not return to Poland due to the agreements made at the YALTA Conference held from 4–11 February 1945 between Winston Churchill, Franklin D. Roosevelt and Joseph Stalin. My father had no option in not returning to Poland; if he had, the chances are that he would have been imprisoned and possibly executed.

In March 1946, the British Foreign Secretary Ernest Bevin stated that the Poles could not be maintained in Britain, which led to an anti-Polish campaign by the TUC (Trade Union Council) and leading unions to turn public attitudes against the Poles. This resulted in many seeking resettlement in the USA and in Australia. Those who had no alternative choice returned back to their homeland of Poland, where later it was rumoured that many were killed or simply disappeared.

Why he did not return to England where my mother was living at the time is a complete mystery to me to this very day. Whatever the reason may have been, my father made his way to Tegelen in Holland and took up a job on the Dutch railway.

As years go by, you tend to reflect on the lives of the people that are close to you or have had a significant bearing on your life, and I often think of my mother now that she has passed away. My mother was born on 29 September 1926 in Linskill Villa, St Andrews in Scotland and was the only daughter of James Wilson, her father who at the time was a Post Office Linesman, and Joan nee McKenzie Robinson, her mother, who had sadly died at the young age of 39 years. The death of her mother must have been devastating for my mother who would have been just ten years old at the time. To compound her feelings and to make matters even worse, her father was to marry Rita Fraser just nine months later.

At a guess, with the loss of your mother at such a young age and finding yourself with a new mother, a lot of conflicts were brought into the family. From all accounts, my mother was a very well educated young girl and attended St Andrews College. She could speak French and Latin, and later she learned to speak and write Polish as competently as any Pole. The only time I heard her talking about work was when she recounted her experiences as a Dental Nurse/Assistant. I have no knowledge of how her relationship developed when she met my father, but I do know that there was no love lost between her father and my father, which would have been quite understandable seeing the age difference. I heard that on one occasion my grandfather had walked into a room on a fourth floor with Rita and found my mother alone with my father and although they were doing nothing at the time, he grabbed my father and pushed him out of the window but managed to hold onto him by his feet. Apparently, it was only the screaming of both my mother and Rita that stopped him from throwing him down onto the street below.

Looking back or rather, trying to imagine the situation at the time, I think my mother was looking for some relationship, and with the looming war pending, she must have felt pretty lonely.

She once – no – she told this same story many times, about the time during the war years when she was sitting in the dining room with one of her relatives; it may have been her grandfather, who had died and was lying in his open coffin, on the dining room table. While she was sitting in the room, a passing German plane dropped a bomb close by. When the bomb exploded, it shook the room so bad, that the body in the coffin shot up into the sitting position and almost scared the life out of her. At the time, anyone who was listening to this story would have had a good giggle and a laugh as they saw the funny side. Later on in life, you ponder what must have gone through her mind at the time and it would not have been pleasant.

Once she had met my father, I suppose a great change must have come over her, as she now had somebody to confide her thoughts and put her trust in. A trust that I am sure, with hindsight, she regretted in later years. Shortly after meeting my father, my mother became pregnant with my eldest sister Sandra who was born on 29 April 1942, in Dundee. I do have a copy of my mother's marriage certificate that showed that she got married on 12 May 1943, in St Clement's in Dundee. At the time she was employed as a café cashier.

Once married to my father, she was issued with a 'Certificate of Registration' under the Aliens Order of 1920. This certificate was in force until 9 February 1946 when she was exempted from registration. This small booklet contained all the addresses of the houses that she resided in, and there are quite a few addresses. Every change of address had to be reported to the local police station and given an official stamp. From this booklet, I can see that my mother moved into Nethermains Cottages on 30 April 1944 when my sister Sandra had just turned two years old, and my mother must have been eight months pregnant with me. Why was she moving around at that time? I don't know. To make matters worse, shortly after I was born and within one day of my father leaving for the war in Europe, she moved to an address in Bridlington in Yorkshire.

Again she moved around the area of Bridlington quite a few times before returning to Scotland to her father's home in Lochee, Dundee. Exactly what happened during those turbulent times, I don't know, but I'm sure they could not have been good times.

I am told that while living in Lochee, both my sister and I were being looked after by Rita, while my mother was out working. Rita also had two sons who were to become my uncles. Ian was born in 1939 and Frazer in 1942.

The war had come to an end but my father had not returned home, apart from the time he was on leave from his unit for a short period before returning to Germany. For some unknown reason, my father failed to return to Scotland and to my mother after his discharge from the Polish Army.

At some time in early 1947, my mother who was pregnant at the time found out that my father was working in Holland and made arrangements to go and find him. On 20 March 1947, she bundled both my sister and me into her arms and made her way to the docks at Harwich to board a boat to Holland. We arrived at the Hook of Holland on 21 March 1947.

Chapter 2
HOLLAND / ENGLAND

My memory of what happened once we landed in Holland is not so clear as at the time I was still under three years of age. But I can recall quite clearly living very close to the banks of the River Maas (La Meuse) near Tegelen. We lived in a small village in Limburg in what must have been an old factory in quite an isolated area, as I cannot recall seeing any other houses nearby. Again from memory, I cannot remember seeing any other people around, but I did have a young friend in a boy called Teo, who was about my age. We used to play in what was a sandpit just outside the building that we lived in and an old room at the top of a tower that we had to climb a ladder to get to. This room was tiny with two or three windows in it and the only furniture adorning the room were a small table and a couple of chairs. Thinking about this place now, I can see that it was used by the factory owners as a watchtower for spotting barges on the river for the transportation of their goods. From rummaging around the factory and looking through boxes, I discovered that they used to make the paper clips that are used in A4 Binders.

Going back to this small room, this was possibly my favourite place as I used to play in there with Teo and also to hide from my mother. It is also the place where I first recall getting an electric shock. I suppose I must have been around the upper age of four years at the time, but this is a memory that embedded itself in my mind as if it was yesterday. In the centre of the room there was a light bulb dangling down towards the table on a piece of electric cable, with the light switch by the door. The light bulb did not work so one day I got hold of a chair and put it on the table and climbed up to the bulb. I got the bulb out and checked out the socket and – how should I put it – I started dancing on the chair. Somehow or other I let go and got down from the table and chair, not hurt or afraid, but yes, in shock. For some unknown reason after that experience, and rather recklessly, I used to repeat the same actions for fun. Since then I have never been afraid of electricity even though I now understand its full dangers. Even now I still experience electric shocks while being silly and too lazy to turn off power supplies when doing any electrical repairs on sockets.

I recall that I used to walk up a long track to meet my dad when he returned home from work on his bicycle. He would stop and sit me on the handlebars and cycle the rest of the way home. Once home, I would go through his shoulder bag that he took to work each day with his sandwiches and a bottle of milk. He never drank his milk and always brought it home, by which time it would already have turned sour. I don't know why but in those days I just loved sour milk.

Once my father took me and my sister Sandra to town, possibly a day or two before Christmas and I saw my first Christmas decorations with buildings all lit up. I also met my first St Nicholas and Zwarte Piet with his bag of apples. In my eyes, St Nicholas looked like he was ten feet tall in his red and gold gown with his big hat on. I had never seen anything like it, nor like Black Peter who had two sacks with him, one full of apples and the other one empty. I was told that he put bad boys and girls in the empty bag and took them away. He terrified me, but as I was a good boy in those days, I got an apple.

Well, I say I was good, but Sandra told me that I once threw her into the river and as punishment my father locked us both in the dark cupboard under the stairs. I never did like dark closets after that. I was also told that at one time I had disappeared, or went missing, and nobody could find me. After searching for me, for many hours, I was eventually discovered in the middle of some crossroads directing military vehicle convoys. I was ably helped and assisted by members of the Military Police.

As a young boy living in Holland, I was oblivious to what was going on around me. I used to go out to play wearing my lederhosen breeches or short leather trousers and my wooden clogs. Speaking was a bit confusing, as my mother used to speak Polish to my Father and English to my sister and me. My dad mostly spoke Polish, and my friend spoke Dutch. No wonder I used to stutter and get tongue-tied, but I did learn Double Dutch, as I always spoke it. Well, that's what I was told.

Not everything was honey and roses in those days. My mother gave birth to my second sister Annette on 5 May 1947 and my first brother on 25 September 1948, who was born in the local nunnery. The family was growing fast, but I guess that money problems were getting bigger and with my father being just a worker on the railway lines, not much was coming in. This probably resulted in the breaking up of my parents' relationship with the result that my father left and made his way to London in January 1949. Again my mother, being the strong-willed woman that she was, was not going to give in. With the help of a local family priest by the name of Pater (Father) Donders, she arranged transport to England.

I remember the night of 14 February 1949 well. It was quite late at night when an Army Red Cross Ambulance pulled up outside our home, and both my sisters, brother, me and my mother got in the back with some bags and bits and pieces before it pulled away and headed for the docks. We were put on a boat or ferry and off it went, heading for England. I vividly recall that on the ship we were in a large cabin with my mother sitting on a chair, probably comforting my baby brother and younger sister in a pram. I suppose I was a bit bored at the time, not being able to see anything except for grey walls, so I got hold of my sister and went through a door onto the decking outside. It was pitch black outside, and I think there must have been a gale blowing as the wind was horrendous and scary. So we dashed back to where my mum was, and I never moved until we had docked in Harwich on the following day of 15 February 1949.

WELCOME TO ENGLAND

It should be remembered that when we arrived in England, my father was nowhere to be found. My mother was pushing a pram with my five-month-old brother lying inside it, along with my two-year-old sister who was sitting in it. At the same time she was also keeping an eye on both my elder sister and me. Never mind also being burdened by what baggage she had. Did my mother have any money? I don't think so or if she did, it would have been very little.

Did we have a place to go to? No, we had nothing and we were in a state requiring immediate help. Did my mother give up? She was too stubborn to give up; she persevered and somehow managed to get to a Police Station with the result that we all ended up in a top floor room with a bed in it. It also had a fireplace but no coal, and as it was so cold in the room, my mother had no option but to take my wooden clogs and put them on the fire. In today's world with the refugee situation, I can well and truly empathise with what they are going through. I do not know the details of what happened after landing in Harwich, but I do know that by 20 September 1949 we were living with my mother and father who had reunited and living in what was called a flat, at 15/19 Eaton Place, London SW1. To live in this same house in today's time, it would cost you millions of pounds sterling. When we moved in there it was known as a 'wash house' or in some cases as the 'work house'. I could define it as the worst place possible; dirty, falling into disrepair and housing many of the down and outs of London who were in a similar state as ourselves.

London in the early fifties was not a nice place to live in. The war had only finished four years ago. Most of the buildings were in a state of dereliction after suffering some of the heaviest bombings of the war. Food and monies were at a premium, as was shelter from the cold. My father was out working all the hours possible, and when he came home, we both used to go out with a wooden trolley looking for wood to burn in the fire. One day we were lucky and stumbled onto an old road that was made from wooden blocks that were stuck together and covered with a light coating of tar. We soon discovered that with a lever we could pry them apart quite easily, and stack them on our cart. We used what we needed and sold the rest. They made great fires, and I can still see, in my mind, the blue flames from the tar. This was illegal and we had to keep an eye out for the police, but London at that time was invariably covered in thick yellow fog or smog, as we used to call it, which at times made it difficult to even see your hand in front of your face. Kensington and Chelsea were not recognisable as the same places that they are today.

On 30 January 1950 my mother gave birth to my third sister who was named Barbara, but at that time the primary spoken language in the house was Polish, so she was called Basha; a name that I am sure brought a lot of controversy into her life as she grew up. There were now five children and our parents living in this so-called flat. It consisted only of two small rooms. We had to share a kitchen and a toilet with three or four other families, and as for having a bath, it was a case of getting the old metal bath or large basin, filling it up with water from the tap and heating up some water in a kettle or pot to warm the water. How we survived I do not know, but almost a year later my mother and father had qualified for a council flat, and on 6 September 1950 we moved into No 37 Campbell House W12. What a change! It was a three bedroom flat on the third floor with a sitting room, a kitchen and our own toilet and bathroom. Even better still, it overlooked the grounds of Queens Park Rangers football club. It was sheer heaven; both my sisters shared a bedroom while my baby sister slept in my mother's bedroom and my brother shared a bedroom with me. This was a temporary arrangement – as the years passed I ended up with a further three brothers sharing my room. We also had a sitting room with a large window which overlooked Bloemfontein Road and quite a large park with sandpit, swings, slide and roundabout, plus trees and a grassed area that we used for picnics. Also in front of the flats was an open-air swimming pool.

By stretching your head out of the window and looking to the right, you could see Wormwood Scrubs Prison at the end of the road. Walking out the front door and going to the end of the balcony, you could see right into the football grounds of Loftus Road. The flats were served with a lift, and there was also a chute for the rubbish. But to cap it all, we had our very first radio. Forget TVs, it was a few years before I even saw one and many years later before my parents owned one. The radio was a big highlight in my life, listening to music, singing and yes, even the Archers, along with the many stories that they used to broadcast in those days. It should also be noted that on Easter Day, my father would not allow the radio to be switched on as he saw this as a day of hymns and prayers.

It was here that my life started to take off and the next seven years saw the building stones of my foundation and shaping of life beginning to develop. I went to my first infant school called Ellerslie Road School which was situated right next to the turnstile entrance to the QPR football ground. It was only a small school and the only memory I have of it was when somebody had thrown a tennis ball over the wall into the football ground. I, along with a few others and a teacher went around seeing if we could get in through the gate at the side of the grounds to recover the ball, only to find the gate locked. Being who I was in those days, I decided to climb over the fence, and with the help of a few others who lifted me up, I grabbed the top which had barbed wire running along it. The wire barb ripped through and tore my middle finger as I fell back. I still have the scar to this day.

To me, these were the days of courage, adventure, and exploration. It was also the place where I started going to Saturday Morning Pictures. It used to cost sixpence for about three hours of entertainment with films like Flash Gordon, The Keystone Cops, Abbot and Lou Costello and how can you forget Roy Rogers? I used to enjoy going as we also used to get a big block of sweet 'Honeycomb' at a cost of 3d (pennies), which was delicious. Every now and again we also used to have a mobile cinema which was mounted in the back of a large truck that I can only describe as a furniture van that came around and set up in the area between the two blocks of flats. There were no chairs or benches to sit on so you had to sit on the ground.

I soon made friends with a bunch of kids, once they realised that I was not a German or a Jew, or an outcast from some foreign land. The war was still fresh in the minds of many parents and this was conveyed in the way many brought up their children. Most people with foreign names were seen as a threat to their way of life. Once I had gained their trust, which was normally after being in a good few fights, I was treated like all the other kids although it was hard at times.

When I look back at the games and adventure we immersed ourselves in, my hair stands up on the back of my neck thinking about the dangers that we put ourselves through in those early days. One of the most dangerous things we used to do was to see how high we could climb the wall on the corner of the flats, which were built in such a way that the corner brickwork used to jut out with the bricks overlapping each other, making the perfect ladder effect for feet and hand holds as we climbed in a vertical straight line. We all used to go up, I guess around the twenty foot plus mark, carrying a bit of chalk and marking the target for the next person to try and reach. I think we used to be scared but could not show fear, and we never thought of the consequences if we fell. When our parents realised what we were doing, they got onto the council who sent workmen out with ladders and erected a barrier on the corner of all the flats to deter us children from climbing these walls. The scheming, however, did not deter us.

We then set our minds to climbing the walls surrounding the QPR football grounds. We found quite a few ways of getting in. During the weekdays when it was quiet we used to have the run of the grounds apart from the watchman, but we could all run faster than him and as far as I remember nobody was ever caught. Within the ground there used to be a few huts built out of corrugated sheets of metal that were used as snack bars. I say snack bars, but they only had packets of crisps, some sweets and bottles of soft drinks which the owners used to sell during football matches. These became a target for us and were easily broken into, and we used to help ourselves to whatever we could fill our pockets with. We never took much, because as to get out of the grounds we had to climb a 10–12-foot corrugated metal fence and drop off the other side onto the outside pavement. As I got older, I used to suffer a sort of guilt complex over this, but to help ease my conscience, I always have, to this very day, been a QPR supporter. Outside the football grounds near the flats was a big open area that was used as a car parking area when there was a football match. This was a great adventure area where we used to try to find cars with unlocked doors to see what we could find inside. It was also the time when taxis only had two doors for passengers and one for the driver; where the fourth door should have been was an area for luggage where you could climb into the driver's seat. These taxis never had ignition keys in those days, and you started the engine by pressing a button. It used to be fun, starting the engines, putting the car into gear and moving forwards and backwards.

When not getting into trouble I would play plenty of games with my mates, which included running competitions, football matches, cricket matches, three-legged races, sack races, hopscotch and hide and seek. On one occasion while playing cricket in South Africa Road as usual, an older boy who lived next door to me raced his bike towards me, which is what he always did, usually swerving at the last moment to avoid hitting me. On this occasion, I tried stepping out of the way only to walk into him. We collided with my right leg going through his front wheel. He went flying up in the air while I was dragged to the ground. As my leg went through his front wheel breaking quite a few spokes, the pointed end of one of the spokes hit my knee with the result that a big knob of flesh and skin was ripped from my knee. I can see it to this day; a spoke with a big lump of flesh on its end and my knee revealing a gleaming whitish blue kneecap bone where the skin and flesh should have been. The scar is still there for all to see.

Another craze in those early days was making our scooters from old planks of wood and using ball bearing rings as wheels. I must say they used to be very noisy when a few of us gathered and raced them down the pavements. If we were not making scooters, we would be making carts with wood from orange boxes and old pram wheels. We used our feet and rope to guide them. These were fun days.

Living in the area of the White City was a fantastic adventure playground. At a young age, I had no fear of travelling around and exploring the area. When not at school, I would go out early in the day and not return home until the late hours of the night, frequently to a good hiding from my dad and being sent to bed with no food. My dad was a great disciplinarian, and I was often belted on the bottom with his belt, a slipper or even a bit of wood. It hurt, but I don't ever think I learned the lesson. My brothers also suffered the belt, but they must have learned as they were never hit as much as I was.

I used to go to Wormwood Scrubs which was a massive grass area just behind the prison and behind Hammersmith Hospital, which was used by the Parachute Regiment to train their parachutists who used to jump out of Barrage Balloons. It was also used as a landing area for parachutists jumping out of planes. In the fifties, it was not unusual to see flight after flight of military aircraft flying in large formations over this area. After watching the Parachute Regiment's training, my mates and I used to walk to a side road by the Prison and yell out to the prisoners who used to yell back and wave out of their barred cell windows. I never dreamed that one day I would enter the prison.

The Scrubs area was also used once a year by the famous Chippenfield's Circus. As a youngster, I always looked forward to this as I used to go there early in the morning and help out by feeding the animals. In those times we had tigers, lions, bears, zebras, gorillas and many other types of animals. I had been particularly fond of an elephant which, if I remember correctly, was called Mary. I used to feed her and clean out her pen of old straw. For my troubles and help, I used to get a free ticket to watch the circus in the big tent in the evening.

Another of the big attractions in the area was the White City Stadium. Again it played a big part in my childhood. Every year it hosted the Military Searchlight Tattoo – an event that brought together the military forces from the four corners of the world. I would go down and stare in awe at the sights to be seen. I also used to relish meeting and talking with the servicemen from all over the world, as well as handling the weapons. Seeing the smartly dressed members of the Indian Army, including the Sheiks with their beards and wearing their turbans along with their magnificent horses, as well as all the many different uniforms of all the military services. I think it was here that the thoughts of wanting to become a soldier first entered my mind.

Just opposite the stadium on the corner of South Africa Road, there used to be a large army camp which used to house the Royal Artillery. This was one of my favourite adventure training areas as it had an assault course, small shooting ranges and lots of overgrown shelters which at some time must have been used for storage of ammunition and other stores. We used to break into these grounds and play all our favourite games like cowboys and Indians, the English against the Germans. It was great fun while it lasted but along came the BBC, who bulldozed the place to the ground and built the BBC Television Studios. The Army still had some military ranges behind the prison that we used to go to, looking for empty ammunition cases and digging up the lead bullet heads which we would screw together to form a bullet. We used to take them home and polish them up. I once found a box of 303 live bullets and gave them to my dad, but have no idea as to what happened to them.

On 22 May 1954, just a week before my 10th birthday, I went to the White City Stadium and spent over two hours listening to the Evangelist leader Billy Graham; a meeting which was attended by some 65,000 people. It was an event that could have changed my life as for some time after I had the yearnings to become a priest. Thankfully it never happened. Apart from this event and the tattoos, I also went to the stadium for school sports days and to watch Track and Field Events.

It should be remembered that at this time there still were many bombed and damaged buildings around, and on one occasion I went to explore an old bombed out church on the West Way Road (A40). Both my mate and I went down into a waterlogged cellar and found a coffin with the remains of a body in it. We got out of there fast, having been scared out of our wits.

Four months after moving into Campbell House on 7 December 1951, my second brother Ryszard, also known as Richard, was born. I recall that I, along with my brothers and sisters, were all told to sit in the sitting room and to stay quiet while awaiting the outcome of my brother's birth.

Two months later I discovered that King George VI had died and informed my mother of the news. She remarked that she was wondering why the only music that was being played on the radio was Military Dirges as the country went into mourning.

The following year my fourth brother Ronald was born on 28 May 1953, a few days before the Coronation of Queen Elizabeth II on 2 of June 1953.

I watched the coronation ceremony on a black and white television at the home of Mrs Regis, who was a friend of my mother. On returning to the flats, I was amazed to find tables and chairs along with a stage being set up. At a guess, there must have been over 50 six foot tables between the two flats surrounded by chairs. There was no room for any washing lines; mind you, there was no laundry to be seen anywhere. Where the washing lines used to be, the ropes had all been replaced by red, white and blue bunting and balloons. It trailed everywhere, including on the balconies. Later on, all the children who lived in the flats sat down to a great party with cakes, sandwiches, sausage rolls, biscuits, ice-cream, orange juice and lemonade while being entertained by clowns, Punch and Judy, along with acrobats and people walking on high stilts. I do remember it was a fantastic occasion. I later learned that my mother had been paying an extra 1d (penny) a week with her rent money towards the costs of the event.

With seven children in the house, it was beginning to get too much for my mother, and she needed some peace and quiet as she used to suffer from asthma. One of the solutions to relieve this problem was to send both Sandra who was eleven at the time, and me who had just turned nine years old, to Scotland to stay with her father and Rita. My father took us both to King's Cross railway station and put us on a train after having paid someone to ensure that we changed trains at Edinburgh for Dundee, where we were met by my Granddad who was better known as 'Daddy Wilson'. I still remember that journey, wearing short trousers and a cap on my head. Both my sister and I also had a label tied to our coats with the destination address on it. We travelled to Edinburgh on the 'Flying Scotsman'. I also remember going over the Forth Bridge for the very first time. Both Sandra and I had settled into my grandfather home, which was quite strange for us as we did not really know my Daddy Wilson, his wife Rita and yes my two uncles, Ian and Frazer (my mother's step-brothers), who both kept referring to me as a Sassenach. Luckily Isobil, my mother's step-sister (my aunty) who was two years younger than me, took me under her wings and looked out for me.

The next task was to get my sister and me into the local Liff Road junior school. This was a school for boys and girls with separate playing grounds that were divided by a small wall. The boys were not allowed in the girls' playing ground and vice versa. Unfortunately, I was nearly always late for school and to make up for the lost time I used to jump the wall into the girls' playing ground before crossing another wall into the boys' playing ground. I used to get caught quite often which resulted in my being dragged to the Headmaster's Office and becoming acquainted with the Scottish form of punishment, known as 'the strap'. For people who do not know what the strap was, it was a leather strap about three inches wide with one end having two or three strips cut about 2–3 inches long. It was administered by the Headmaster raising it above his head and bringing it down with some force, with the cut side onto your outstretched hand facing palm up. It was painful. When you got back to the classroom all the children used to giggle. I received it quite a few times but then it was understandable as I could not understand the broad Scottish dialect and at the same time I was seen as a 'Jerry' or as a foreigner with a strange name.

School in Scotland was not a pleasant experience, possibly due to the fact I could not understand the teachers. When the children talked to me in their broad Scottish accents they were as bad, if not worse, than my Scottish aunt and uncles. Mind you, they probably could not understand me when I spoke in my English/Polish gibberish, along with my stutter. I think this is one of the reasons that I started to play truant from school on quite a regular basis. I used to get a beating from my Daddy Wilson when he found out, but his belt was about four inches wide, so it did not hurt as much as the strap which I got when I turned up at school again. It was not fair in those days as I used to get two punishments for one offence but, at the same time, I enjoyed myself while playing truant.

I used to spend the day exploring the area around Lochee and walking along the canal near a factory that made crisps. It may have been Walkers or Smiths Crisps; I'm not quite sure, but they did smell nice. I learned a lot while exploring. Apart from recognising and naming all the birds, I could also name the trees and quite a few plants. I learned about using burdock leaves that were used to rub on bare skin to take away the stings of nettles. I also learned how to catch fish from the canal using an old bicycle wheel rim with a piece of sacking tied to it, which was connected to some string. This was lowered into the water and sometime later raised to the surface of the water. If you had any fish on it, they could not escape because the sacking used to sag in the middle as the water was draining out. In Scotland, I think everyone was too poor to buy nets. I frequently took the fish home in a jar; that's how they found out I had been playing truant and I always had to throw the fish away.

Shortly after arriving in Scotland, I found out that the Queen and the Duke of Edinburgh were going to parade down Kingsway, now called Queensway as part of their Coronation Tour. This was something that I was not going to miss, and as it was taking place on a typical school day, I decided to play truant and go and watch the parade. I did not know that the parade would be held in the late afternoon and that all schools would be closed by then. Anyway, I found a spot where the parade was to pass and stood there for hours. Sometime in the late afternoon, an old car, possibly an old Austin or a Morris 8, stopped where I was standing beside a large gathering of spectators. The driver poked his head out of the window and said that he apologised for the Queen being delayed, but she would be coming down in her carriage shortly. As he drove off, one of the spectators had recognised the driver and shouted out, "It's the Duke of Edinburgh! It's the Duke of Edinburgh!" That's when everyone started cheering.

We could see him stopping at different spots along the road passing on the same message to the other spectators.

It was later confirmed that it was indeed the Duke of Edinburgh who had stopped to inform the spectators. This was the first of many occasions in which I had contact with the Duke of Edinburgh. Later I saw the Queen and the Duke as they passed me in their carriage, accompanied by her military escorts on horseback to much cheering and applause from the gathered crowd. I went home after the parade, probably starving and not looking forward to a good telling off and maybe a belt when I told everyone that I had seen the Queen.

One of the big highlights of our stay in Scotland was when we went down to Cupar on holiday, where my Daddy Wilson had an old double-decker bus which had been converted into a caravan or do you call it a busavan? It was parked in a field, miles away from anywhere next to a single line railway track. In the distance, we could see the main road between Perth and Cupar and used to watch the blue line coaches going up the hill. There was a 'burn' – in English a small pool fed with fresh running water, maybe about a mile or so away down the railway track that we had to go to every day to fill up our buckets with clean water for cooking and for getting a wash. There was also a dairy farm within the area where Ian and Frazer used to go and deliver milk to outlying houses. I used to go with them at times and was introduced to life on a farm by helping to clean out the cowsheds and feeding the cows. I also learned how to put my hand down into the mouth of a calf and have it sucked. When I helped in delivering the milk, we used to take out two or three crates of bottled milk on a small trolley going up and down narrow roads and tracks, which took quite a few hours to deliver.

I learned a lot about nature during my time there and can remember a lot of it very clearly even though sixty-odd years have passed. I remember my Daddy Wilson showing me how to get the butter out of the thistles that grew along the railway embankment and the fear that I had of bats. Both Ian and Frazer always used to tease me about the bats. One evening, while lying on our beds on the upper floor of the bus, they kept on telling me that there was a bat under the bus, scaring the living daylights out of me all evening. It was only the following morning that they put me out of my misery by taking me to look under the bus and to draw out a cricket bat, all the while insisting that they were always referring to the cricket bat the previous evening and that they could not understand why I was so upset. Now I can laugh about it, but if I had been bigger, I would have beaten them both up.

At the burn (pool) there used to be kingfishers and lots of other birds, along with flying dragonflies of all colours and sizes. The big honey bees and the odd lizards here and there were a far cry from the streets of London, and yes, plenty of nits and midgets that used to bite you whenever they could. I should point out that the time spent at the caravan was in the middle of summer and the weather was warm and sunny most of the time.

Rita also took me into the small market town of Cupar where I used to love standing on the bridge overlooking the fast flowing, shallow river watching the salmon and trout in all their colour swimming in the clear water. Rita also used to treat me to sweets and crisps and other bits and pieces which led to an everlasting, genuine bonding.

Other memories I have of Scotland on that occasion are going out to work with my Daddy Wilson, who was a Charge Hand with the local Post Office. He was responsible for putting up telegraph poles with his gang. Once he took me up to the top of the Law Hill and showed me the telegraph pole he had erected there. This is a place that I grew to love as the views were magnificent. Looking at photographs of the place now, I can see the changes that have been made. The telegraph pole is no longer there, and neither is the old, red painted WWII sea mine which must have been about twenty feet in diameter if not more, with lots and lots of percussion detonators sticking out of it. I remember that it had a small slot in it for collecting coin donations. There were also quite a few telescopes around the top of the hill for viewing the River Tay and the surrounding area. You had to put a one penny piece into the telescope to use them. I also used to love hanging onto the backs of the tram cars that used to run on rails around the town of Dundee.

I do not recall how long both my sister and I stayed in Dundee, but it must have been quite some time as I well remember Ian and Frazer dressed as jockeys and Isobil dressed as Sleeping Beauty – or was it Snow White – going out singing. Ian had an excellent singing voice which was very high pitched. He had to sing for his mum, dad and us before he was allowed to go out with the others to do their trick or treating. I also learned how to burn cork bottle stoppers to make soot to put on their faces to try and disguise them before they went out. All face makeup was very expensive in those days.

Dundee still is alive in my memories, but before moving back to London, I must mention that in the fifties around Lochee, I still remember the man who used to walk the streets with his big stick switching the lights on and off, on the street lamp posts.

Chapter 3

LONDON

I cannot recall the exact date that I returned to 37 Campbell House, but it must have been in late September or early October. Both Sandra and I must have returned with Daddy Wilson and Rita as they took us both to the Earl's Court Stadium to see Gene Autry and his Wild West Show. It was a brilliant show which included real live red Indians and cowboys and not forgetting Champion, the Wonder Horse.

The following year my brother Julian was born at home on 24 October 1954, and I do recall being ushered out of the room along with the rest of my brothers and sisters while my mother gave birth. Noisy. We all sat on the stairs, listening to all the groans and squeals of pain, as my mother gave birth to our new brother. There were now ten of us living in the three bedroomed flat and it was getting crowded. My brothers and sister were now aged between twelve down to less than one year old. My mum and dad still had one bedroom between themselves plus a cot for the newborn Julian. The girls shared one room between the three of them while I shared my room with my other three brothers. I still slept by myself in a single bed while Leonard and Ryszard shared the other single bed and Ronnie slept in the top drawer of a chest of drawers.

Money was still very tight in those days with my father working all hours at the Dayton Bicycle Factory. To help make ends meet, my father, who was excellent with his hands, used to make little trolleys to sell around the neighbourhood. These were designed as ducks for children to pull around on a piece of string. He also used to make small wooden guitars which were very popular as Rock and Roll music was just hitting the streets. In the meantime, my mother took to making children's sponge toys out of multicoloured sheets of foam, usually in the shape of rabbits. These were very successful, and we sold them in their hundreds. My sister Sandra, along with my dad and me were responsible for selling these items. My mother was also entitled to Family Allowance which was about two shillings and sixpence for each child; that's twelve and a half pence in today's money. In those days there were no housing allowances or any other social benefits that you could claim. You had to work for the money you had, and nothing was free apart from the bottles of cod liver oil and orange juice which you got from the National Health Service.

Both my mother and father were excellent cooks who knew how to make a little food go a long way. Forget the food of today; that was non-existent for us. For us, breakfast consisted of porridge made from salted water served to us in a soup bowl, to which we used to add some milk and a sprinkle of sugar. If we were lucky, we also got a knob of Stork margarine on top. In Scotland we only got salt sprinkled on top. This used to be followed by a slice of toast with some mixed fruit jam spread on it. Tea was typically served in an old jam jar as cups never lasted long in our house. I do not recall having dinners unless I was at school. So it must have been a sandwich or a roll or even a biscuit for lunch. Both my mum and dad took turns in preparing the evening meal, as this was normally the main meal of the day. Some of the meals that we enjoyed were quite unusual, so I will mention some of these and how they were made. I will spell the names out as I pronounce them, or as near as possible as most of these were Polish origin.

The first one is 'Snaps' which we had for breakfast and even as an evening meal, depending on the money situation at the time. This consisted of a couple of slices of plain bread, placed in a soup plate and covered in hot milk with a sprinkle of sugar on top.

One of our favourite meals was 'Perush-ki'. This was made out of flour and water dough, which was rolled out to about a quarter inch thickness and then cut into four-inch squares. On this, we would put about a tablespoon of the filling which consisted of mashed potatoes with fried onions. You then wet the edge of the pastry square and pulled one corner over to the opposite corner, crimp together the two edges and prick the top a couple of times with a fork. When all is done, place them into a pot of boiling salted water for about twenty minutes.

These would be served straight from the pot onto a plate, with a sprinkle of some fried onions and margarine, or oil, in which the onions were cooked. Any leftovers would be fried whole the following day until crispy and served with HP or Tomato sauce. If we were lucky, we sometimes had a mushroom sauce spread on top. It was very cheap to make and tasted great.

Another treat we used to have – and it was always my father that made this dish – was called 'Gal-ompi'. This consisted of a large cabbage blanched whole in boiling water to allow the leaves to soften in order to remove as whole leaves. These leaves were then filled with a mixture of cooked rice, fried bacon and onions. The leaves were then rolled with the ends tucked in and tightly placed in two or more layers in a pot, immersed in water and left to simmer for about thirty minutes. Once ready, the would be served two or three on a plate with tomato sauce. Delicious.

A third dish, again generally cooked by my father, was a dish called 'Plact-ski'. This consisted of a mixture of grated raw potatoes, finely chopped raw onions, flour and water, salt and pepper to taste. It was mixed to a relatively thick consistency but runny enough to cover the base of a hot frying pan when shaking and moving it about. The mixture was poured into a lightly oiled frying pan to a depth of about a quarter of an inch and cooked until golden brown on one side, then flipped over to achieve the same texture. These were stacked on a plate before serving. We would add tomato or HP sauce. It was a meal in itself with no side dishes required.

On one occasion my father created a ball of mince-meat and onion, flavoured with various spices and deep fried them. They tasted great, and all my brothers and sisters asked him what they were called. He had no real name at the time but as it was the time of 'Rock & Roll' he simply called them Rock & Roll. They became the most favoured foods of our young days. I also now know the real reason behind the name. The 'Rock' stood for them being hard, and the 'Roll' stood for them rolling off the plate when trying to cut them with your fork and knife.

One of the best soups that I have ever eaten was what we called 'Clus-ski' soup. It was very easy and cheap to make. It consisted of half an inch diced, raw, peeled potatoes, chopped raw onions, with a thick flour and water dough rolled into one inch balls and all placed in a pot of boiling water and cooked for about twenty minutes. This was served in soup bowls with a knob of Stork margarine and a drop of milk. Fantastic and very popular. It would taste even better today if you were to change the last two items to butter and cream.

My mother was great at making pies and cakes of all shapes and flavours, and I used to enjoy sitting with her and watching. Best of all was licking the spoon with the cake batter on it. Most of the meat pies were made with minced meat which by far was the most common meat that we used to eat. One of the pies I mostly enjoyed used to be filled with just a mixture of fried onions and baked beans.

The most standard of meals in the evening used to consist of shepherd's pie, cottage pie or plain old mince and potatoes with a few vegetables. Chicken was not very common and we only had turkey on Christmas Day. The only fish that we used to have regularly was kipper, and that's only because our dad liked them. Cod, plaice or my favourite rock salmon all in batter were a rarity, as were chips. We never had fish during the week except on a Friday as, believe it or not, my father was quite religious, and he believed in his religious teachings. On special occasions, along with my sister Sandra, I used to go to the Fish and Chip shop in the small line of shops down South Africa Road and get ten portions of chips which used to cost 3d a portion; that's old pennies, not new. In today's money that would be just over one penny or a total of two shillings and sixpence. Twelve and a half pence. I am mentioning the cost in both old and new coinage so that anyone who reads this can relate to the differences in cost across different decades. On extra special occasions we also got some battered fish which we used to share and, if we were lucky, we got a pickled onion. Pickled eggs were, in most cases, a step too far. So were the hot dogs.

Other common foods that we had to eat quite often were beans on toast, jam on toast and sometimes even egg on toast. On occasions when money was very tight, we used to have just fresh bread with sugar. Cornflakes were a rarity as were Rice Crispies. On quite a few occasions the larder was bare, so we had nothing apart from the teaspoon full of cod liver oil that we had every night without fail.

My brother Leonard was always hungry, and on quite a few occasions he would raid the larder and steal whatever food he could find. He used to stand inside the larder and close the door where he would eat the best part of half a loaf of bread with each slice sprinkled with sugar and sterilised milk. I did not mind him doing it, but I always got the blame and a belt around my ears from my mother or father. One thing I can say with pride is that neither I nor any of my brothers or sisters could be called fat.

As I have mentioned, my father was quite religious and used to respect religious festivals such as Lent, Easter and Christmas. He also abstained from meat on a Friday. So on Good Friday, my mother would boil up lots of eggs in different coloured water which we would then decorate with faces. She would then collect them together, and during the night when we were all asleep, she would hide them all over the house for us to find on Easter Day. Sometimes it took hours to find them, and we were not allowed to eat them until they had all been found.

On Christmas Day, my mother and father would always find a turkey to cook with all the trimmings. It was a meal that we looked forward to every year as we only had it once a year. Again as money was so tight, presents at Christmas for me used to consist of a sixpenny piece all wrapped up in coloured paper and a pack of playing cards. This was also the time we got some new clothes for the coming year, such as a pullover that my mother had just finished knitting and some new socks. Maybe even a new pair of short trousers. On one occasion I got a new bike from my father's factory. I can still remember quite clearly my mother taking me out and teaching me how to ride the bike. I used to sit on the saddle and pedal away, while my mother would hold the back of the seat and run beside me. It did not take me long to learn and I later used the bike for going to school. To be allowed to use your bike for school, you had to take lessons on the Highway Code and pass a riding test taken by the local policeman.

We often went to the park opposite the flats for a family picnic where we used to be treated to a bottle of Tizer or some 7Up Lemonade, sandwiches, sausage rolls and fairy cakes made by my mother. We also used to buy broken biscuits from the local shops as a special treat.

On my return to England from Scotland, I had to go to a new school which was Coverdale Junior School in Coverdale Road, close to Shepherds Bush Market. It was the school that I felt was the most prejudiced towards me because of my surname. It was here that I got into quite a few fights and got the cane on more occasions than I can remember. One of my problems was that I was left handed. The teachers never liked that and always insisted that I write with my right hand. Every time they caught me writing with my left hand they would rap my knuckles with a ruler.

I believe that I was not very well liked as I enjoyed learning at school and was more advanced that the majority of children at the school. In fact the teachers could not keep up with me. In reading, for example, I was a fast learner and used to read all the comics; be they The Eagle or the Hotspur, the Beano or the Dandy. I also used to read all the girls' comics from a very young age. When I was introduced to my first books at this school, it was unbelievable. They used to give us a book to take home and read as homework, usually just a few paragraphs, and I would read the entire book. The following day, students had to read out a small excerpt in front of the whole class, which I found very easy. I also used to get bored listening to the others trying to read out a story that I had already finished. This used to be misinterpreted by the teacher who thought I had no interest in reading. I was either told to wake up or sent to stand in the corner facing the wall for not paying attention to the lesson. Once they had learned the reason for my failure to show any interest in their lessons, they started giving me many books to read and treated me like a star pupil.

Other subjects that I had a flair for were history, geography, and mathematics. I would like to point out that as a young child at that time I had a distinct advantage over the youngsters of today. The reason I say this is because, like many of us in those days, we never had television, computers, X Boxes or the internet. If it was raining outside and we had to stay in, it was a case of playing board games such as Snakes and Ladders or maybe Ludo. If you were lucky, your parents would have bought you the game of Wembley or the other game in which you went to jail if you landed on the square. Oh yes, Monopoly! If nobody wanted to play with you, you got bored, and that is where all my reading was put into practice. To me, maths was like a puzzle, and I was very good at it. I was later rewarded for my knowledge of maths by getting my brother Ryszard interested in the subject at a young age and in later life he took it to a greater stage when he went to University.

I enjoyed school but what made it even better was that I was entitled to free dinners. We also got a free bottle of milk at school and on some occasions, you got chocolate flavoured milk. The bad thing about school was that it was quite a long walk to get there and coming from a somewhat poor family, my shoes often had holes in the soles. I often had to cut cardboard and place it in my shoes, which was okay when it was not raining. I also used to end up with holes in my socks which my mother was forever mending. My mother tried her best in clothing us and apart from making many of my sister's dresses she also used to knit pullovers and jumpers for us boys. I was quite lucky as the eldest boy, as sometimes I got new clothes, which were handed down to my younger brothers as I grew out of them. Up until the age of eleven, I was still wearing short trousers.

I recall in my early days at Coverdale having to go swimming for the first time at Lime Grove Swimming Baths. I had no swimming trunks, so the teacher had to borrow a pair for me. The lads who I was with duly noted this which resulted in them constantly asking me if I could swim, to which I would only reply in the affirmative as I did not want to be seen as a wimp. Not a good thing to do. When we got to the swimming bath and upon seeing the size of the pool and all that water, I was terrified when they told me to jump in. I hesitated, so they jumped on me, picked me up and tossed me in. I almost drowned before I was pulled out and it taught me a lesson that I would never forget. After that, I learned to swim but only with a board in front of me, which I never let go of.

Later on, I would go back to Lime Grove Swimming Pool not only for swimming but also for my first boxing match when the pool was covered with wooden planks, and a boxing ring was set up.

Apart from the usual Physical Training that we carried out on more or less a daily basis within the school grounds, we also used to board a coach which took us to a sports field once a week for a sports afternoons, where we would get involved in track events or play football.

I enjoyed the ups and downs of school life, but I did enjoy playing truant even more.

Since my school was close to Shepherds Bush Market, it was like going into a great big playground. I think this is the place where I learned how to steal. Initially, it started out as a dare with a few of my mates to see who could get an apple or an orange from the stalls without being seen. This was too easy to start with and as time progressed we began taking other bits and pieces, normally it was something to eat. On occasions, we used to get chased but never caught. To both me and my friends it was a great big game.

I used to play truant quite a bit which allowed me time to explore the area quite well. Sometimes I would go to the cinema that was next to the Empire Theatre and wait by the exit door at the side of the cinema for somebody to leave and then sneak in. In those days they normally showed two films; a B-rated film followed by an interval and then the main feature film. The entire show used to last around three to four hours. It was a good way to spend an afternoon or early evening. Later I took to going to the Empire Theatre and watching live drama or comedy events which I did enjoy.

On most of these occasions, I used to pay to get in. It was not unusual to ask total strangers to take you in as children were not allowed in unaccompanied but this never proved to be a problem provided you gave them the admission fee first. I did not go that often, as I seldom had any money.

I had a mate called John who lived in the flats opposite me and who was my primary partner in crime; he was the same age or a little older than me. I cannot recall him having a father, and his mother was a very small woman and quite frightened of him. She never liked him being in the house and always gave him money to get him out. If we were together, she would give him additional money so that we could both go to the cinema. We both used to go exploring together; one of our favourite areas to explore was Holland Park. The houses and apartments here were very expensive and occupied by very wealthy people. You could tell they were rich by the carpets and wall decorations when you entered the doorway. We never stole from these places; we just explored them up to the roofs. If anyone stopped us, we would tell them that we were collecting old newspapers. This may sound strange in today's time but back then, collecting newspapers and bottles was a good way to earn some money. We would bundle the papers up and take them to the local scrap merchant who used to pay you for them by weight. On occasions, we would be invited into some of these posh houses and given tea, biscuits and even some pennies. I can well understand it now, as I am sure we looked like a couple of scallywags or urchins.

When my mate and I wanted to go to the Empire Theater and we had no money, we used to go to Shepherds Bush Green where the Red Double-Decker buses used to take a break. The buses used to park up and the bus drivers and conductors used to go to the front bus and gather around for a smoke and a chat. They never paid any attention to us lads playing on the steps of the bus to the rear. The trouble was that we kids knew that the conductor kept a small brown case on the shelf above the luggage compartment and that within this case he kept a small bag of coppers totalling either two shillings and sixpence or five shillings. I'm sorry to say this, but when they were not looking, we used to take it. Over the years we did this quite a few times. We were never caught, although I do recall being chased a few times. I still do not understand to this very day, why or how these conductors never learned to lock and secure their cases.

Sometimes when I walked to school, I used to go down Warbeck Road which came out in front of my school. Halfway down this road on the right-hand side lived an old gentleman who, at some point in life, had lost both his legs. He lived alone and as far as I know looked after himself. He was always dirty with overgrown hair, a rugged beard and moustache and dressed in rags. He used to crawl to his so-called garden wall in front of his house with a tin box and beg all who passed him for a couple of pennies. I became a good friend of his and, along with some mates, we used to go around houses collecting old newspapers and bottles for him. He used to invite us into his house which was a real mess filled with bundle upon bundle of newspapers and bottles. The place stank something rotten, and at times you could even see rats crawling about. He used to make us tea and even gave us biscuits. He never had any cups, so we had to drink our tea from old jam jars which were not very clean, but then again we never had any fears over a bit of dirt. He used to enjoy our company and talked about many things; I just wish I could remember what we used to talk about. He also used to give us money from his tin. I sometimes wonder whatever happened to him.

Living in Campbell House and knowing the surrounding area was an experience that I will always remember. It was an experience that children of this modern age will never know. An age where it was not uncommon for children to go to school with a catapult in their back pocket or a sheath knife stuck in their belts. We also carried penknives in our pockets along with marbles, elastic rubber bands and even conkers on a string.

Things were soon to change as I learned that we would be moving to a new house outside of London. I was apprehensive at this news as I thought that moving out of London would mean living in the sea.

The family must have moved to our new house in Carpenters Park in Hertfordshire in mid-1955. I recall the day we left Campbell House as my brothers, and I had to sit in the back of the furniture van. Luckily it was a nice sunny day when we set off on a journey that appeared to last for hours, going down roads with big fields on either side, many of them with cows and sheep in them. We did not see any cows and sheep in London, so this was quite new to some of my brothers who had never seen a live cow or sheep before. Finally, we arrived at our new home: No 1 Kenilworth Gardens, Carpenters Park, near Watford in Hertfordshire. A big three bedroomed house with a big front and back garden. My three sisters still had to share a bedroom while I shared my bedroom with my three brothers. The only difference we had was the beds as our two single beds had been replaced by one double sized bed. This meant that we used to sleep two up and two down. It's not as bad as it sounds but I did have to tell one of my brothers on some occasions to "stop biting my toes." We all used to enjoy having great pillow fights in that bedroom. Thankfully Julian was still sharing a bedroom with mum and dad.

One of the biggest events in moving to our new house was the day that we got our first television. It was black and white as colour TV was not around at the time, but I think we had a 17" screen which was the biggest screen available. There was only one television station which was the BBC. Unlike today, programmes were only shown from late afternoon until around 10:30pm in the evening. It used to start with children's programmes such as Sooty or Bill and Ben, The Flower Pot Men, followed by a serial like The Railway Children. This was normally followed by the early evening news. From about half past eight in the evening, the programmes were typically aimed at the older generations, with programs like Dixon of Dock Green or even one of my favourite programmes, War in The Air, being aired. My brothers and sisters were regularly sent to bed around half past seven or eight o'clock. As Sandra and I were older, we were allowed to stay up a bit later to watch TV, providing the programme was suitable for children. Sometimes when War in The Air was on, my dad would send me up to bed as he did not think it was suitable for me to watch. When the last programme of the evening finished, it was always followed by the playing of Britain's national anthem, God Save the Queen. Then the TV screen would go black with a white spot in the middle and then go blank. That's when the TV was switched off.

My new school was quite some way from the house, which meant that I had to either ride my bike or walk. The school was called Hampden Park Senior Boys and Girls School. It was here that I started wearing long trousers for the first time. As in all the schools that I went to, there was discrimination to start with; again mainly due to my surname being Zawadzki. It was a great school, and as I had no friends to start with, this stopped me from playing truant. I excelled in my entire subjects and was in the highest class for my age. I was introduced to other classes such as art and cooking. I never looked forward to drama classes or music classes even when given the triangle to start with. As for the recorder, my mother would not let me play it in the house, not even to practice. I tried the tambourine and even the cymbals but now when I look back at these times, I only wish they had bagpipes. I think I would have been good at that as even today they tell me I am full of wind.

The school had a large area devoted to gardening. This is a sector that I used to spend a lot of time in, learning about growing plants, mixing manure and the compost heap. Between here and my garden back home I learned a lot for later use. My father was also a devoted gardener, and every part of the garden was put to full use, mainly in the growing of vegetables for our consumption. The only time I did not like gardening was when my dad used to insist that I do the weeding first before going out with my mates to play. Like the school gardens, everything that we grew was used either in our kitchen or sold off to local friends.

One of the nice things about the location of this school was that it backed onto the LMS or London-Midland-Scottish railway lines which were used by the English Electric Company for testing their new Deltic which was a very powerful diesel-powered train engine. It used to run past the school every day and used to hoot its horns as it was passing, much to the delight of all who were present to watch. This engine was what enticed me into the hobby of collecting train numbers and back to playing truant.

Unlike London, where everything was on your doorstep, you had to go quite a long way from your home to get involved into any type of adventure. Around us, there were golf courses, fields and woods plus houses and a few shops. So life was a bit dull. Collecting train numbers was a great way of getting out. Initially, my mates and I used to go down to the railway lines and sit by the track which was very well used. It was also the place where the trains used to pick up water for their steam engines from the trough between the railway lines. At times there used to be three or four engines approaching and crossing in front of us from both directions which meant some of us had to rush and cross over the lines to get the numbers of the trains passing on the other side. They would then come back over to where we were, and we would swap train numbers. Thinking about it now, it was quite dangerous at times.

From the side of the track, we eventually went to Carpenter's Park Railway Station and paid a penny for a platform ticket where it was a lot more comfortable apart from every now and again running over the footbridge when two trains pass simultaneously. From there the platform ticket used to get us to Watford and from there all the railway stations became our oysters for just one penny. Mind you, hiding from the train ticket inspectors used to be quite daunting at times.

Both my mother and father continued making the 'Sponge Clowns and Duck Trolleys' which went down quite well within our new area. At the same time I was introduced to 'scrumping' which to the uninitiated means going around the area and looking for apple orchards and plum trees. Once found we would get into the grounds somehow and collect all the windfalls (the fruit that had fallen on the ground) and place it into bags. If there were no windfalls, we used to throw sticks into the trees to dislodge the apples or pears and even the plums. At all times we had to keep an eye out for the owners as they did not take kindly to us for scrumping their fruit and we got chased quite a few times. I only remember my brother Leonard ever being caught. He had to give all the fruit that he had bagged back to the owner and was thoroughly berated, before crying his eyes out and being sent on his way. He was quite happy when he re-joined us as we had gotten away with quite a haul. All my brothers and sisters used to enjoy it when we went scrumping as we all shared the apples, pears or plums out. If we had any spare which we normally did, mum would make pies or crumbles with whatever fruit we had. Nothing was wasted. The apple fritters were a great delight to behold.

As the area where we lived was surrounded by woods and fields, my father and I would go out collecting wild mushrooms. People who used to see the mushrooms that we collected would look at them in disgust and tell us they were poisonous or even called them toadstools. Mind you the ones we picked never looked like the mushrooms that you bought in the local greengrocers. They were all colours, shapes, and sizes. Many of them looked like sponges when you turned them over, but when cooked they tasted a lot better than the traditional mushrooms. I was also taught the secret of telling the difference between an edible mushroom and a poisonous mushroom, and it's very simple. All edible mushrooms contain sugar which is eaten by a multitude of insects. By examining the stalks of an unrecognisable mushroom for any insects activity, you can tell if it edible or not. If there is evidence of any bugs eating the specimen you are looking at, it means that it is clear of any poison and is edible for human consumption as insects do not eat poisonous plants. If you find no evidence of bugs, stay clear as it's always better to be safe than sorry.

At times we used to collect so many mushrooms, that we had to convert our dining room into a drying room. We used to string the mushrooms together, hang them from the ceiling and dry them out. To help us to do this, we also collected lots of wooden tree stumps and logs from the woods to keep the grated fire going for extended periods of time until all the mushrooms had been thoroughly dried out. The only problem we had was the room smelled very musty, but the mushrooms did taste good.

Outside the front door of the house was a large lawn grass area which was an ideal area for playing football or any other game. We all played our games except for when the policeman who lived opposite our house was on night duty. He did not like the noise us kids used to make when he was trying to sleep.

This area was also a place where a group of adults used to gather every Sunday afternoon to sing praises to the Lord and teach us children quotes and passages from the Bible. They also gave us kids a bit of paper with a quote on it at the end of their meeting that we had to learn by heart and recite to them the following week. If we had learned it correctly, we used to have a card punched, and once we had received a given amount of punches, we would be given a small present, generally a book. I am not sure if they were members of the Baptist or Mormons faiths and although I was brought up as a Roman Catholic, I did enjoy going to their meetings. Another bonus in attending their meeting was that they used to hold small parties or dinners in their homes and we would often get invited to participate. All was above board with the invites as they used to talk with our parents and seek permission to be allowed to take us to their homes as some of them lived a fair distance from our houses. They used to lay on cakes, sandwiches, ice-cream and jellies along with soft drinks, we also played games like 'I Spy' and ended up with a sing-song before setting off back home in a car. In those days it was even considered as a privilege getting into a car, never mind being driven in one.

One afternoon in early 1956 while I was still eleven years old, I was playing football outside the house, and during the game I must have been kicked in the leg. I never felt any pain at the time, but later in the evening I felt an excruciating pain coming from my leg and ended up crying and screaming at the same time. My father must have called an ambulance, as I was rushed to Shrodell's Hospital in Watford. This was the start of an extended period of time in the hospital. From all accounts, the doctors could not diagnose my condition, and after administering injections for pain relief which from my memory did nothing to relieve the pain, x-rays were taken which also showed no abnormalities. I continued crying and screaming while I was awake and kept on falling into unconsciousness. From all accounts, this lasted more than one month during which time I was receiving two injections per hour every hour. Throughout this time I was suffering from pain, fever, and unconsciousness. I was told that my father used to visit me every night after he finished work and used to sit by me. On occasions, I could remember seeing him there, but I could not remember ever talking to him.

After some time, my fever eventually went, and the pain in my leg started to subside. I was still receiving injections for pain every hour which caused a lot of problems. These problems arose from the facts that they were finding it hard to find a place on my body to continue injecting me. My arms, legs, back and the cheeks of my bottom, were completely black and blue with bruises from the injections that I had received since being admitted to hospital.

From all accounts, the doctors still did not know what my problem was, but I was feeling quite a bit better and was in a position where I could sit up and start to eat regular food again. I became quite popular with the nurses, and when I reached my twelfth birthday, they insisted that I should remain in their ward and was not moved up to the men's ward which was standard practice. It was here that I first started taking an interest in members of the opposite sex. I cannot recall talking to girls apart from my sisters, but the nurses changed all that for me. They were fantastic, and I will always remember the name of one of them, who was called Barbara. I used to call her Basha which she found hilarious. Even to this day, I can still see her in my mind. She was of medium height with a slim and well-shaped body. A beautiful face with large brown eyes and eyebrows, and short, dark brown straight hair. She also wore large brown glasses. She also looked like a nurse, dressed in her dark blue uniform, her white apron, a small white cap on her head and black silk stockings, unlike today's nurses who appear to be so clinically dressed with very little colour.

She was always there for me, whatever my needs. She used to bring me books and comics to read and even play games with me when her duties allowed. On occasions, she used to stay with me after she had finished work. If it were possible, I would love to seek her out and thank her for being there for me, as without her I do not think I would have survived. As I was slowly improving my father was not always available to visit me and as far as I can recall no other member of the family ever visited me while I was in the hospital. I made friends with the other children who were in the ward along with their parents and visitors, but they never lasted long as they were discharged quite soon after they arrived.

I was still bedbound and experiencing some pain in my leg after having been in the hospital for over four months, when I was told that I was to undergo an operation. I was not told what the operation was, but I know my dad was worried. Lucky for me the day before the procedure, I took a turn for the worse and was diagnosed with having pneumonia. The operation was cancelled and it was only later that I realised how lucky I was to get pneumonia, a disease that has ended many lives.

I do not know how long I had to wait for my recovery from pneumonia, but when it cleared, the pain along with the poison that I did not know about in my leg had also cleared. I made a full recovery and no longer required to undergo my operation, which I later found out was to have my leg amputated. The only problem I had now was that I had been bed bound for over four months and had lost the use of my legs. Over the time spent in the hospital, I know that the nurses used to massage my legs on a daily basis, so I was lucky; all I had to do was to learn to walk again.

It took the best part of a month with specialised therapeutic nursing staff to teach me to walk again. First, it was learning to stand and putting weight on my legs followed with balancing and then moving my leg while trying to walk. Thinking about it now, I was like a newborn baby taking its first steps.

Once I had started walking again, the doctors decided that I should be sent to a convalescence home to practice my walking skills and to recuperate from the months that I had spent in the hospital. I was to be sent to a convalescence home in Broadstairs, Kent, for a month.

Just before going, all the nurses and doctors took up a collection for me and gave me about twelve pounds for spending money. It was the largest amount of money that I had ever had in my life. My father came up to say goodbye as he was not going to see me for the whole time I was at the Home. I was then put into a car and driven all the way to the home.

I guess that I arrived at the St Mary's Convalescent Home for Children sometime in July or August as it was quite warm and sunny. It was quite a big house with large dormitories for the boys and girls and a large eating hall. The place was run mainly by nuns who used to be very demanding and strict. At 12 years old I think I was one of the older boys there at the time. There are two main things that I remember about the place. After the midday meal we had to go and sleep on the cots outside on the veranda and breathe in the sea air. The sandy beach was very close to the veranda, with a constant breeze blowing in from the sea. The other thing I remember fairly well is that there was a carpenter's shop where the elder boys used to learn carpentry, mainly making small tables or light stands. I was taught how to make a sailing ship which I was quite pleased with. We also attended lessons on reading and maths which was taken by the nuns.

I also had to take a lot of exercises to improve my walking skills but was restricted from being too adventurous in games like football and running. I used to go and walk on the seashore as the sand was good for exercise. I also used to get into trouble for answering the nuns back and spent quite a bit of time in solitary confinement or standing in the corner facing the wall.

On occasions, we all used to be marched around the town of Broadstairs as the nuns went out with their begging bowls while we were shown off to the general public. We were often given sweets or even a cake or an apple on these occasions.

The area of Broadstairs is a beautiful location which I thoroughly enjoyed as it was all new to me, but I was always looking forward to going home as I had not seen my mum or my brothers and sisters for over six months.

Chapter 4

CARPENTERS PARK TO THE BRITWELL ESTATE

I returned home to Kenilworth Garden from the convalescent home sometime in late 1956, and I guess I was treated like the long lost son. Initially, I had to take things easy and was not allowed to be too active, so I spent a lot of time in the garden or helping out in the kitchen and learning all the tricks of the trade in cookery. I also helped my mother out when she carried out any redecoration in the house. I have already mentioned that my mother was a very intelligent woman; she was also a very far-seeing woman with a great talent for interior design. She used to carry out all the home decorating, including hanging the wallpaper and painting. I often helped her hang the paper, usually by pasting the back of the wallpaper and handing it to her while she was up the step ladder. She also taught me how to paint, and it was normally me that had to paint the floor skirting boards. My mother never did like getting down on her knees to do any painting.

I continued my schooling, taking it quite seriously and studying hard, which I enjoyed. I was rewarded by the school on quite a few occasions by winning books on school presentation days and at other events. The only competition I had at school was the girls. Although I did not have much to do with them, most of them were bright and intelligent, and if I was ever stuck on a subject, they were the only ones who I would turn to for help. I still used to get into trouble on occasions when involved in a fight or for taking an air pistol to school, which was a relatively common occurrence at the time. As I have mentioned, penknives, sheaf knives, catapults, ropes and air guns were familiar playthings for us boys in the fifties and were not frowned upon or prohibited in those days. If you were caught fighting, you often had to report to the gym after school with the lad you were fighting, where you would have to put on boxing gloves and fight him again under the supervision of the sports teacher. I often went home with a black eye after these events.

I still enjoyed trainspotting which was my primary outdoor activity and which meant that I still played truant but not as often as I used to. I remember that I did go into Watford on some occasions mainly to find the hospital that I was in. I did locate the hospital but was always too frightened to go in. Looking back now, it's something that I will always regret. I never did see my nurse Barbara again. On most of my visits to Watford, I used to walk to Carpenters Park then onto Bushey and finally to Watford, before returning home the same way. If I was lucky and I had no punctures on my bicycle wheels, I would cycle.

Another of my pastimes was going out with one of the boys I knew with an old pram that we had salvaged from the local rubbish tip. We would go to the local railway lines and collect the coal that had fallen off the trains' coal tenders. At times this was not such an easy job, especially with a pram. The railway embankments were quite steep which meant that we had to struggle to reach the lines. We would then follow them until we came across a lump of coal and some of the lumps were huge. We then had to take the coal back to the pram. We continued doing this until the pram could hold no more coal and then we would struggle to get the pram onto a good track or pavement before setting off to sell it to the local neighbours. On occasions, we would refill the pram a few times until it got dark. When we never managed to sell the last load, we would take it home, much to the pleasure of my mum and dad. I always returned home looking like a black scallywag and in desperate need of a bath. These were the only times I ever had a bath and the water all to myself.

I was never really interested in girls before I went to the hospital and, having fallen head over heels in love with my nurse Barbara, I had to find a replacement. She was not too far away; in fact, she lived next door and was a friend of my sister Sandra and around the same age of fourteen. Her name was Vera Peet.

The only trouble was that since we first met when we first moved in, we were always fighting between us and calling each other names. In fact, to tell the truth, I had no experience in talking to girls even though I had three sisters at the time and all I ever did with them was to indulge in in-house fighting. I was now at that age where curiosity about girls was starting to be felt. Like a lot of other lads in the same age group, I was starting to learn about hormones. Sex education did not exist at this time in schools and any mention of it was strictly taboo. It was the time that I started taking an interest in 'Playboy' and other magazines especially the ones with naked women in them. Every now and again my mother, brothers or even sisters used to find them under the mattress. My mum would blow a fuse and have a right old going off at me, calling me all the names under the sun. I never told her that I sometimes found the same sort of books under the mattress where my dad slept in his bedroom.

Sandra and Vera often went out together, and I never knew what they got up to, but on many occasions, I used to hear my mother yelling at her and telling her that if she ever got pregnant she would be thrown out of the house and the baby would be put into care. My sister never liked me talking to Vera; maybe she thought I would split them up and then again she was two years older than me. One evening my sister Sandra scuttled all hopes of me getting anywhere with Vera when she caught me at the window at the top of the stair that allowed a full view into Vera's bedroom. I had noticed that Vera had gone into her bedroom and switched on the light, but had forgotten to close the curtains. As I was watching her take off her jumper, Sandra had come up the stairs unnoticed just as Vera was about to take off her bra. Looking out the window and seeing what I was looking at, she immediately started screaming and banging on the window to catch Vera's attention which she did; the result was that Vera looked aghast and rapidly closed the curtains. I don't think Vera ever spoke to me again after that.

As Christmas approached, my mother was pregnant yet again and my fifth brother, Marion, was born on 28 April 1957. This meant that the house was getting crowded and Julian was about to move into and share our bedroom with the rest of the boys. My father was still the only person working, and money was still very tight. It was felt quite a lot in the bedroom especially when the bedrooms got quite cold. We never had enough blankets to cover ourselves and had to resort to covering ourselves with our coats and huddling even tighter together to keep warm. Space within the house was now at a premium, so it was no surprise when my mother and father gathered us all together and told us that we were leaving and moving to a new house.

I do not recall the exact date that we moved into No 56 Doddsfield Road, Britwell Estate, Slough, Bucks, except that it was in 1958, but I do remember the commotion when we moved in. The first thing that happened was the local paper sent a reporter round to the house to interview and to take a photograph of us all. A few days later the front headline story in the Slough Observer was 'Britwell's Biggest Family Moves In,' which gave a brief description and a photo of the whole family.

The house was a big four bedroomed house with a large side garden on the right of the front door as you looked at it and a smaller garden to the left next to the main road. The house faced a large open area with a large tree in front of the front door. It was pure heaven to us kids for apart from the four bedrooms, we also had two separate toilets, a large bathroom, large kitchen, dining room and a big living room. The first task that my mother took on was the painting and decorating of the whole house along with the more common of chores like feeding the kids, washing and ironing, and her never-ending job of knitting and dressmaking. It was not unusual for my mother to be carrying out room decorations into the early hours of the morning while all my brothers and sisters slept. In fact, at times she never did sleep. This overworking used to have extreme effects on her health at times with asthma attacks which resulted in her being bed bound for quite a few days, and on occasions being rushed to the hospital. My second eldest sister Annetta would take over running the household, and she used to love it. She was a typical tyrant when she was in charge. I think even my dad used to keep out of the way.

Meanwhile, both my dad and I turned our hand to the garden. First, we dug a vegetable patch which consisted of half the garden and then laid the remainder to lawn but not before digging a large dugout that was covered in corrugated sheets, earth and grass. When we had finished, it looked like an old bomb shelter. It would have made a safe bomb shelter for the whole family if required but the main reason for building it was for growing mushrooms. We also planted six trees, four of which were apple trees and two were pear trees. If my memory serves me well the apples were called Cox's Pippins and oh boy, did they taste good!

I was now fourteen years of age, and I still had to go to school. The only school available for me to attend was the William Penn Boys School. This caused my mother and father a few concerns as money was still a rarity in the house, and I was required to wear my first school uniform. The outfit consisted of a black blazer edged in silver with the school badge on the breast pocket, grey trousers, black shoes and a cap in black and silver. Not forgetting the white shirt and tie. It was not long before I started to have problems both with the staff and the other boys that attended the school. Again I went through the whole racial name calling which turned into fights and me visiting the headmaster who went by the name of Mr Merchant. Now Mr Merchant was a tall bloke and well over the six-foot mark, which meant that when he swung the cane, you felt it. I received my first caning on either the first or second day at school. This had a very adverse effect on me and my schooling with the results that I spent more time playing truant than attending this school. I was constantly in trouble with my maths teacher who was an ex RAF Squadron Leader and pilot who used to fly Spitfires during the 1939-1945 world war. He sported an enormous typical RAF handlebar moustache and was ultimately used to discipline, but for some unknown reason, he could not instil it in me. This used to result in my meeting the headmaster on quite a few occasions and me having a very sore hand.

My schoolwork started to go downhill as I was not paying any attention to the teachers and my grades suffered. I was shunned by most of the boys at the school and also became a target for the school monitors. Most days, I used to turn up late for school, and the school monitors used to delight in putting my name down for school detention, which I think I did most days. I do not recall ever making friends with any of the boys at this school. The only good thing at this school was that I got free school dinner meals which my mother did not know about as I had told her that I had to pay for my school dinner's daily. This gave me about one shilling a day to spend how I wanted to. Normally on crisps and sweets while at school and some food while playing truant.

While playing truant, I was always by myself. I would set off for school and then when I was almost there, I would change directions and walk away. Initially, I would explore the area around the house looking out for apple and pear trees in people's gardens and then go further afield to places like Burnham Beeches where I discovered a small permanent fairground and a small zoo or what would now be called an animal farm. I found the local rubbish tip down a small narrow lane leading from the Beeches back to the Britwell Estate which became a major attraction to me while living in Slough. I spent a lot of time exploring Burnham Beeches, building hideouts in the ferns, going down to a large pool and catching newts and looking for slow worms and adders. There was quite a bit of wildlife in the area such as badgers, foxes, rabbits and squirrels along with a great variety of birds. At that time I could name all the different birds and even their eggs which I used to enjoy collecting during nest hunting. To me, Burnham Beeches was a different world.

On nice warm days, I would take a book there, find a nice comfortable spot and lie on the ground and read my book all day before returning home.

I would also walk into Slough Town Center and explore all the cinemas and try to get in for free at the theatre exits or go to Woolworths and other large places to see what I could get away with. I think it's called shoplifting in today's society. As time went by, I started to explore places further afield, like walking all the way to Reading after having gone through Maidenhead and walking all the way back. On occasions, I would walk all the way to Heathrow Airport Terminus and back. Walking to Windsor and Eton was a piece of cake as the distance was not so great, which allowed me lots of time to explore the area. Mind you, I did get home quite late on some evenings which used to lead to a good telling off from my mum and dad, and I still got the belt.

On most of these adventures, I was always on my own and never got into any trouble. The majority of the time I was just sightseeing although I spent many hours watching people whether they were working on building sites, loading and unloading vans and trucks or people just working. By watching people in their every day works, you have a tendency to learn quite a bit and pick up a few tricks of the trade.

During the early part of living at 56 Doddsfield Road, it came as a bit of a surprise to the whole family when we were all told that we had to tighten up our belts as Mother was expecting another baby. Sandra was told that she was to leave school and to look for a job to help support the family and I was told that I had to go and get a paper round.

Much to my surprise, I found an early morning paper round job with the local Post Office/Newsagents in Farnham Royal. The pay was quite good considering wages in the late 1950s. I was to be paid twelve shillings and sixpence (12'6d) for delivering papers seven mornings a week. In today's money that would be sixty-two and a half new pennies or half a Euro. The only downside I had with this paper round was the 6:00am start. Once I had been shown the paper round route that I was going to service, I soon got down to doing the job. The course I was given was Blackpond Lane. A road that was lined with many old houses with large gardens. Many of the houses were set well back from the road with large spaces in-between. It was an interesting route, and I made many friends with the people that I delivered too. I used to get tips, oranges and apples; even cakes on some occasions. If it was not raining or snowing, some of the residents used to come and wait for me at their gate. From the wages that I used to receive every Sunday morning, I had to give my mother ten shillings and kept the remaining two shillings and sixpence for myself. I always felt rich on a Sunday morning.

In early November my mother was rushed to the Canadian Red Cross Hospital in Taplow where she gave birth to my fourth sister Angela on 10 November 1958. I now had five brothers and four sisters.

Although I did not spend too much time at William Penn, I always kept up with my school work as I still had ideas of attending college and later on going to University. I still read all the books I could get hold off. I had already read the entire collection of Biggles along with all the James Bonds books that were out at that time, and hundreds of Westerns. I spent many hours at the local library where I mainly concentrated on history and geography books which I used to book out and take home. Along with my maths including geometry and algebra, I was doing quite well although my end of year school report showed otherwise. Luckily for me, a new school was just about to open on the Britwell Estate called 'Warrenfield Fully Comprehensive School for Boys and Girls'. Somehow I managed to get a transfer to this school for my last scholastic year. Unknown to me at the time, Mr Merchant would take over as the Headmaster, and my old maths teacher had also transferred to the school.

Over the past few years, I had watched the building of the new school taking place in what used to be greenbelt farmland and always wondered what kind of school it would be. I was not disappointed when I went through the doors for the first time dressed in my brand new school uniform. The school was ultra-modern, and everything was new from top to bottom. Classrooms were all well designed as were the science labs, woodwork and metal craft rooms along with a large kitchen area designed for cookery lessons. There were also special places for art and pottery along with a place for music lessons. Outside there was a school garden for the growing of fruit and vegetables and the sports field was designed to cater for all your sporting needs.

I do not remember the name of the class I was put in, but I do know that it was the top level in the school at the time. It was also the first class where I encountered girls that I noticed in the same age group as myself. As this was the first day that the school was to operate as a school, everything was a bit of a shambles. Many pupils were to meet for the very first time and moving from classroom to classroom was a bit of a problem. Being in the senior class in the school resulted in many of us seniors being appointed as school prefects, with me being one of the ones selected. This led to a significant change in my outlook on life. I was now in a position of responsibility and to be fair, I think it went to my head. For the first time in my life people were looking up to me, and I felt important.

This brought about a change in my attitude to schoolwork and to playing truant. In fact, I stopped playing truant. I started to shine in my school work and also in the eyes of most of the school teachers.

For the first time, I was becoming popular with both the boys and girls who used to come to me for help with their schoolwork. As I have mentioned before, I was never actually female orientated while at school; well, how could you blame me, I had four sisters, but that all started to change. First, there was the art teacher; she must have been in her mid-twenties, tall, shapely with short dark hair, who always dressed in the latest fashions including a miniskirt. She always gave me a lot of attention, but I am sorry to say only in the classroom and while doing painting or drawing which she always encouraged me in, with the result that I was quite a good artist in my younger days. Yes, I did fantasise over her, which was quite normal for a boy of my age. There was also another girl that I used to fantasise over, she was the same age as me and a bit shorter, but there any similarities stopped. She was an absolute stunner, apart from being beautiful she had short dark hair, the most beautiful eyes and a figure to die for. Her name was Barbara Townsend, a name that I will never forget. As her name was Barbara, yes you have guessed it, I used to call her Basha, and she used to love it. Apart from my nickname of Basha, she also had the nickname of 'Beetle'. I was never romantically involved with her as she had many boyfriends but we were good friends.

Once I had settled down at this school, I got very engrossed in all subject and started to shine in my school work. Possibly to such an extent, that my old maths teacher from William Penn wrote me a glowing report stating that he had never seen a pupil make such a big leap in learning in such a short time. With this came a lot of interest from my teacher in what kind of future I could see myself in once I had left school at the end of the term. They all said that I should apply to go to the Slough College of Further Education and then apply to go to university. I was elated by all this support from my teachers and one day I mentioned to my mother that I would like to go to college and then go onto university. This led to a significant argument that lasted for many weeks where she kept telling me that she could not afford to send me to college or university and that I had to get a job as soon as possible to help support the family. I finally gave up my dreams of going to university but still kept up with my schooling.

As my fifteenth birthday was coming up, I used to spend a lot of time with my friends either going to the pictures or to see live pop shows and even going to the local dances and meeting up with the girls. I suppose I was a typical teenager of the time and moving into the period of 'Mods and Rocker', 'Rock and Roll' and shuffleboards.

I was now at that age where boys are known to start to rebel against everything and nothing, and I was no exception. As I have mentioned my father was quite a strict disciplinarian and keeping a family of four girls and six boys in line was no easy feat. On one occasion, I must have done something which was wrong in my father's eyes. He grabbed me and took me into the kitchen and closed the door to give me a good old belting. As he started to beat me, I thought to myself, this was not right, so I turned around and faced him and at the same time I punched him. I am sure you all can imagine the screams and shouting that took place, causing my mother to rush in and stand between us until things had calmed down and I was sent to my bedroom. I was not proud of hitting my father and was in deep anguish for some time, but the result was that my dad never hit me again and to some degree, we both started showing a different type of respect towards each other. Discipline was still practised with prevalence in the house, and my father was probably closer to me than ever before to such an extent that we started going out together by ourselves to places such as the cinema and even to church.

On occasions when not out with friends and having nothing better to do, I used to sit on a bench by the small table by our front door with family members and play cards or just having a general chat while watching the world go by. One day while sitting there, a fairly tall and attractive blonde girl walked pass while walking her dog and somebody made a comment which she heard. What the comment was, I have no idea, but she turned around and said something before she turned around and carried on walking her dog. I had never seen her before, but over the next few weeks, she used to walk the dog past the house every day at around the same time.

I started to look forward to seeing her every day and was also trying to build up the courage to talk to her. My brothers and sisters had noticed my attention to her when she walked by and started badgering me to speak to her knowing that I was very shy of talking to girls. Finally, I got up the courage to stop her by the table and asked her what the dog's name was. She replied, "Beauty." Then I asked her what kind of dog it was, and she told me it was a Columbus Spaniel. She told me I could stroke the dog if I wanted to and that led to a short conversation and I found out her name was Joan. After a short while she had to go, and as I watched her go, I knew I had fallen head over heels in love with her even if I never knew what love was.

Chapter 5
GROWING UP

When I reflect back on my family life, I have always considered it to be quite normal and fairly common to all the other families that we were surrounded by, but looking back on life now, I have a tendency to say no, it was not that normal.

Large families were quite common in the early twenty century up until the start of WW2, but when it ended in 1945, people's attitudes changed which was entirely understandable. The war took its toll on the lives of many thousands, along with the casualties that were maimed and injured. Those returning from around the world's conflict zones, along with our home victims, required constant attention. There was a brief boom in the birth rates to start with, but this slowly began to decrease as people started to come to terms with the destruction of their surrounding areas. Thousands of people were homeless and at the same time many refugees from war-stricken countries were also taking up residence in the UK. There was a large-scale shortage in accommodation to such an extent that old military bases that were no longer required were repurposed to accommodate the many thousands of homeless persons.

At the same time, food rationing was to remain for quite a few years after the war. It was not the time to start big families, and very few could afford it.

One of the good things about being a member of a big family is that you always had your brothers and sisters around you and thus little time to feel bored. With my father constantly being away at work to the late hours of the evening and mother spending her time cooking and making dresses for the girls, providing she was not home decorating, it left plenty of time for us kids to get into all sort of trouble. It was quite normal for the boys to gang up on the girls be it in pillow fights, hair pulling or even checking what they were wearing under their skirts, to the mundane jobs of nappy changing and feeding the youngest brother or sister, to rocking the cradle or pram to get them to sleep. We also had our daily chores like trying to keep our bedrooms clean and tidy, and that was a big headache in itself. As we got older, the household chores got bigger. All my brothers and sister knew how to make a cup of tea from a very young age and had a good inkling on cooking. Ironing and mending our clothes was quite common especially the ironing bit which was quite comfortable with the introduction of the electric, regulated iron. When I first started ironing, you had to put the iron on the gas stove to heat it up while covering the item that you were about to iron with a wet cloth to stop it from getting dirty from the soot on the iron sole plate.

My father spent most of his time working, be it in his full-time job or his part-time job. He used to work as many hours as possible which included a lot of overtime. When not at work he would spend time relaxing in the garden growing his vegetables or doing woodwork and making furniture or other bits and pieces for around the house. He also spent many hours playing with us kids, be it piggyback rides to rumbling on the ground with us kids on top of him, to playing card games. For complete relaxation, he would go to church or to his Polish Club and meet up with old Polish friends.

On my mother's side, it was completely different. She had very little time to relax as in her first twenty years of married life, she was either pregnant or raising a young family. As I have mentioned, times were very hard, and money was a rare commodity. Apart from having to find the means and ways to feed and dress the entire family, she also had to cope with looking after the family health. Health issues were very common in the forties to the early sixties mainly due to the influx of immigration from the four corner of the world. Many new diseases were being discovered along with the more common ones like measles, chickenpox, whooping cough and scarlet fever. It was very seldom that the term 'cancer' cropped up, although pneumonia was quite a common, deadly disease. Colds and flu were still as prevalent then as they are today. Yes, all my brothers and sisters including myself were not immune to catching these common ailments.

Fleas or head lice, as known today, were a very common ailment. It was so common that the school nurse used to come around to check our hair for fleas every week at school. If she found any, the affected students were sent straight home and not allowed to return until they were clear.

My mother spent many hours with us kids, combing out fleas with her metal comb onto a sheet of newspaper where we would have to squash the live insects with our fingernails.

Raising a large family also brought my mother strain and stress with the result that she suffered from asthma attacks, some so severe that she used to end up in the hospital. On occasions, she used to take a break away from us kids and get away to Scotland or the Isle of Wight for a bit of rest and recuperation.

As us kids grew older, we used to take away some of the stress from our mother by carrying out some additional household chores, thus allowing mum to indulge in one of her true passions in life, which was reading. I am sure that I inherited my passion for reading from her; we also shared the same interest in books. One of her main passions in reading was anything to do with the occult and spiritualism. It's possible that she took it to the extreme as later she used to get caught up in séances and the Ouija board. Did she ever make contact with the other side? I will let you decide on that, but things did change in my life. I have reproduced in this book a letter that I penned a few years ago that may be out of time but which I think is relevant at the date of writing.

My story of the strange goings-on at 56, Doddsfield Road, during my younger days

Now that I am relaxed and fully into the "retirement" mode of living, I finally have some time to reflect on some of the more interesting parts of my life that many of my brothers, sisters, nieces, and nephew might find of interest. The following is an accurate account of events that happened in my younger days while living at 56, Doddsfield Road. (It was renumbered 72 at a later stage.)

As my brothers and sisters will recall, living at 56 was a big highlight in all our lives. Mum, Dad, six brothers and four sisters plus Trixie, the dog. A couple of budgies, not sure if we had any cats around at the time, but we did have a hedgehog in the garden, and of course, two unwanted strangers which many, if not all in the house, were unaware of at the time. Yes. The house was fully occupied.

My story of events started when I was about fourteen or fifteen years old. At that time I would consider myself an average lad with all the attributes of a teenager of the late fifties and early sixties. Except for one thing, I used to be scared shitless when I was alone in the corridor between the kitchen door and the top of the stairs, more so at night when the lights were off. To say I was scared was no exaggeration and of what, you may ask? At the time I had no idea. In the evenings when we all used to congregate in the sitting room watching television, I used to make up an excuse for someone to go upstairs with me so that I did not have to walk in the dark corridor by myself. Even at the age of eighteen, I was still going through this dread of being alone in the dark, so much so that I used to take Angela up to bed and she was only a few years old at that time. How bad did it get? Well, if I had to venture into the corridor by myself in the dark, I used to make a dash for the kitchen light switch to turn on the light before switching on the hall and upstairs lights. The point I am trying to make here is that it was further for me to go to turn on the kitchen light than to switch on the corridor light switch, but for some unknown reason, I hated going past the kitchen door in the dark. Throughout these times I don't think I ever mentioned this to anybody. If I had, all my brothers and sisters would have been calling me all the names under the sun. They would have had a field day. Thankfully at eighteen I joined the Army and got away from that house, but the story still carries on.

In my early days in the military and while carrying out my recruit training, I still went home for the weekends and the atmosphere in the house was still the same; I still could not stand being in the corridor in the dark. I was always glad to leave the house. In early 1963, having completed my recruits training, I was posted to Malta. A few years of sheer bliss. After about eighteen months in Malta, North Africa, and Cyprus, I thought it was time to go back home on leave. What a mistake. I never told anyone that I was coming home on leave as I thought I would surprise everyone, but I believe that I was the one who got the surprise. I still remember this as clear as daylight. I arrived at the house in the early hours of the morning, around two to two thirty; the house was fully dark as everyone was in bed. Knowing that the back door was never locked, I entered the house and went into the sitting room and was greeted by Trixie. The open fire embers were still glowing, so I put on some more coal or coke before settling down on the settee for the night and the big surprise for all in the morning when they got up. Yeah, tell me about the surprise. I was just dropping off to sleep when I was alarmed by somebody coming down the stairs. Not wanting to scare anybody for thinking that there was an intruder in the house, I shouted out, "It's only me, I'm here on leave from the army." Silence greeted me. I shouted out again and the silence persisted. I thought to myself that I must have imagined somebody coming down the stairs. So I settled back down again. A few minutes later I heard those heavy footsteps coming down the stairs, loud and clear. At the same time this fear came over me and the hairs on my neck were sticking out. I jumped up and yelled at the top of my voice, that it's only me on leave from the army. I switched on the corridor lights. Seeing nobody, I then proceeded to wake up the whole house. What a surprise. I'm sure my brothers and sisters will recall the event. Still I never told anyone what had woken me. It was still there, this unknown fear.

I experienced this strange fear in the house up to the mid-seventies when everything changed. Before going any further, I would like to remind my brothers and sisters of other strange happenings in the house, which I am sure they will all recall. Do you remember that mum used the dining room as a bedroom for quite some time especially when she was suffering from an asthma attack? Also on some occasions, she used to accuse Leonard and Ronnie of going into the room while she was asleep and placing a pillow over her head and attempting to suffocate her? She used to be quite adamant in these claims although both Leonard and Ronnie always denied this. These were outlandish claims, but knowing the facts behind these events now paints an entirely different picture.

It was not until the mid-seventies that I found out the reason behind the mysteries of 56, Doddsfield Road. Again, I remember the occasion quite well. I was sitting in the sitting room alone in the house with mum when I turned round to her and said, 'The atmosphere in the house has gone and that it feels quite normal now." To which she replied, "What do you mean?" I then told her about all my experiences and fears that I had in the corridor over the years. She was very surprised at this as this was completely out of the blue and she had no idea of my involvement in what she was about to tell me.

Apparently, mum had a couple of friends who were psychics and involved in the paranormal activity, who came round to the house one day. On entering the house, one of them said to mum, "You have a couple of spirits in the house." After some talk, these two psychics agreed with mum that they should hold a séance and try to make contact with these two spirits. They held a ritual, not in the house but twenty odd miles away in Reading where they made contact with the spirits, with the following results.

In 1939, dad was in the Polish Army, during what was called the 'September Campaign 39' when he was taken as a prisoner of war by the Russians along with some of his comrades and friends and placed in a POW camp. Before or during his escape from that camp, two of his friends were killed. These two men did not know that they had died and stuck with dad. It would appear that these two spirits, who could not communicate with dad, blamed my mother for stopping dad from speaking to them and consequently, on some occasions tried to suffocate mum, just to get rid of her so that dad would start talking to them again. It was only when they were both told that they had died that they left dad and the house alone.

For my part, I never saw them, but I did feel their presence, and it's an experience that I will never forget.

That's it. Maybe next time I will tell you the story of my involvement in a manhunt for a murderer who cut his girlfriend's head off with a machete in the jungles of British Honduras and how I slept on somebody's grave.

The above is all correct and written as I remember it.

Leon Zawadzki.

The above is not the only ghostly story to come out of Doddsfield Road. My mother told me on one occasion that while her stepbrother, my Uncle Ian, was down from Scotland on a short break, he had a strange encounter. My uncle Ian used to like his beer and he was always betting on horses. So on this particular Saturday, he had gone down to the local bookies to place a bet on a few races and then he went to the local Ex Servicemen's Club to have a few pints of beer before making his way back home. My mother and other members of the family were sitting in the living room and heard him come in through the front door and go upstairs to his bedroom. A few minutes later they all heard my uncle having a raging row, a row that lasted around twenty minutes on the subject of horses, races, and jockeys. The row got so heated that my mother and the rest went to the bottom of the stairs for a closer eavesdrop, only to find my uncle charging down the stairs as white as a sheet and falling into their arms. Once they had calmed him down, they asked him who he had been arguing with. He replied, "With Dad." It was this realisation which resulted in him flying down the stairs. His father had been dead for over two years. Was it the drink or did he indeed see his dad – my granddad?

By all accounts, the house at Doddsfield Road holds quite a few unexplained mysteries, and my mother used to play on it, to such an extent that it was not long before she earned the nickname 'the old witch' by close members of the family. No wonder, as she did scare some of them, and I am not just talking about the children. She would often tell us that she could see people standing behind us.

So just where is the normality in our family?

My sister Sandra started work in a food canning factory and decided to become a vegetarian after having seen the way stewed steak was cooked and canned. She also started taking up with boyfriends and she liked motorbikes. The first boyfriend she had was a MOD, (a term used for a moderate person) who came along with his Lambretta. He was a tall, lanky, well-dressed lad who was not very well loved by any of my brothers and sisters. I didn't like him either. One day, Annetta came up with the perfect solution to separate them when they were both sitting in the living room. She asked them both if they would like a cup of tea. Sandra said no, and he said yes. Annetta then proceeded to the kitchen to make him a cup of tea, but instead of pouring it into a cup, she poured it into his crash helmet which he had placed on the sideboard in the corridor. He was too engrossed with Sandra to remember his cup of tea, and it was completely forgotten.

The light was not on in the corridor when he was leaving; he just grabbed his helmet and walked out of the front door before putting it on. It was quite messy, and his language was quite loud over our laughter when he stated that he would never come back. He kept his word and Sandra was not very happy.

It was during the late summer of 1959 that I had my first real encounter with Joan and her dog, Beauty. We were both still at school although my days of schooling were fast approaching the final days. Joan went to a public girls' school and always looked stunning in her school uniform. On our first true date, I asked her to go to the pictures with me in Slough which was quite a headache in itself. I never had any money and apart from my school uniform, I never had any decent clothes. On top of that, I had still never shaved and had lots of bum fluff on my chin. So the only solution I had was to grab my father's cut-throat razor and to have my first ever shave. I had seen my dad doing it so many times and he always made it look so easy. Luckily for me it was relatively easy, and I did not suffer any cuts. I felt I had done a good job and felt quite proud of myself. My next task was to grab hold of my father's best shirt, which was a gold satin shirt that he only used on special occasions. I made sure that I had given it a good ironing along with my drainpipe jeans. I even polished my black shoes. My final task was to see if I could scrounge some money from my mother. I managed to get some money and can tell you that it was far less than ten shillings, maybe around five? In my eyes, I looked good for my first date. As dates go, it was great although we never even held hands on that occasion.

Although I was a very shy lad, somehow or other we just got on, and our relationship just seemed to grow and grow. Initially, we just used to go out walking together, accompanied by her dog. It was not long before she took me to her home and introduced me to her mother and father, who both accepted me into their home and even allowed me to go into Joan's bedroom. Whatever people may think, just forget it, it never happened. We just used to talk and listen to her one and only record, which was Pat Boone's 'Love Letters in the Sand'.

As our relationship grew, she became a regular visitor to our house and was accepted by all my brothers and sister as well as my mum and dad. Joan was my first girlfriend, and at the time I was deeply in love with her. It must have been noticeable as my mother was always telling me not to get her pregnant because if I did, I would be thrown out of the house. When I look back on my relationship with Joan, I always come to the conclusion that I must have been an idiot. I'm sure people would not believe me if I told them that it took me the best part of four months before I plucked up the courage to kiss her for the first time. I still remember that first kiss like it was yesterday. I was walking her back home from my house in the late evening down a short dark alley, holding her hand, when we both just stopped and kissed. As my lips touched her lips, it was like getting an electric shock. I don't think we spoke for a good few minutes after that as we were both in a daze.

At the age of fifteen, my days at school ended and I was quickly tasked with finding a job. An apprenticeship would have been the ideal but the pay was only around ten shillings a week, and my mum and dad were desperate in trying to get additional monies into the household. So I found a job in a company known as Cooper's Mechanical Joints, which specialised in the manufacture of gaskets.

I well remember my first day at work, turning up dressed in my old school uniform of grey flannel trousers and my brown school jacket and tie. I was quite smart, in fact too smart for the job that I was about to undertake which involved moving gasket parts from one location to another. During my first day at work, I was also to learn that many of the workers started to think of me as a snob. This assumption about me was to remain throughout the years, although I do not consider myself such. Initially, I figured it was due to my dress when I first turned up and then learned it was from the sound of my voice and the way I spoke. I know as a youngster that I had a stutter which at times I found quite embarrassing; this used to hold me in check and I used to spend a lot of time thinking before I spoke. I had no real accent and people found it difficult in trying to pinpoint as to where I came from. This is quite understandable with the Polish/Scottish connection. Throw in the Dutch connection, and maybe the London accent plus maybe a few other UK connections and you will understand where I am coming from. I would also like to mention that I was never one for using swear words in my everyday conversations although I could swear along with the best when required. I was always taught to be polite when speaking and always put this into practice. So I do now understand where the snobbish connection comes into my life.

As a first job, working at Cooper's was an eye-opener. For the first time, I was involved to some degree with real working class people from all over the world. I met many Poles who knew my father and with my Polish name they had a tendency to take me under their wings. Apart from telling me their wartime experiences, they also told me what their everyday lives were like since settling in the UK. They also taught me how to use the 50-tonne press machines and how to put gaskets together. It was not long before I was operating my own press machine and exceeding the speeds of many experienced operators. To top it all, I was earning around three pounds ten shillings a week. My mother allowed me to keep the ten shilling and the rest went into the house kitty.

I was now rich, with ten shillings a week. I could now take Joan out and buy her some chocolates or take her to a show at the Embassy in Slough or even to the local dance hall. I even had money to accompany her to the Cruft's Dog Show in Earls Court along with Beauty who was being put on show. Now that was an event that I will remember. Being a Columbus Spaniel, Beauty was a big heavy dog that used to slobber everywhere. He was also very powerful and quite a handful. To get him from Slough to Earls Court meant that we had to take him on the Local Bus Service, and bus drivers and conductors were not very keen to allow a big dog like Beauty on board. Somehow we managed to persuade them to let us board their buses on the understanding that we went on the upstairs deck and remained at the rear of the bus. Getting Beauty upstairs was a headache in itself but well worth it. On arrival at the dog show venue, we had to book him in and then it was a case of grooming him which took a few hours before Joan was called to show him off in the ring with all the other dogs in the same class. He did not win, but we were both delighted with the reception that he had. We then spent a good few hours going around all the other dog exhibits and even had time for a soft drink and some hot dogs before making our way home. The hot dogs could not have been very good as Joan was sick on the bus on our return trip. We returned home very late in the evening, and I do remember we were both exhausted.

My relationship with Joan was good, but due to my shyness even after six months, I had still only kissed her. I know that she wanted to go further as she often asked me if I had ever given a girl a French kiss or if I knew what it was. The answer was always no. She also talked about love bites and mentioned that one of her friends at school showed her, her love bites on the top of her inside leg. She used to work me up, and in addition, she would sometimes read extracts from books like Lady Chatterley's Lovers, but my shyness always used to get the better of me. I was just too scared to touch her. I never even got around to touching or fondling her breasts in all the time I knew her.

After having gone out with Joan for around nine months she left school and took an office job in the same factory that I worked in, Cooper's Mechanical Joints. I was not very pleased as on occasions she had to leave her office and walk around the factory floor delivering papers or wage packets. When that happened, all the men would let out wolf whistles and make derogatory remarks. It became even worse when they found out that she was my girlfriend.

After a short time, I could no longer put up with her working there so I gave her the option of seeking another place of work or that I would quit my job there. She wanted to stay, so I handed in my notice and left. After I had left our relationship started to break down and she found another boyfriend at work, resulting in my first ever break up.

As the family moved into the dawning sixties with the thundering Rock and Roll music beating out from all doors and windows, my mother had given up on having any more children and decided to take her first part-time job in almost twenty odd years. The job she took was working part-time at Weston Biscuit Company on the Slough Trading Estate. She worked from 6:00 pm to 10:00 pm Monday to Friday. And that's where the problems started. We never owned a car at the time and the bus service to her place of work was somewhat erratic, to say the least. The distance from our front door to the factory was around two miles or a half hours walk, but my mother was not renowned for walking at the best of times. Her solution for this was that she would ride my sister's bike halfway to the factory with either me or one of my older brothers or sisters running alongside her until she had got to a distance where she was comfortable to walk the remaining way. She would then hand over the bike to me or whoever to ride it back home. After work, she used to get a lift with one of her workmates, thank heavens. Apart from the fact that we used to get knackered and out of breath running alongside her and then having to cycle uphill on the return journey home, it also played havoc with our free time.

With my mother going to work, significant changes were being made at home as both mum and dad were out working till late evening and very seldom seen during the week. Annetta took over the reins of running the house, looking after my younger brothers and sisters as well as taking over the preparation of the evening meals. Nobody would interfere with Annetta or even argue with her as she had one hell of a temper if she got upset. Sandra used to come home from work at around 6:00 pm only to rush upstairs to get changed before rushing off to meet with her latest boyfriend. In my case, I also got home from work at around six to quickly scoff down any food I could find before going out with my mates. Very seldom did I get changed as I never had anything to change into unless I was going out with Joan, which meant I had to borrow my dad's shirt yet again.

One of the good things about my mother working at Weston was that every week they would have staff sales of all their products that never passed their set benchmarks. Mainly misshapen or broken biscuits not fit for general sales. This resulted in my mother bringing home many Wagon Wheels and chocolate covered marshmallows which at the time was one of the most famous biscuits on the open market. Any chocolate products were a big treat for us; now it became a weekly treat that we all looked forward to.

With my father still working all the hours possible along with me, my sister and now mum working, money started coming into the house with the result that we could now afford to get our first family car. A beautiful two-toned green Renault Frigate with the registration number NDM 143. A number plate that we could never forget as my mother always referred to it as "No Damn Money 143". This resulted in the start of my love affairs with cars. Getting our first family car also brought with it a load of problems. The only person in the household with a driving license was my father, but he had not driven a car or a vehicle in over sixteen years, so going out with him was an experience that I would not wish on anybody. My mother could not stand to be in the car if he was trying to drive which resulted in the car standing idle outside our front door for weeks apart from being cleaned. This resulted in my mother taking up driving lessons with a male colleague from her work as at the time she could not afford to take up driving lessons with a driving school.

This triggered the beginning of a breakdown in the relationship between my mother and father as he began to get jealous seeing my mum paying attention and spending more time with this chap who went by the name of Phil. It was not long before my mum learned to drive the car and quite often she would ask me to jump into the car with her and she would take me for a ride around Burnham Beeches or even into Slough or Maidenhead. She also taught me the ins and outs of driving and the Highway Code. She had still not taken a driving test and only held a provisional license, but she felt comfortable when I was in the car with her even if she was only using me as an excuse just in case she was stopped.

The tension between my mother and father was still rising as she still went out with her male colleague on driving lessons, a tension that I must have escalated when I came home one evening and told them that I had given up my job at Cooper's Mechanical Joints. As the anger in the house was rising, my father agreed with my mother that she should take a week's holiday with a drive up to Scotland with Phil, my mum's work colleague and driving instructor and that I should also go as company.

At the time, Phil was seen just as a friend of my mother. He appeared to be quite a decent married man. In fact, he often came round to the house with his wife, and she got on well with everyone including my dad. Maybe it was because she always brought sweets and biscuits when she visited. Was there anything going on between my mother and Phil? As far as we were concerned, they were just friends.

The trip to Scotland was quite impressive for me as I had a few pounds in my pocket. I also got the opportunity to drive the car with my mother in the backseat. She was not very happy with me driving, but Phil told her to give me a chance to do some real driving. Maybe she was worried because she knew that I had no driving license what so ever. After we had visited my Granddad and family in Dundee, we drove to St Andrews to visit my Aunty Ester and Uncle Bill.

At the time my Uncle Bill was the Regimental Sergeant Major of The Gordon Highlanders stationed in St Andrews and it was only fitting that he should take me on a tour of his barracks. He also signed out a rifle from the arms kote along with some live ammunition and took me to the firing ranges behind the camp and proceeded in giving me my first weapon instructions on how to aim and fire a rifle. By all accounts, I did quite well, and he was very surprised with my shooting ability. I am sure that it was at this time that I started to get a hankering to join the army. I think I upset my uncle once and that was when I referred to his kilt as a skirt.

I think I also embarrassed my mother while sitting around the table having a meal with them when I blurted out how nice the margarine tasted, only to be told it was butter. Well, how was I to know? I was only sixteen and had never had butter before in my life. Says a lot about the 'Echo and Stork' margarine of the times.

Yes, that trip to Scotland was an eye-opener, and I learned a lot.

On returning home, I started looking for a new job and surprise, surprise! I found a job at the Weston Biscuit Company where my mother worked part-time. I began working in the biscuit department that made the Wagon Wheels and marshmallows on a two-shift system. The department consisted of what is best described as three conveyor belted machines approximately two hundred feet long. One was used for the production of Wagon Wheels and two for the manufacturing of Chocolate or Coconut Covered Marshmallows. My primary job initially was to keep the women supplied with the correct biscuits at the head of the conveyor belts along with keeping hoppers supplied with desiccated coconut flakes and the flow of the marshmallow and chocolate. After a short time, I was given the responsibility of looking after one of the complete lines of production which meant that I had control of the machine speeds and the women who worked on the machine from start to finish. It was entirely reasonable for the men who were controlling the production lines to swap over machines from time to time so that we all knew how to operate the other machines and the different products.

I was working shifts from 6:00 am to 2:00 pm and 2:00 pm to 10:00 pm from Monday to Friday which alternated every week. This meant that every other week I was working when the part-time workers came in for their evening shift from 6:00 pm to 10:00 pm, including my mother. I think she hated working on my line as every time she was working on it, I used to turn up the speed and had to keep telling her to keep up. I got my own back on her for all the times she used to tell me to go and wash or dry the dishes or all the other housework that I had to do. Who says revenge is not sweet?

Working at Weston's was quite an eye opener especially the bit about having the women under your control. But after a relatively short period, the job became very mundane and the getting up early in the morning for the early shift started to become a problem especially if I had been out or had a few drinks the previous evening. I must have been there about a year when I decided that I had had enough and started looking for a new job.

Within a short period, I found employment with a paint factory called Blundell's & Spence where I trained to become a colour matcher. It was a specialist job that required a natural inclination, and although colour matching may sound and look easy, you had to have excellent eyesight. Lucky for me I did have good vision, and it was not long before I learned to look for the black in a yellow, or a red in a green along with all the other combinations. The primary job was to match up small quantities of paint to an exact match to a colour, for example matching paint for a car that had scratch marks or was involved in some other mishap to a standard that you could not see the difference between the old and the new paint once it is applied. A point to remember is that the colour of a car changes over time with simple things like fading due to weather conditions and age.

I found the job challenging at first, but once again after some time it became boring and did not present any new challenges. It became mundane, and I could see no future in the job. I needed to find something more challenging.

Meanwhile, things at home were changing. My sister Sandra changed her job and started working at the famous Mars Factory and met her latest boyfriend called Fred who had a decent motorbike and to whom she was to get married a few years later. With my sister working at Mars, life got even better as she was entitled to buy Mars Bars and all the other products at staff sales. Life was good, we now had Mars Bars and Wagon Wheels and the chocolate started coming out of our ears, but for all that, we all remained skinny in the family.

Fred was a great guy who did his National Service in the 'Royal Green Jackets' (RGJ) and he was also a great motorbike addict. We clicked quite well, and it was not long before he started taking me out on his motorcycle and giving me driving lessons. I well remember on one occasion sitting in the driving seat of his bike, holding onto the motorcycle's handlebars with him stretched across me; his hands also on the handlebars while I was accelerating down the roads around Burnham Beeches. It must have been quite a sight, and thankfully there were no police around at the time. He also spoke about his time while serving in the army, which used to get me thinking.

Apart from motorbikes, I used to enjoy cars, and on occasions, I would take my dad's car when he was at work, and my mother was not around. On one occasion when I had taken it along with some mates, I was driving along Slough High Street and seeing that there was nothing of interest going on, I decided to stop before turning the car around. I pulled up just past a No Entry signed street and then proceeded to reverse into the road to turn the vehicle around. I then pulled back onto the High Street to move forward in the opposite direction. Within seconds a police car overtook me and indicated for me to stop. My mates and I were shitting ourselves as two policemen started walking towards us. On reaching us, the policeman nearest to me said that they had just watched me turn the car around by entering a No Entry Street which was illegal and as 'This is Slough Police Courtesy Week' they would like to bring it to my attention. They then wished us a pleasant evening and to drive carefully before turning around and walking away. There must have been a great sigh of relief from all of us in the car as nobody had a driving license and no car insurance would have covered us. Somehow my mother found out about this, and after a good telling off for taking the car, we both agreed that I should buy a car for myself and get a license.

Getting a car was not that easy as money was still a big problem and the cars that I liked were expensive. My mate had just bought a V8 Pilot, and that cost him £25. It was a big car, but the only thing it had going for it was that it would run on paint thinners from Blundell's & Spence. I looked at and went out in an SS Jaguar, but the owner wanted £40 for it which was way out of my league.

Again Triumph TR2 and 3's were around the £30 mark so, in the end, I settled for an old Morris 8. It cost me £20. What fun I had with that car! I learned the engine and mechanics ins and outs and spent many hours searching in local scrap yards for spare parts. I took up driving lessons with Haynes School of Motoring, and although I failed my first driving test, I still drove that car all over the place, much to the anguish of my mother.

I spent most of my spare time with my mates, and although we were friends with a few girls, I was still very shy and did not get involved with them. If it was not for the cars and motorbikes, it was down to the local snooker hall. As for drinking, neither my mates nor I really got into it; even smoking was not really on our hit list. On one occasion I along with two mates decided to go to France for the weekend and what an adventure that turned out to be.

We all made our way to Dover by train and went to the seaport terminal to catch a ferry over to Calais. Initially, we were just going to explore Calais but somehow ended up at the railway station where we decided that we would go to Paris. We found a train that was heading to Paris and somehow ended up on it with no tickets. We had no idea how far or how long it would take to get to Paris as we thought it was only a short distance away and again we had no tickets. As time passed, the journey appeared to stretch into hours and then along came the train conductor who wanted to see our tickets; with the result that we had to pay for return tickets that took almost all the money that we had between us. Eventually, we arrived in Paris and took to the streets on a quest of exploration. We took to the sights and went to the Arc de Triomphe and the Tomb of the Unknown Soldier. We walked along the Champs Elysees and visited the Eiffel Tower. We also saw many places of interest along with the River Seine. Initially, we had enough money for a cheap hotel in Calais but with the cost of the train ticket, this was now out of the question. As night closed in, we made our way back to Paris Railway Station to wait for the first train back to Calais. We found a bench to park ourselves on and fell asleep only to be roughly woken by heavily armed Gendarme who told us to get out of the station. We moved outside where we found a café open and went in for a cup of tea. My mates had coffee. It was the most expensive cup of tea that I had ever had. It cost me ten shillings in French Francs or the best part of a day's pay at the time. The return journey was not remarkable as we spent most of it sleeping, but we were delighted to get home.

Reflecting back on the early years of 1960–1962, I suppose I was doing the usual things that a teenager would be doing, I still spent many hours reading, going out with my mates, being introduced to beer although I think I only got drunk once or twice. I was still scared of the dark and was still haunted by what I did not know at the time. And yes I was still shy, bashful and a virgin.

One of the biggest highlights of my life occurred during this period. It was an event that I will never forget. I, along with my mother and father and a few of my brothers and sister were sitting in the living room watching television when there was a knock on the front door. Annetta went and answered the door, and then came back into the room shouting, "There is an old man at the front door with two suitcases. I don't know what he said, but I think he is speaking Polish." My father got up to see who it was and then came staggering back with a shocked look all over his face and said it was his father.

As you can all imagine, pandemonium was let loose. My father had not seen his father in over twenty years and to find him on his doorstep without any warning was the biggest surprise of his life. It must also be made known to the reader that at that time, travel between Poland and England was not usually allowed. The next few weeks saw a lot of change and turmoil at 56, Doddsfield Road. My grandfather arrived with the clothes on his back and nothing else apart from the two suitcases which were filled with nothing but apples. This might sound strange but before he left Poland, he was told that we did not have apples in England. On his return to Poland, he took quite a few bananas as he had never even seen a banana in his life, let alone tasted one.

Apart from the joys of meeting my grandfather and learning more on the ins and outs of Poland, I also believe it was around this time that my mother first heard about my father having a wife in Poland. This was kept a secret from my brothers and sisters including me for many years but now gives me an insight into the rapid deterioration reflected in the relationship between my mother and father.

Chapter 6
THE BRITISH ARMY

With the ending of the WWII in 1945, the entire civilised world was still living in fear of one sort or another. It was thought by the military leaders and the politicians the world over that WWII was the war to end all wars, but that was not to be. The Malayan Emergency ran from 1948 to 1960, while the Korean War of 1950 to 1953 also took its toll on the lives of many members of Allied Countries. Apart from many minor conflicts all over the world, there was also the Cold War between the East and West that was to last from 1947 to 1991.

After the end of WWII, the British armed forces were severely reduced, but with the increasing tensions around the world the British Government came up with the idea to reintroduce National Service from 1 January 1949. Additional changes were made, stipulating that all healthy males between the ages of 17–21 would be subject to serve within the armed forces for two years apart from those employed in essential services. This practice was to remain in effect until the last call-up for service on 31 December 1960. The last National Servicemen formally left the Armed Forces in May 1963.

As I had just turned eighteen, I used to reflect on my past life and the direction that I wanted to pursue. I had to get away from my run of the mill existence as my mother always told me that if I did not change my habits, I would end up in jail. At the time there was a great call going out to join the 'New Regular Army', and this did appeal to me. I made some inquiries at a local Army Recruiting Display in Windsor and made arrangements to attend a formal interview and medical assessment in Reading. I participated in the interview and medical assessment at Brock Barracks in Reading on 7 September 1962. During my interview, I was supplied with lots of information on the different units and roles within the army including requirements to pass before being selected. At the time I was more inclined to join an infantry battalion and had seen a lot of promotional material for a regiment that was recruiting before being posted overseas to Malta. I was interested in this unit and was later recommended to serve in this unit in the Regular British Army. It was only when I returned home later in the day that I mentioned to my mother that I had gone for the interview with the intentions of joining the army. She was not amused and for some time did not believe what I had done. I had no further information and no clue as to whether I would be accepted. This led to a few in-house arguments resulting in my mother suffering a severe asthma attack a few weeks later and ending up in hospital.

On 15 October 1962, I received a telephone call and was told to be ready in one hour as an army Land Rover was being sent to my home to take me to Brock Barracks. I was also told to pack a case with my clothing and washing and shaving kit. All of a sudden I was in a complete quandary thinking of packing a suitcase – with what? I found a brown paper bag and put some bits and pieces in it, but apart from the clothing I was wearing, I had nothing. There was nobody in the house apart from my youngest sister Angela and my brother Marion. My mother was still in hospital while the rest of my brothers and sisters were at school and my dad and Sandra were both out at work. I tried to explain what was happening and explained that I might not be back home that night as I was off to join the army.

At Brock Barracks in Reading, I went through a more thorough interview and was again asked which regiment I wished to join in the Wessex Brigade. I stated that I would like to join 'The Duke of Edinburgh's Royal Regiment' (Berkshire & Wiltshire) and I was accepted. I was then formally sworn in with my allegiance to Queen and Country and given the Queen's shilling. I then signed my enlistment papers and the Official Secrets Acts and became a member of the British Armed Forces.

While at Brock Barracks, I also met some other lads enlisting and who were to become great friends over the coming years. Once all the swearing in had been completed and papers signed, we were all given a one-way rail ticket to Honiton in Devon, bundled into the back of an army lorry and whisked down to Reading Railway Station.

I think it was only when we had all gathered on the platform of Reading railway station, waiting for the train to take us to Honiton, that the realisation started to hit us.

We were all a bit dazed and at the time we could see no way out. On boarding the train carriage we all made ourselves comfortable and started to get to know each other while eating the food packages that we had been handed in Brock Barracks. Nobody knew where Honiton was or how long it would take to get there but the anticipation of what was to come could clearly be seen on everyone's faces and it was a bit scary.

We arrived in Honiton a few hours later and from first impressions it resembled a small town with one main road running through it. There was nobody there to meet us, so we had to ask for directions to Heathfield Army Camp. Lucky for us it was only a few miles down the road and we all had to walk. Again, lucky me, I only had a small paper carrier bag to carry, and I was not the only one. As we approached the camp all we could see were wooden huts which in all likelihood would be our homes for the coming months. It was not long before we entered the camp by the main gate and greeted by a lot of shouting. To this very day, I still can't remember what they were trying to say. Was it a greeting or what? Maybe they were welcoming us to the British Army?

We were stopped at what was to become known as the Guardroom, and our names were all taken before we were ushered into a large, barn-like, wooden building where we met other lads who had also just arrived from around the UK. After some time it was deemed by someone that everyone had arrived, and we were formed into three ranks totalling around forty odd recruits. We were then greeted by what we now know as the Regimental Sergeant Major (RSM) whose name I can't recall, by a lot of shouting before getting lined up and spaced out while all facing the same way, before being handed over to the Commanding Officer of the camp. After he had officially welcomed us to Heathfield Camp, we were all told that we would be referred to as 80 Platoon. He then preceded to hand us over to our Platoon Commander.

At this point, I would like to mention a few facts on the unit that I had joined. The Duke of Edinburgh's Royal Regiment (Berkshire & Wiltshire) was formed on 9 June 1959 with the amalgamation of the 'Royal Berkshire Regiment' (Princess Charlotte of Wales) and the 'Wiltshire Regiment' (Duke of Edinburgh's).

The Royal Hampshire Regiment, The Gloucestershire Regiment and the Devon & Dorset Regiment all formed 'The Wessex Brigade". Heathfield Camp was the main training camp for all recruits at this time for these regiments and was staffed by a mix of regimental soldiers.

Once the Platoon Commander had finished with his talk, we were all handed over to the Platoon Sergeant who divided us into four groups that were called sections. Each section was then assigned a Full Corporal and a Lance Corporal and from then on, should I say, the fun began? First, we were shown a room in a wooden hut that was to become our accommodation. This consisted of ten single metal beds, each with a bedside table and a six-foot metal locker. Within the room, there were also two large iron enclosed stoves for heating. Just outside our room was the bathroom and toilets later to be known as the ablutions. Now the fun was really about to start as we were doubled over first to the bedding stores to collect our mattresses, pillow, sheets and blankets, which was some distance from our hut and we had to carry everything back in one go. From the sidelines, it must have been hilarious to watch as bits and pieces were dropped and the struggle to pick the fallen item up from the ground ensued while at the same time being shouted and yelled at and told to move faster by the section corporals. Once our bedding was in our rooms, we were all rushed off to the Quartermasters stores to collect our clothing. Inside the stores we were confronted by at least half a dozen storekeepers and as we went past them they all yelled out, "Size!" If you did not know your size, they would make a quick appraisal of you and shove shirts, shoes, trousers, etc. into your hands.

Most of the items given to you were either too large or too small, but once we got back to our hut we managed to swap items around and in most cases everything worked out well. As the evening was fast approaching, we were all told to grab our knife, fork, and spoon (KFS), along with our issued metal mug and make our way to the cookhouse. For most of us, it was the first hot meal of the day and in some cases the first hot meal for days. It was an excellent introduction to army food although the tea tasted funny.

The first evening in our hut was spent getting to know the kit that we had just been issued with, and making friends with the other lads. Not such an easy job as I found it quite hard to understand some of the lads especially those who had been brought up in the farmlands of Devon or Dorset. Even the guys from Somerset were difficult to comprehend. A lot of talking had been done until late into the evening, and most of us were completely exhausted. Many of the lads were just starting to realise just what they had signed up to and were already missing their homes and families. On the contrary, I was overjoyed. I had my own bed and did not have to share it with anyone, and I also had my first pair of striped pyjamas. I went from never having a pair of pyjamas in my life to being the proud owner of two pairs. I slept well that first night in the army.

Our first night in bed did not last very long as at 05.30hrs or half-past five in the morning we were all woken up by a lot of screaming and shouting from our two corporals who went along the two rows of beds and started tipping them over while the occupants were still asleep. This was to become a recurring event that was to last for many weeks.

Over the coming weeks, we were taught discipline, drill and all the other aspects of becoming a soldier in the British Army. It was hard, and as the weeks went past, many of the lads who initially started out with us began to drop out, deemed unsuitable for military life and were discharged. In my case, I adapted to military life quite well and used to shine in weapon handling. I also proved to be an excellent shot on the 7.62 SLR, and the LMG along with the 9mm SMG. Apart from the military skills that I learned quite well, I also got the opportunity to improve my education and took my Army Certificate of Education Class 3 which was the educational qualification needed to rise to the rank of full corporal. Our field training was cut short due to the UK suffering from the most severe winter weather conditions that would not be surpassed over the next fifty odd years. This resulted in us going out rescuing sheep and cattle from the surrounding fields and helping the locals to keep roadways open. It would appear that the whole of the country had come to a standstill.

Throughout my time at Heathfield Camp I got to know the ins and outs of the other lads as one of the things that you have to learn about is bonding. Everyone had his reason for signing up to join the army, and in many cases there was no real choice. Many came from broken families. Quite a few had problems with the police and were given the choice of either joining the army, going to a Borstal Home or even ending up in jail. Again many could not get a civilian job due to their poor level of education. I was quite surprised at how many could not read or write.

There was a great variety of personalities, from the chap that could not stop dancing who got the nickname of Dancer to the chap that could not stop whistling. The latter knew most of the bird calls and as you can guess he was nicknamed Birdie. We also had a few who thought they were the toughest men alive and were always looking for a fight. Some were very timid while others would have made a good stand-in for Samson. We had the dirty ones who would not wash and even the ones that used to wet their beds, one even went as far as messing his bed and sleeping in it and not only once. On occasions such as this, we would secure him in his mattress and drop him, mattress and all into a bath filled with freezing water. On the whole, we all looked after each other and if something or someone was wanting, we would all sort it out as a group. We also had some who were definitely gay.

At no time was I shown any racism towards me due to my name but at times I did feel slightly uncomfortable mainly because of the way I spoke. I still had my stutter, but I was also seen and categorised as being a snob. I was never involved in any personal fights, but I would go in to help break up a fight. The only time that I suffered any problems was on a night when a few of my mates had gone out drinking and returned to the hut quite late and woke me and a few others up. I got a bit irritated and told them all where to go, at which they all pounced on me, stripped me naked and blackened my balls with boot polish. I was not amused at the time. They all apologised the following morning, and I do laugh at it now.

I did have a few problems with my surname, the main one being that nobody could spell or pronounce it. It also contributed toward my being a witness on payday along with always being last in line for my pay.

Yet it was not always about work and training. We had our sports which included football and boxing along with basketball and volleyball. For the first three weeks of recruits training, we were not allowed out of camp, but we did socialise in the NAAFI. We had a payday every week; my pay was around £6.00 per week and I felt quite rich. Once we were let out of camp in the evening, we used to go to the local pubs in Honiton where we all took to the local Scrumpy and the Devon cheese. Scrumpy or Devon Cider must be the best cider in the world. It was strong and it tasted so so good. It was also the cause of too many headaches. I also recall the occasion when the British Army was to replace the traditional BD or Battledress with a new smart uniform called No2 Dress which we were issued with before the majority of the British Army had even seen it. This was an occasion where a few mates and I got dressed up in our new uniform and made our way down to Exeter City to show it off. Not knowing Exeter or where to go, we found a dance hall and decided to go dancing. What an experience. There was us, all smart young soldiers dressed to the nines and there were the women. I'm sure there was no one under the age of fifty and at that time anyone over the age of thirty was considered old, if not ancient. But it was an experience as they did all the asking.

Once we had reached and passed our initial basic period of training we started having a free weekend, and most of the chaps, myself included, looked forward to the end of our last period of training on Friday. We would forget about the evening meal and dash to our accommodation, get changed into civilian clothing before rushing to the railway station in Honiton and getting a return ticket to our hometowns. I well remember the first time I returned home. I was greeted with open arms from all my family members and our dog Trixie just would not leave me alone. My mother had returned home from the hospital, and although she was still angry with me for joining the army while she was in the hospital, she fully understood why I had done it. She was a bit worried when I told her that when I had completed my training that I would be posted to my Regiment in Malta. I, along with my parents, brothers and sister had never heard of Malta before, and we had no idea of where in the world Malta was. It was only once I had done some research in the local library that I could explain and calm my mother's fears that Malta was a small island in the Mediterranean Sea at the bottom of the shoe of Italy and not in darkest Africa.

In January of 1963, I had passed my recruit training program and was transferred to the holding strength of the Depot's Headquarter Company. On my first parade with HQ Company, I along with other members of the company were lined up in three ranks and stood to attention in front of the company offices. Where we were greeted by the Company Sergeant Major (CSM) Warrant Officer 2nd Class (WOII) Collins. His first words to us were, "I'm looking for a smart, intelligent and happy looking chap to come and work in the company office." He then proceeded to walk down the ranks and stopped in front of everyone and carried out an inspection. When he stopped in front of me, he said "You look smart, intelligent and happy. What's your name?" To which I replied, "Private Zawadzki, Sir." He then shouted out at the top of his voice "What? Gore blimey, Fred." All on parade just burst out with laughter and my nickname of Fred was born. A nickname that is still in use today and will be with me until the day I die.

The days that I spent at the depot in Honiton will always be remembered with great affection as I made many friends there. Friends that left the depot to join their Regiments, many of whom I never met again although in some cases I have some knowledge of their army careers. I also found out why the tea tasted so bad. It used to be laced with bromide, a substance that controlled your blood pressure and stopped you from getting an erection.

I was informed that I would be leaving the UK to join my regiment in Malta on 26 February 1963 and was entitled to two weeks embarkation leave before going. I was also told that I was entitled to a free return rail ticket to anywhere in the UK. I opted to get a return ticket to Dundee in Scotland to visit my Daddy Wilson, Rita, my uncles and aunt. A journey that I made wearing my No2 Dress Uniform. I only spent a few days in Scotland and well remember taking my Aunty Isobil to the cinema in my uniform. I never saw her as an aunt as she was two years younger than me. I also recall losing my return railway ticket, so I had to go to the local Black Watch Barracks to get a replacement ticket. I then made my way back home to spend my remaining days with my family before making my last return journey back to my camp in Honiton prior to my flight to Malta, on 26 February 1963.

MALTA

On 26 February 1963, I along with a few mates were driven to Heathrow Airport where we embarked on a BEA flight to Luqa Airport in Malta. The aircraft was a four-engine prop Vickers Vanguard. The journey took approximately four and a half hours plus a refuelling stop in Nice, France. This was the first time that my mates and I had ever been on an aeroplane, and I suppose our heads were buzzing. It must be remembered that in the early sixties, air travel was still a significant novelty and very few youngsters of our age had ever flown before. I think that flying up in the clouds was like a dream coming true. In the early afternoon we landed at Luqa Airport in Malta which at that time consisted of one runway, an old dilapidated wooden hut as an airport terminal and a small airport control tower. We were met by members of our regiment and taken to St Patrick's Barracks in St Andrews. On arriving at the barracks, we were all taken to what was to be our accommodation for the next few weeks and told that we were to join 6 Platoon B Company, which was the battalions' continuation training platoon.

No sooner had I placed my suitcase on my bed, when there was a bit of a commotion as the CSM of B Company came charging in shouting out, "Where is Pte Zawadzki? Where is Pte Zawadzki?" Jumping to attention, I shouted out, "I am Pte Zawadzki, Sir." The CSM came up to me, grabbed my hand and started to shake my hand while at the same time speaking in Polish. I could understand parts of what he was saying and I know that he was a bit disappointed when I told him that my Polish was not so good. Everyone in the room was as surprised as I was at this greeting by the CSM. He was greeting me for being the first Pole to join the Regiment from recruit training. I learned this shortly after my first meeting with the CSM whose name was Tony Smelzer, who had joined the Royal Berkshire Regiment during WW2 after having been conscripted into the

German Army. It was also rumoured that he was awarded the Iron Cross II Class at some time during his service against the Allied Forces. I do know that he took part in the Italian Campaign with the 2nd Polish Army Division and was involved in the 'Battle of Mount Casino'. Over the next few years, we both shared a lot of his old memories between us and I do know that he looked out for me when required.

As I settled down into military life within my regiment, I started to notice the distrust, jealousy and the racism that was being shown by the officers, WOs, NCOs and the other ranks towards each other. I believe that most of the distrust happened when the Royal Berkshire Regiment and the Wiltshire Regiment were amalgamated in 1959 into the 1st Battalion 'The Duke of Edinburgh's Royal Regiment' (Berkshire & Wiltshire). Most of the Officers, along with all the Warrant Officers and Senior Non-Commissioned Officers as well as the majority of Junior Corporals and Lance Corporals were raised and served in either of these two units before the amalgamation and were still worried about their promotional aspects and their future career prospects. It should also be remembered that less than twenty years had passed since the end of WW2 and quite a few serving members had participated in that conflict. There was also the last group of National Servicemen still serving in the unit, many of whom could not wait for the day of their discharge to come so that they could hang up their boots. Racism could also be seen, mostly against non-white persons. Jealousy also started to be shown toward new recruits especially if they showed some sort of superior educational qualification as again, before the establishment of the New Regular British Army; education was not a priority for joining.

Initially, no racism was shown towards me, but that was to change in the years ahead. My biggest problem was that nobody could pronounce my name and that included the officers. In most cases, I was just called 'Z' or even 'Private Z' and then in some cases 'Fred Z'. I knew who I was, and so did everyone else.

After spending around six weeks in continuation training, I was considered a fully trained soldier and posted to 7 Platoon in C Company as a rifleman. My army life was about to start in earnest. The platoon was considered as being the hardest and possibly the best platoon in the battalion. The men were rough, hard and in some cases mentally insane. I would also go as far as saying that a few of them were in love with themselves and even bent, or as we used to say in those days, "faggots". Many could not read or write and at times when talking to them, it was like talking to a brick wall. The one thing we all had in common is that we all looked after each other. If anyone were to pick on a member of the platoon for whatever reason, they would have to deal with the consequences from the whole platoon as one. The real meaning of the Buddy Buddy System was indeed brought into focus which endures to this very day.

Everyone knew his place within the platoon/section and discipline was very strict. All Non-Commissioned Officer's (NCOs) were addressed by their ranks and familiarity was frowned upon. Even the senior private soldiers demanded a certain amount of respect, and you would know about it if you ever went over their heads.

It was not long before I got to learn the ins and outs of my colleagues and started making friends, many of who I remained friends with to this day. I soon settled down to the routine of everyday military life with the training program, regimental duties and the straightforward bull shite. Life was good, providing you knew your place.

St Patrick's Barracks was a purposely built barracks complex, constructed in 1938 to accommodate the ever-increasing military personnel allocated to Malta. It was also used as a hospital during WW2 and came under attack by the Axis Air Forces on a number of occasions. At times it was a bit eerie as many stories were told of the number of deaths that the building had witnessed over the years. There was also a small Military Cemetery just outside the Main Guard Room Gates. Although the barracks formed part of a larger Military complex, it was still quite a distance from the local civilian establishments.

In the 1960s Malta's population was just over 300,000. It was also a very religious country and to a certain extent dominated and controlled by the church. Censorship was rampant and it was a fact that if you were seen kissing a girl in the street, you could be arrested. English newspapers were censored and page 3 of The Sun was not allowed. Most, if not all decent girls, had to be home by nine o'clock in the evening. The average wage in Malta was around £4.00 per week and in most cases it was only the men who went to work while women stayed at home and looked after the house. My, how things have changed. For a person like myself, I found Malta to be fascinating. The island's history pre-dates Stonehenge and the Egyptian Pyramids by thousands of years and has been part of many dynasties through the ages. To me, it was like walking into the history books, and I still have that feeling today.

Most of my army mates had very little interest in the history of Malta; they were more interested in getting drunk and chatting up women. The first part was easy. Within the barracks, we had our NAAFI which was open until 10:00 pm each and every evening. There were also quite a few bars all over the island; the nearest one, 'Ma Blake's', was only about fifteen minutes' walk from the barracks and a very popular venue. The biggest problem associated with going out in the evening especially if you were living in barracks was that you had to dress up. You had to wear a long-sleeved shirt with collar and tie and were not allowed to wear jeans. You were also required to book out of barracks at the Guardroom and inspected by the duty Guard Commander. The problem for most of us in those days was that apart from owning our own military clothing, we had very little civilian clothing. Borrowing shirts, trousers, and shoes was a very common occurrence.

Once you had passed the scrutiny of the Guard Commander, you then made your way to Spinola which was the nearest place of any night entertainment. To get there, you walked two to three miles, got the local bus service that cost a 1d which ran every hour until the last bus at 10:00 pm or got the local horse-drawn carriage known as a 'Garry'.

The principal place of entertainment was Valletta, the capital city of Malta. I will not go into the details of Valletta but will mention that every evening between six and nine o'clock, it was like all the young eligible girls and boys in Malta would gather in the main street called Kingsway and walk up and down in big groups, shoulder to shoulder.

It used to be so crowded that it would take you the best part of half an hour to cover five hundred yards. By 9:00 pm, the street would become deserted as all the girls would have disappeared home. The only people remaining on the streets would in most cases be servicemen or shopkeepers locking up their establishments.

The only remaining place of entertainment in Valletta was the notorious Strait Street. A street that had established itself as a den of iniquity, a place of bars and prostitutes and which was frequented by servicemen from all over the world. It was the only place you would find a woman after 9:00 pm. As for finding a lovely, young lady? Forget it. I do not think I ever saw a pretty young woman down that street. I, along with many of my friends, used to go to Strait Street on regular occasions mainly for the cheap drinks and the everyday entertainment with jukeboxes, the local musical instrument players and small groups. On most evenings you could guarantee to see a fight or a big punch-up between units and the different services. As for the women, all they wanted was for you to buy them drinks with the promise of a dance. If you wanted to go further, it was going to cost you. In my case, I was still a very shy person when it came to women. It was entirely reasonable to spend many hours in the bars, slowly getting drunk while enjoying yourself before the dreaded return journey of trying to make it back to the barracks and getting changed and ready for First Parade. A return trip that typically meant walking around ten miles back to camp as there were no buses after ten in the evening. The chance of getting a lift from a passerby was extremely unlikely as you very seldom saw a car on the roads after ten in the evening. Mind you, in the sixties there were very few cars in Malta. To this very day, I still do not know how long it used to take me to walk from Strait Street in Valletta to St Patrick's Barracks in St Andrews. I was never late for First Parade although I may have had a terrible headache while on parade at the time.

During my first year in Malta, I again took up some driving lessons with the aim of getting a Maltese driving license. After a few lessons, I was ready to take the driving test which was supervised by the local Police. There was no comparison to a British driving test. Maybe it was for that reason that I passed it the first time. Armed with my driving license, it was not long before I was out hiring cars for the weekend and exploring all the nooks and crannies of Malta. I was in constant demand by my mates as few had a driving license.

On New Year Eve 1963/4, a buddy of mine celebrated the New Year with me in Valletta and we both got a bit merry and started the long walk home. On reaching Paceville, we both decided to go to St George's Bay and go for a celebratory New Year's swim. As it was quite a cold night, neither of us could be bothered to take our clothes off and we both ran and jumped into the sea. After our initial shock and boy, oh boy it was a shock, the water was bloody freezing – we got out and made our way back to the barracks completely soaking wet and freezing. Never were a hot shower and a warm bed so appreciated in my young life. It was a New Year event that I can't forget.

On many occasions when the American 5th Fleet was in the Grand Harbor, I along with a few friends would go into Valletta and meet up with a group of American sailors. We would explain to them where the best bars were and also how the Maltese barmen used to charge the Americans over double the price for drinks. We would then explain that we would go up and get all the drinks if they paid for our drinks and how they would save money – an agreement which was frequently reached.

Now the problem with most American sailors is when they have had a few drinks, they start to show off and start saying how they could drink the British Army under the table. This usually ended in a direct challenge to us. A challenge that my mates and I would accept on behalf of the British Army, bearing in mind that they were paying for our drinks. It was also common knowledge to us that while at sea, American sailors were not allowed to consume alcohol so they were more liable to get intoxicated a lot quicker than us. Once they were completely intoxicated, we would pick them up and tell the bar staff that we were taking them back to their ships. Now this is the naughty bit and on reflection I know I did wrong but what the hell, it was normal in those days. Once we had taken the sailors around the corner of the building, we would take their wallets, watches and cameras which were normally top of the range cameras and anything else of value, but before heading to the local pawn shop, we always checked that they were comfortable and just sleeping it off.

I was told later on that when the American 5th Fleet came into Malta, all sailors who were disembarking from their ships were given a card which described the do's and don'ts while in Malta. One of the Don'ts was spelt out as 'Do not fraternise with members of 'The Duke of Edinburgh's Royal Regiment'. I honestly do not think that they paid any attention to this card as the abuse continued up to the end of our tour in Malta.

As I started to settle down to being a member of 7Pl C Company, for reasons unbeknown to myself, I was selected to go on a Junior Non Commissioned Officers (JNCOs) Cadre – the first one to be held by the regiment in Malta. This was not only a shock to me but also to my fellow mates who had seen far more service than my six months. I was not happy at the time as I wanted to be closer to my new friends while enjoying myself. This was the start of a six-week intensive training programmed to become an JNCO, and my heart was not in it. I completed the course, and for all intents and purposes, I did well finishing quite high up in the listings. At the end of the course, I was told that I had passed the course, but I was not being recommended for promotion due to the limited time I had been in the army and the number of people that would be upset if I was seen to be promoted. Then the bolt out of the blue was struck, for the first and only time in my service career, I was asked if I would be interested in going for a Regular Commission as an Officer. I was told that it would take around two years and would also depend on me reaching the eligible education level. I replied that I was not interested in promotion at the time or applying for a commission. Interview over. Over fifty years later, I applied for my service records and for the first time learned that according to my service records, I had failed my NCOs Cadre and details were completely different to what I had been told.

Shortly after the end of the JNCOs Cadre, two fellow members who were on the course with me and due to be promoted to Lance Corporal with whom I had become friends with, were killed in a horrific car accident in the area of Balluta Bay. Both were best friends with each other and belonged to B Company. A few days later funeral arrangements were being made, and it transpired that C Company would be duty Company at the time of the funeral and that they would be required to provide the burial detail and guard. Members of B Company were not pleased with this, as they wanted to bury their own. Our CSM was very stubborn and insisted that as we were the Duty Company on the day of the funeral, C Company would carry it out. I was selected as one of the pallbearers and ended up practising with others by carrying a six-foot wooden table between us as a substitute for a coffin.

On the day of the funeral, I along with the rest of the funeral party dressed in No 3 Dress, set off in two 1-tonne Austin trucks that were highly bulled up for the occasion to the Hospital in Mġarr to collect the coffins and contents. We then returned to the Pembroke Military Cemetery where a full military ceremony took place with all members of the Battalion present. It was a very moving ceremony and the first one that I was deeply involved with.

As C Company was Duty Company that day, it also had to provide the evening guard, and yes you guessed it. I was also on guard duty that night. During the late evening/early morning, I was on sentry duty at a sentry box that was about two hundred meters from the cemetery boundary wall in quite a desolated and dark spot away from the barracks. Throughout my two hour stint on sentry and remembering what had occurred earlier during the day, all I could hear coming from the direction of the cemetery was a scrapping sound as if someone was trying to dig his way out of a hole. It was quite scary at the time and to make matters even worst, the film that was showing at the Australia Hall at the British Servicemen's Cinema that night was the movie called 'The Premature Burial' starring Ray Milland. Yes, it was a scary time for me and previous paranormal activities in my life did not help.

As Malta was somewhat restricted in size towards military training, Libya was designated as a military training area as we were soon to find out. I made my first acquaintance with the RAF Hastings cargo plane which had a carrying capacity of around seventy odd men. I along with members of my platoon boarded one at RAF Luqa which then flew to King Idris airport near Tripoli in Libya, North Africa. From the airport, we then made our way to an Old Italian fort sixty odd kilometres away in Tarhuna in the back of a 3-tonne Bedford truck. It was not a very pleasant journey as sand kept blowing into the back and the roads and track were quite bumpy. At the old fort the accommodation was a disaster. It was here that I was first introduced to what was to become known as 'thunder boxes' or an essential substitute for a toilet. It consisted of a large screened room which had a pit around thirty foot long, six foot wide and no telling how deep it was, covered by a wooden structure that resembled a long oblong box with thirty odd holes for sitting over while relieving yourself. No privacy and no flushing and the stench was unbearable. The funny thing is that at times it was hard to find a seat.

The training in the North African desert was hard and exciting. Mainly we concentrated on section/platoon/company attack with me acting as a section, 2nd in command (2i/c) most of the time due to my having attended the JNCOs cadre. Again the Buddy Buddy system came into the full meaning of relationships with your comrades. Water was always at a premium, and it was always shared between mates, as were the salt tablets that we had to mix with the water. Digging trenches and sleeping in them was a bit of a problem. We never had sleeping bags in those days – only a blanket and a ground sheet. At night time the only light you had was the light from the stars and what a most beautiful sight that was. With the coming of night, the temperature would take a nosedive. Usually, we would be moved out in the very early hours of the morning while it was still pitch black and while shaking the sand out of your damp blanket, we would jump back in alarm at the sight of blue static electricity flashes on your blanket. During the day we were plagued with flies as they were everywhere. It was sad seeing the flies congregating on the faces of the local children, especially around their eyes and mouth. They were so used to it that they did not even bother to brush them away with their hands. Flies were not the only problem as scorpions were very common as were the vast diversity of spiders and sidewinder snakes. Chameleons became a favourite with the lads, and many were brought back to Malta along with quite a few tortoises.

Many live firing exercises and demonstrations were held with 2inch mortars firing high explosive (HE) and smoke bombs, along with the 3-inch mortar again firing HE and smoke rounds. The support Anti-Tank Platoon also gave a demonstration firing HE and armoured piercing (AP) rounds from their Mobats. I also had the opportunity to fire live 3.5-inch Rocket Launcher rounds and hitting the target. Presentations were also given on the Vickers Medium Machine Gun which was coming to the end of its service life.

The training and exercises in Libya were very hard and demanding, but the rewards were also most welcoming. On the conclusion of one exercise, the battalion settled down into a makeshift tented camp by the shore of the Mediterranean Sea close to the ancient city ruins of Leptis Magna for a few days. While there, I took the opportunity to visit this old Roman Empire City and was amazed at the structures and extent of excavations that had taken place. I spent quite a few hours exploring the site, and I know that my imagination was working overtime trying to visualise the town 2,000 years back in time. I spent a lot of time going over the grounds of the Amphitheatre which was such a splendid site that it has never been surpassed to this day for its sheer beauty.

During my spell within the confines of the fort in Tarhuna, I noticed that someone had written a poem high on the wall in the 'Cook House', which I memorised and still have buzzing around my head to this very day. It's a bit rude, and I have written it as it was displayed.

ISABELLE COX

Here lies the body of Isabelle Cox

Who gave 2000 men the Pox?

Soldiers Sailors and Men of Honour

Fought like fuck to get upon her.

They fucked her standing

They fucked her lying

If she had wings

They would have fucked her flying.

But here she lies

But not forgotten.

The smell of her cunt

Was fucking rotten?

On returning to Malta, it was back into the regular routine of Duties, Regimental Parades, and everyday training along with the usual sporting events, except for one significant change that would change and challenge my army career.

After a short period of serving with 7 Pl. C Company, I was transferred to the Signal Platoon in Headquarter Company along with others from the three rifle companies. It was here from day one that I realised that I was up against a brick wall but never realised by just how much. Many in the Regiment saw members of the Signal Platoon as the Intelligencia of the battalion, which is quite understandable seeing how many members reached the rank of RSM and even went on to getting commissions and achieving high ranks. There was a competitive atmosphere even if nobody ever commented on it.

Unfortunately, in the eyes of some it was taken to an extreme that brought out racism and hatred that was overlooked by the majority and experienced by a tiny minority. In my case, it was my Platoon Sergeant who showed his hate towards me from day one, for what reason I do not know as I had never met or had any dealings with him till the day I joined the Signal Platoon. He was a Wiltshire man who served in the Wiltshire Regiment. He was against anyone who served in the Royal Berkshire Regiment or came from a different background, and he hated foreigners. He never liked officers and what they stood for but knew how to bend over for them. With my name Zawadzki, I was already at a significant disadvantage with him. He could never pronounce my name and started referring to me as the 'Polish Count' to others, but when he was out of earshot of others when addressing me, he used to drop the 'o' in Count. He always referred to coloured members of the platoon as 'black bastards' followed by their surname. I do not recall him having any friends even with the other senior ranks. To me, he was a complete loner who was only seen when required to be seen.

I successfully carried out and passed my signals cadre and for my endeavours was given the job as the 'Batman' to the Signal Platoon Commander. It was not a job that I liked, but I suppose that he must have taken my personal presentational standards of dress into consideration. I had a good working relationship with him, and we soon learned each other's traits. I believe this also contributed toward the Platoon Sergeant's dislike towards me.

On one occasion just before a big Regimental Parade, the Regimental Signal Officer (RSO) gave me his boots, belt, sword and scabbard to bull up, or to highly polish. Not a problem until one of my roommates came into the room and seeing the sword on the bed, he grabbed it and started waving it about as in a sword fight. I quickly grabbed the scabbard and using it as a sword began to defend myself. During the ensuing fight, the small strap that secured the scabbard within the belt holster was cut off. Having no means to fix it, I just placed the scabbard back in the belt frog with the sword and handed all the items back to the RSO without mentioning the unsecured strap. The following day while carrying out a battalion practice drill parade with the officers and just after having done a 'Present Arms', the order came to 'Shoulder Arms' which required the officers on parade to return their swords back to their scabbard. Unfortunately for the RSO, when he tried to replace his sword in its scabbard, the unsecured scabbard flew across the parade ground much to the laughter of all present apart from the RSO as he was deeply embarrassed. This episode resulted in me losing my job as the RSO's Batman.

In early January 1964, a situation in Cyprus started to escalate between the Greek Cypriot EOKA irregulars and the Turkish Cypriot population. My Regiment was placed on immediate standby to fly out to Cyprus. As tensions grew the battalion was tasked to fly to and secure Nicosia Airfield with the result that we flew out on 9 February 1964 in RAF Britannia aircraft. On landing at the airport, it was a case of shovels and pick as we dug slit trenches around the airfield. After a period of around four days erecting fences and filling sandbags, most members of the signal platoon and the remainder of HQ Company took over the role of a Rifle Company and were deployed to Nicosia, while the rest of the battalion were deployed to places of strategic importance.

My first place of deployment in Nicosia was attached to the Drums Platoon tasked with the responsibilities of securing Electra House which was part of the Cypriot tele-communication establishment. Mainly we were deployed on the roof as lookouts as it gave a commanding view over the surrounding areas including Paphos Gate which was the entrance to the Old City. You also had a good view into the local police station. It was not uncommon at night to see the blue flashes of electricity as used in torture coming from the police cell windows.

On one occasion while I was on the roof late at night, I saw a car stop and a man get out. The car drove away while the man walked towards a bike by a wall. On reaching the bike the man opened a box behind the seat and took out a pistol and pointed it in my direction and fired. By the time I had rung the field telephone and spoken to the duty operator, the man had jumped on the bicycle and pedalled away as fast as he could. I got a bit excited at the time as I had never been shot at before. I never returned fire as I was armed with a Sterling Machine Gun (SMG) and the chances of hitting him were very slim. He was never caught.

Cyprus was an exciting tour and at times quite scary. Most of my duties consisted of Guard duties outside military or government buildings like the Turkish Secretariat, where the occupants had all been murdered including some in the bath. Now that was a bloody mess. The only thing left alive was the pet dog which we took under our wings. I was also involved in many patrols in the old town centre along what became known as the Green Line, which was drawn up to separate the Greek Cypriots from the Turkish Cypriots. I was also involved in the escorting of Turkish Cypriots with their furniture vans and trucks going into the Greek Cypriot territory to collect oranges and lemons from their orchards. Freshly picked Cypriot oranges are the tastiest oranges in the world.

I was almost shot at on an occasion when I was sitting in the back of a Land Rover as the radio operator while out on patrol during a school march demonstration.

While driving along the road next to hundreds if not thousands of chanting students, I was punched in the back by a total stranger. Sitting opposite me was the Provost Sgt and the CQMS, both of them veteran and relatively old soldiers. Both were armed with SMGs as was I. Seeing me being punched in the back, their immediate action was to start shouting while cocking their SMGs. On hearing the commotion in the back, the RSM, who was sitting in the front of the Land Rover with the driver, told the driver to put his foot down and to get us out of there fast. This resulted in both the Sgt and the CQMS almost falling over each other with cocked SMGs. Luckily for me; they never had their fingers on the triggers. This episode led to an enquiry into the incident, and orders were given that no Land Rover or any other type of vehicle should ever leave base without being accompanied and escorted by a second vehicle.

On 22 March, the battalion was relieved by the 2nd Regiment Royal Artillery and the Canadian Royal 22nd Regiment who later became the first troops of the new United Nations forces in Cyprus.

The battalion eventually moved to a tented camp in the Famagusta area before leaving for the return trip back to Malta on 1 April in RAF Hastings.

Initially, no recognition was given to the regiment for its contribution to keeping the peace in Cyprus apart from words of praise, although all who served under the United Nations received the UN Medal. This was eventually overturned in 2015 when the General Service Medal with the Cyprus 1964–65 Bar was issued. I received my medal 51 years after the event, but it took me over 70 years to get my father's medals from his involvement in WWII.

Back to Malta, it was back to the same old routine with the additional information that Malta was to be granted Independence from the United Kingdom. It was also the time that the battalion was initially put on standby for the troubles in Aden normally referred to as the Radfan Uprising of 1963–67. This was later rescinded as consideration was taken off the battalion's recent role in Cyprus.

I had now been in the army for some eighteen months and had settled down to military life quite well. I had achieved one of my ambitions in becoming a marksman on the 7.62mm Self Loading Rifle (SLR) and an excellent shot on the Light Machine Gun (LMG) which reminds me of the occasion when I was firing the LMG on the ranges under the supervision of the range officer who happened to be my RSO. On his command, "20 Round in groups of 3 to 4 rounds fire!" I started to shoot. Shortly after he yelled out, "Stop!" "Z," he yelled at me again, "I said groups of 3 to 4 rounds, not 1 to 1½ rounds." This brought out screams of laughter by all on the range and even ended up being mentioned in our Regimental Magazine. I mean, how can I even fire ½ a round?

I had also passed my Signals Cadre and knew how to send messages in Morse code. I had also lost my stutter and learned to swim. I had also made friends with a girl, and although I spent a lot of time with her swimming, that was all there was to it although many thought she was an intimate girlfriend and I must say I never put them right. I later met a girl from Paola who I thought I was in love with, but my shyness always got the better of me. One day I had hired a car out with a mate, and we met up with her and her friend and went out for a drive and a meal. In the evening I had found a spot in the Marsa Sports Complex to park up the car. My mate was in the back with her mate while I remained in the front, with her. After some small talk we snuggled up towards each other, and I actually kissed her. It was while we were kissing that I got the shock of my life as she put her tongue in my mouth. I had never experienced it before, and I was turned on to such an extent that I started fondling her breasts. I was going crazy as this was completely new to me and I would have gone further if it was not for the two Royal Military Policemen who stopped by my car in their Land Rover. After asking me if I had permission to be on the Marsa Sports Ground, they told me to move my car off the military property that I was parked on. I got the impression that they thought I was a young officer and just wanted me to move after having interrupted my fun. What a bummer. If they had not come along, I do not know what could have happened. The relationship never lasted long, and I put that down to my shyness and nothing more.

The 28 May 1964, however, will always be a memorable one. I was in Valletta along with a few friends and we went to a place called the Prego Bar where we noticed a few girls. One, in particular, caught my eye and I took a shine towards her.

Apart from her being stunning, she had the most beautiful brown eyes that I had ever seen. I started talking to her. Her name was Josephine and she was out celebrating her 18th birthday. We started chatting, and I told her my name was Leon. As it was getting close to the nine o'clock home time, I made arrangements to meet her the following day at 7:00 pm.

Chapter 7
JOSEPHINE

On 29 May 1964, which was my twentieth birthday, my first exposure to the phrase 'what's in a name' started to take off in a big way. I had arranged to meet Josephine in the evening on what was to be our first official date, but for some reason I was running late and met up with her half an hour later. She was not amused, in fact she did not even want to talk to me. During the time she spent waiting for me, she had noticed some of the lads I had been with the previous evening and asked if they knew where I was. Unfortunately for me, she had used my name, Leon, when asking about me. While attempting to chat her up, my so-called mates told her that my name was Fred and that I had been lying to her. I cannot blame my mates for this as they only knew me as Fred. Over fifty years later, many of my old buddies still call me Fred and if I mention Leon, they become thoroughly confused. Many who, like myself, had a nickname, reverted back to their normal birth names after leaving the services and have become complete nobodies.

Josephine thought I had lied to her by giving a false name and it was only after some time had passed that she realised that I had been telling her the truth. Over the next few weeks, as I got to know Josephine a bit better, my heart started to warm to her in a big way and I think it was for this reason that my shyness began to kick in again. I learned that she worked in a shop by the indoor market in Valletta with her mother and uncle. She had been raised by her granddad and grandmother along with her aunt and uncles and lived in Floriana. She had an elder sister and two younger brothers who used to live with her mother. Her father had left her mother and moved to England with another woman with whom he also had children.

When I met Josephine's mother for the first time, both Josephine and I were walking down Kingsway in Valletta. Quite by accident we bumped into her mother as she was walking towards us. On seeing her, Josephine stopped and pulled me up in front of her and introduced me to her. Her first reaction was to look at me before raising her finger and drawing it across her throat while saying, "If you hurt my daughter ..." and that was it – she walked away. Josephine was not amused, and neither was I.

A short time later I was taken to her home and introduced to her father's brother and sister and treated to a meal. Her grandparents had passed away recently, and she was now being raised by her uncle and aunt as she did not want to go and live with her brothers and sister at her mother's house. I found it quite a strange situation but was told that it was quite common in Malta. Her uncle Gianni and aunt Sunta, both brother and sister, were unmarried and neither were they in any form of relationship with anybody. At the time, her uncle was a uniformed member of the Customs Department and quite easily spotted on the occasions when he used to follow us, just to see what we got up to. The whole family were devoted churchgoers, and it was not so long before I started to attend the Sunday church mass with Josephine.

After a short period of time, I was accepted by her uncles and aunts on her father's side of the family and invited to meals at their homes. Josephine still had to be in by 9:00 pm, but I was allowed to stay till 10:00 pm before making my way back to the bus stop to catch the last bus back to St Patrick's. Sunta was a fantastic cook and how she managed to cook the meals on a primus stove and an Aladdin heater. I just don't know.

Josephine's mother used to visit the house. Over a period of time, we started to get to know each other along with her brothers and sister and again slowly accepted into her family. Initially, there were dark suspicions shown towards me by her mother, and they never disappeared.

I recall one evening sitting around the table with some members of the family and being asked if I wanted a beer, which I refused. I was then asked if I wanted a Coke to which I replied, "Yes, please."

Josephine's uncle took out a bottle from the crate, opened it and poured it into a glass, before passing both bottle and glass over to me. As I was eating my meal and drinking from the glass, I eventually got the bottle to refill my glass, only to find the Coke was not coming out of the bottle as the neck of the bottle was blocked. Holding the bottle up to the light, I got the shock of all shocks. Inside the bottle, I saw a giant, dead, pickled lizard. When I showed it to Josephine's uncle, he took one look before rushing out, retching. On my part, I just told everyone present that it was the first bottle of Coke that I had ever drunk "with real body in it." This resulted in a stampede to the door as others also started to be sick. It was also the time they began to learn that I had a strange sense of humour.

As our relationship developed, I used to take Josephine to the local cinema, and we used to sit in the back seat and have a kiss and cuddle. Josephine was as shy as me, but she started me back onto french kissing, and it was also her who took my hand and placed it on her breast. I was back in heaven, but we never progressed any further over the next year on that side of our relationship. Not that we did not want to, but our upbringing, in particular the influence of religion when it came to sexual relations, deterred us.

While courting Josephine, military life was to some degree put on the back burner. However, with the forthcoming of the granting of independence to Malta on 21 September 1964, drill was the main training agenda. It was a case of drill, drill and more drill, along with all the bull that came along with it. I had participated in many ceremonial occasions in front of the public as a whole with themes such as 'The Queen's Birthday Parade', the 'Opening of Parliament,' plus parades for special dignitaries along with the two most significant Regimental Battle Honours of Maiwand and Ferozeshah Parades. But this was going to be the parade of all parades, and I was looking forward to it.

Just before the big day, I had a fungal nail infection on my big toe that had gone septic. I had no option but to report sick to get it treated but due to a big CO's inspection of best boots and other dress items on that particular morning, my platoon sergeant would not allow me to attend the morning sick parade. During the CO's inspection, in the Battalion Dining Hall and while I was standing to attention with my No1 Dress hat on, best boots in my left hand and belt and bayonet frog in my right hand, the pain in my toe was so intense that I blacked out, which caused me to fall forward while still in the position of attention and hitting the floor with my chin. Once I had recovered, I was asked by the CO and the RSM what had happened. I explained about my toe and that I had tried to report sick but was refused permission to attend morning sick parade by my favourite Sgt. He was promptly summoned, and I was taken to the Medical Centre for treatment. I received five dovetail stitches to my chin and the infection on my big toe was also treated. I was also told that I would not be available for the Ceremonial Parade at the square. I was also severely reprimanded for not having attended the morning sick parade regardless having being ordered not to attend. The medical officer also asked me if I had been to North Africa and other places as he had no record of ever having come across my name on his medical files. I was quite proud to mention that I had not been sick or needed any medical attention in the past eight years.

I do not know what was said to my Platoon Sergeant, but I do know he was given a severe dressing down by the RSM.

He was not even pleased when I told him that I had been taken off the parade. When I saw Josephine that evening, she was quite surprised to see me as she had been told of the incident by a couple of my mates. Upon seeing my face with a great big bandage covering my chin, she broke down in tears.

Due to my injuries, I was not on the actual parade in front of the general public, but I did play a role in it. At the time of the granting of Independence, there was a lot of tension between the governing Nationalist Party and the opposition Labour Party, and it was possible that there would be some clashes during the ceremony.

I was detailed to take up a position overlooking the grounds where the ceremony was to be held with a few others, in the capacity of a sniper. Thankfully the ceremony was peaceful, and I was in a unique position to overlook the entire ceremony that was attended by thousands of Maltese spectators. Malta gained its independence at midnight on the night of 20-21 September 1964, and I felt very proud of being involved in the occasion.

As the battalion started to settle down after the Independence Parade, it would be appropriate to mention the noticeable changes that were taking place within the Regiment. All National Servicemen had now been discharged and the army was now a Regular Army. Most regular soldiers who had served in WWII were no longer seen, and very few had seen any active service apart from Cyprus. A better class of recruits were joining up along with many who had gone through Junior Leaders.

These youngsters were also seen as the up and coming threat to many older soldiers as in most cases they had taken and passed the required educational qualifications for promotion. In my case, I had applied for educational courses within the unit but up to that time, I had never been offered a place.

On 2 January 1965, I was flown out to Cyprus as a part of the HQ Company with B Company to come under the command of 1 Gloster at Episkopi. This was a peaceful and calm area and for the short time that we spent there going out on routine patrols and carrying out mundane duties, it was also possible for me to hire an old Triumph Herald car and to go out sightseeing with a good mate of mine. We toured the area of Limassol, Paphos and the lower limits of the Troodos Mountains and saw some breathtaking views and places where ancient history was made. The only problem we had was when we drove into a small village in the foothills of the Troodos Mountains. We were seen by a large group of villagers who, on noticing that we were British soldiers in uniform, decided to approach us in a none too friendly gesture. On seeing this, we had no option but to do a quick three-point turning and get the hell out of there. At the time it was a bit scary, but we had a good laugh after it. Our tour came to a sudden end, and we returned to Malta on 24 January.

I must have been quite pleased to go back to Malta and ask Josephine if she would marry me. She accepted and a short while later we had an engagement party at her house.

In April the Battalion was on the move again, back to Libya. This time we were camped in a tented camp in what was to be called 'Bomba' – an area that was fairly flat, sandy and next to the sea. For some unknown reason, I was promoted to the position of the CO's radio operator. It was a job that I enjoyed. The Battalion's training mainly revolved around company training, again with section, platoon and company attacks followed by a Battalion exercise.

It also involved a Battalion night march led by our Intelligence Officer which turned out to be one of the most disastrous marches that I had ever been on. No, I can't really say that, as I was tucked up in comfort in the back of the CO's Land Rover with my radios.

It started off with the Intelligence Officer who had half a dozen or more pre-set compasses hanging on their lanyards around his neck. He was a bit agitated as we waited for the last rays of sunlight to disappear from the skies to be greeted first by the pitch darkness of the heavens and then to be suddenly bathed in glorious starlight. On being given the 'Go' by the CO, he selected one of his compasses and quickly took a bearing before stepping off. Unfortunately for him, parked directly on his route was a Land Rover. Not a problem you would think, but to him it was. Instead of walking around it, he took the hard route and climbed over the vehicle before continuing on his way. I do not recall how long the march took but I did feel sorry for the marching men. They looked quite knackered after a few hours. I will not make any comment on what they said or called me, seeing me nice and comfortable in the back of my vehicle.

The disastrous march was to continue until the early hours of the morning, when an unmistakably red light appeared on the unseen horizon. On seeing this, our Intelligence Officer assumed that it was a signal lamp put out by his section to guide us to our rendezvous point, so without taking any care and consulting his compasses, he headed straight for it while leading the battalion. After a good few hours of heading for the light that never got any closer and with daylight fast approaching, it was soon realised that the 'red light' was the aircraft warning light on top of the radio tower, quite some distance away in Tripoli. The march was quickly brought to an end and I was told to radio back to send the truck to pick up the shattered men. On the return journey back to camp, the CO made it quite clear that he was not a happy man.

The Camp Site of Bomba was not an ideal location for a tented camp as the surrounding area was dotted by very clearly visible live ammunition left over from WW2. Landmines were spewed all over the area, as were a lot of anti-aircraft shells. Safe areas were marked out by tape and in some cases a bit of fencing. We were all warned not to touch any suspicious looking objects. Unfortunately, a good friend of mine who I had served with in 7Pl C Company never paid any attention to the warnings. He found an anti-aircraft shell and decided to take it back to his tent. Luckily nobody was close by as he tried to dismantle the warhead. It exploded and took his head off. I heard the explosion and saw another friend enter the tent. He was a West Indian when he went in but came out white with the shock showing on his face. My friend never left Libya and was buried in the Military Cemetery outside of Tripoli.

Shortly after returning to Malta, I noticed my name on Battalion Part One Orders stating that I had been selected to attend the second JNCO's cadre to be held in Malta and that I was to report for the entrance tests. When my Signal Sergeant noticed my selection, he informed me that it was a mistake as I was to attend the MT driving cadre on the same day of the tests. I had no doubt of what I was told even though I knew that he neither liked me nor respected me and accepted that I was to go on the MT Cadre. Big mistake. Having attended the first day of the cadre, I was summoned to the Company Office to see the CSM. I was then given a big dressing down for not having attended the JNCO's Cadre's entrance tests. I explained what I had been told and by whom and was promptly told to tell the Signal Sergeant to report to the CSM straight away. I was to report to the officer in charge of the JNCO's Cadre and to take the entrance tests that evening.

I passed top in the entrance exam and was to go on and pass the course with very high grading leading to my promotion to Lance Corporal a short while later. As I was promoted, the Signal Sergeant also got promoted to Signal Platoon Colour-Sergeant.

As our tour in Malta was coming to an end, we had been informed that our next posting would be to Minden in West Germany, within the role of a mechanised infantry battalion in an Armoured Brigade. Training was geared to make the changeover of rolls possible which included many

Signal courses for the future radio operators that would be required for the role. In my case, I was sent on an MT Cadre and taught to drive a Land Rover. Most of our training was taught driving a 1 tonne Humber Armoured Car, commonly referred to as a Pig, on the disused airfields of RAF Ħal-Far and Ta Qali. It was a difficult vehicle to drive with a reversed facing steering wheel and small narrow slits as windows. We were also told that to pass the Highway Code test we had to know everything that covers horses by heart. The reason behind this was that the MT Officer was a mad horse enthusiast and horses came first, not people or vehicles. I passed and was awarded a Group 1 Vehicles Service License which allowed me to apply for my British driving license to go with my Maltese driving license.

I was still going out with my fiancée, Josephine. While talking about being posted to Germany, the subject of marriage came up. Over a short period, it was decided that we would get married on 8 August 1965. It was not such an easy procedure for a member of the armed forces to get married in those days. First I had to inform my Company Commander who also had to give me his permission to marry after first giving me a lecture on the ins and outs of marriage. Then the wheels were set to turn in motion with security and suitability checks carried out both on Josephine and her family as well as my family background. The church also got involved as they were very reluctant in seeing their young girls marry British members of the armed forces, especially in one of their churches. This resulted in me having to attend meetings with a church representative who checked out my suitability for marriage. Once these were cleared, it was a matter of preparations for the big day.

We both opted, or maybe it was the family that opted, for a full Church Service Wedding at the Church of St Publius in Floriana. Neither my mother nor Josephine's mother were euphoric with the announcement of our wedding plans.

The wedding plans were being made mainly in secret by Josephine's aunt and uncle. I was told just to turn up on the day at the specified time. I left it at that and went to Valletta to have a made to measure suit and shoes made for the big day. I also arranged for hired suits for my best man and myself. I had invited my mother to fly over to Malta for the wedding at my expense, but she had no intention of coming over. One of the reasons for her not attending I put down as a fear that I was marrying a girl from a different culture. In fact, I would go as far as to say that she thought Josephine had a dark complexion when the truth is, she was whiter than me. Inter-race marriages in the mid-sixties were frowned upon. With the wedding date fast approaching, friction was breaking out between Josephine's father's side of the family and her mother's side of the family. It was a stupid incident that was to cause a lot of anguish for many years to come.

Josephine was brought up and raised from a very young age by her grandparents, her aunts and uncles while her mother took a backseat, to such an extent that when she emigrated to Australia with her other children, Josephine was left behind. It was therefore obvious that her uncle and aunt who were paying for the wedding, would put their names on the cards when the wedding invitations were printed. This infuriated Josephine's mother with the result that she told all members on her side of the family to boycott the wedding.

On the day of the wedding, I turned up at the stated time with my best man and entered the magnificent church of St Publius with all the lights glaring. I walked towards the altar on the red carpet that had been specially laid for the occasion. The church was full to capacity with guests and spectators as apart from the wedding there was also a full church mass service.

Waiting for Josephine to turn up was quite a scary moment with feelings of trepidation and suspense coming all over me and then there she was, standing at the church entrance dressed to perfection in her white wedding gown and attended by her bridesmaids. As she stepped onto the red carpet, the organ broke into music and one of the top tenors of Malta sang the Ave Maria. From then on, it was the full church mass which was all in Maltese and lasted a good hour in which time I had not even seen Josephine's face. In fact, during the service, I was praying to God that it was Josephine standing next to me and not a complete stranger. When the wedding ceremony took place, and she lifted her veil, I'm sure I let out a sigh of relief.

A short while later I was married, and again the 'what's in a name' syndrome broke out. Here I was, Mr Leon Zawadzki or was it Zawadski or even Sawordski? And now yet another problem was to start over. Mrs Josephine Zawadzka. Yes, that's right. Mrs Josephine Zawadzka. In

Poland, there is a male spelling and a female spelling. In this case, the female spelling ended in an 'a' as opposed to the male spelling ending in an 'i'. Lucky for me that when signing the Church Registry and explaining the spelling differences, they finally accepted the difference in spelling but only because I was a Lance Corporal. This difference in spelling cropped up quite a few time and still goes on to this day. Finally with all the paperwork signed it was off to the cheers from the crowds to the gleaming white open-topped Bugatti car that was to take us on a tour around the island before ending up in Gzira where the reception was being held.

The reception was attended by around three hundred adults and children including many of my army buddies, and all seemed to enjoy themselves although there were many comments raised as people noticed that many members on Josephine's mother side were nowhere to be seen. I think both Josephine and I were in a bit of a daze through the evening and we were both looking forward to spending our first, and yes I will repeat that, our first night together. After we had both changed our clothes and thanked everyone, all my mates plus a few others lifted Josephine into the air and marched around the ballroom. Not wanting to be outdone, the women then grabbed me and lifted me up in the air while someone grabbed my … and almost sent me to the hospital. It was painful.

Our first night of passionate lovemaking was to a certain extent curtailed due to the facts that we were still both extremely shy and, to tell the truth, utter virgins. On top of that we were also both extremely shattered, maybe it was the heat as August is one of the hottest months of the year with the temperatures in the upper nineties. As for any sort of lie in? Forget it. Three of Josephine's young cousins came up to the flat and started ringing the doorbell before six o'clock in the morning and would not go away until we let them in and served them breakfast. I think it was an initiation of "welcome to married life in Malta."

As we settled down in our small flat, we both started to get to know each other, both the good points and the bad points. Josephine took after her aunt and was a brilliant cook, but she could not iron. I gave her a pair of KD trousers that I was to wear on duty one day to iron, only to find three creases along each trouser leg when she had finished ironing. I could just imagine what an inspecting officer would have said if he had seen them. After her first attempt and seeing the result, I never let her iron any of my trousers again and that also applied to shirts. Fifty-odd years later, I often think to myself that she planned it from the outset.

Being married was a big change to my lifestyle, no longer the barrack life lifestyle. Josephine prepared my breakfast in the mornings plus a packed lunch box. I would then hurry and catch the local army transport that took married personnel to work. The driver never waited. If you were not there on time, he would drive off even if he saw you in his mirror. The same applied for the return journey. Most evenings were spent with family members or having a chat with friends over a meal and a few drinks. Televisions in Malta were a rare commodity, and very few Maltese owned a TV. The local cable radio only had two or three channels and was not very good unless you liked church services, local traditional music and singing.

Life was good although I was a bit worried as I had been told that initially I would not be receiving an army married quarter when the battalion moved to Minden in Germany due to unavailability of quarters. I informed my mother that I would be returning back to England on leave with my wife towards the end of November and if she could put us up. I do not know what her immediate reaction was, probably not very good initially I think but thank heavens all communications were by mail. The days of cheap telephone calls, emails and the internet were still a long way off.

In the last six months of our tour in Malta, over fifty members of the battalion married Maltese girls.

On 26 November 1965, Josephine and I said goodbye to Malta and many friends before departing by plane to Heathrow Airport to meet up with my dad who was still driving his old Renault Fregate. Josephine was in a state of trepidation, having said goodbye to family and friends, taking her first ever flight in a plane and with the prospects of meeting my family for the first time. Her first impressions of England were not so great either, as it was cold, raining and we landed relatively late in the evening.

On reaching my mother's house, we were greeted – no, that's not the word. We were met by my mum, brothers, sisters and Trixie, our dog who was pleased to see me as could be seen from the tail waggles and the jumping up and down. I believe the first words spoken were by my youngest sister Angela who, while looking at Josephine said, "You took my big brother away from me." Although a certain amount of friction was shown towards Josephine, curiosity started to creep in and everyone began to talk to each other. I had the best part of a two-month leave to take and hopefully sort out any problems that may arise. As the family gradually moved closer together, Josephine started to explore the shops and sights of Slough. She was quite amazed at the sheer size of supermarkets and the variety of goods on display along with the buses and trains. One of the items that really amazed her was while she was being served her dinner on a plate, was the Brussels sprouts. She had never seen these before in Malta and commented on these as 'baby cabbages' – a name that stuck with my family and her for many years to come. Ok, so again, what's in a name?

Things were not going too bad, as although we never knew it at the time, Josephine had conceived our first daughter sometime during December 1966.

On 1 February 1966, I proceeded to Heathrow Airport and embarked on a flight to Hannover Airport to rejoin my Regiment in Minden, leaving my wife in the hands of my family.

Chapter 8
MINDEN
1966-1969

On 1 February 1966, I flew from Heathrow Airport to Hannover Airport in Germany to start my first tour of duty in Germany. As I had not qualified for a married quarter and as a junior NCO, I was given my own accommodation in the Signal Platoon Lines in the HQ Company Block, which consisted of a room on the third floor with a window overlooking the main ring road in Minden.

Clifton Barracks, formally known as Mudra Kaserne, was built around 1936 for the German Wehrmacht. It was a fully functioning well-designed barracks. Living in the barracks was quite good but evenings became quite a bore. I spent most of my time reading books, studying or writing letters home to Josephine. She was not having a very good time with my family at home, so I took it upon myself to start looking to hire private accommodation for both of us. It was not too long before I found, together with a couple of my mates who were both in the same situation with their wives, a suitable German family who had three bedrooms to rent out within their house, with the use of a kitchen/ dining room and toilet facilities. Having got the clearance from our housing officer, it was not long before Josephine and the others had all moved into the house. It was great fun even if a bit overcrowded and the other two wives were both Maltese. Josephine started to enjoy herself and became good friends with the German landlady. A few months later both Josephine and her friend discovered that they were both pregnant.

With Josephine being pregnant, I jumped the housing priority list and it was not long before we were given our first army married quarters in Bastau Strasse, which was just a short distance from the barracks. To top it all, it was a house with three bedrooms and a back garden. It even had a cellar which housed the central heating stove. The front windows overlooked a quiet road and a stream flowing through open fields. It was regarded by many as one of the best married quarter areas in Minden. Life was looking good.

With the change in our units rolls from garrison duties in Malta to an entirely Mechanised Infantry roll in Germany, many significant changes had to be made and our role within the Signal Platoon was to change quite drastically. Apart from the regular wheel based vehicles, we were now in possession of armoured tracked vehicles known as AFV 432s. Each rifle company was equipped with fourteen vehicles plus attached vehicles. This resulted in many cadres being set up to teach the required driving skills and for radio operators to learn the necessary security and voice procedure. Initially, I helped in the signal cadres and was then told that I was to be attached to the MT Platoon as the Commanding Officers Driver/Radio Operator. Having been the CO's radio operator in Malta, I was somewhat surprised at the appointment as he still had his staff car driver. Later, I found out that this was due to the change in role of the regiment.

Being the CO's driver/operator had its good and bad points and over the years, our understanding of each other was very good. I got to know his ways and, to some degree, the way he thought. He always appeared to want to travel in his Land Rover as opposed to his staff car which meant I was always in constant demand. In his initial months of taking over the role of the CO of a mechanised infantry battalion, he was in constant demand to visit the relevant Headquarters and supporting arms along with reconnoitring the layouts of training and exercise areas. He was also a keen driver who used to take pride in driving, with me in the front passenger seat. As I was a married man and living off the camp, I used to bring a lunchbox and a flash of coffee with me to work, and on many occasions, I would be called out at short notice to drive the CO somewhere. It was very seldom that he ever took a lunchbox with him, with the result that on many occasions I would share my lunchbox. This soon led to him getting a craving for the coffee that my wife used to make, a desire that resulted in either the CO or myself driving round to my house and getting my wife to make a flask of coffee before we could proceed on our journey.

Many of my neighbours used to be quite surprised seeing the CO walking in or out of my front door, and I can just imagine what they told their husbands. I'm sure this also fuelled my Signal Platoon Colour Sergeant's (Sig Pl CSgt) dislike towards me as he lived a few doors away from me.

One of the bad things about being the CO's radio operator was the many occasions that he put me into a compromising situation. When out on an exercise, he always paid particular attention to voice procedures and security, and whenever he heard any bad voice procedure or security errors being made over the air, he would tell me to sort it out and to reprimand the offender over the air. Most of the offenders were the company commanders or company 2i/c, and they did not take kindly to being told off by a Lance Corporal. This frequently resulted in them retaliating against me once the exercise had finished and we had returned to the barracks. In most cases, they would see me and yell at me to come over to them. I would double over, come to attention and salute. While standing to attention, they would then give me a good dressing down for having contradicting their voice procedure on air during an exercise with the result that I would be threatened with being locked up in the local Guardhouse if I did it again. I would try to explain my situation, but they would never compromise. Once I had been dismissed, I would march away and think nothing of it until I next met up with the CO. I would then explain the situation to him, and he always told me to leave it in his hands.

I know that he did deal with it as after a time I was shown lots of respect to my face and to a certain extent most senior officers treated me in a different light, unlike the time when the Sig Pl Csgt was marching towards the CO Land Rover. Seeing the CO's vehicle approaching him with the CO driving and me sitting in the front seat, he did a smart eye's left while saluting at the same time. Seeing this, the CO turned round to me and told me to return his salute as he had his hands full with the steering wheel. I promptly did an eye's left and returned the salute. I also saw the look on the CSgt face and knew that I had not heard the last of this salute. Again as with the senior officers, when the CSgt saw me again, he had me standing at attention in front of him and started calling me all the names under the sun while telling me that he did not expect a Lance Corporal to return one of his salutes to an officer. I explained the situation, again to no avail and again reported the incident to the CO on our next meeting, with the same result that he would take care of it.

My relationship with my CSgt was about to take a further nosedive.

As my regiment settled down after having qualified as a Mechanised Infantry Battalion of the British Army of the Rhine, life started getting a bit hectic with the harsh training exercises that were to be taken on in Company, Battalion or Brigade formations. These exercises would take the battalion all over Germany, into France and back out to Libya. Many different scenarios and situations were dreamed up, and regardless of the weather conditions at the time, all carried out to their conclusions. Being the CO's Dvr/Op, I was seen by many as having a cushy job. To some extent it was as I did not have to do all that marching with a full pack on my back, unlike them.

What they did not see were the occasions when the CO would be visiting a platoon doing for instance, training of disembarking from a helicopter hovering 20m above the ground by rope. While watching, he would turn around to me and tell me to get on the next helicopter and to show everyone how it was done. I would grab my webbing and weapon and get on the next helicopter which would take off and hover about 20m off the ground. For some unknown reason, I was always given the rope first, which I would grab and start to descend. At the same time, the helicopter pilot would raise his craft until the rope was at least three to five meters from the ground. I would have no option but to keep going down the rope otherwise I would feel the boots of the person descending above me on my head and then the unexpected three or more metres unsupported drop. Ouch. It was the same when he visited places where training was conducted on, for instance, the 'Death Slide'. This was normally a rope of one to 200m long suspended from a high point sloping downwards into a valley. You then got hold of a bit of rope which you threw over the suspended rope, and after making sure that you had a firm grip with both hands, you threw yourself off the edge and slid down to the bottom of the suspended rope. Trying to stop was the hard bit. I would like to point out that during the 60s, health and safety issues did not exist. There were no safety harnesses; everything happened at your own risk.

Initially, I found it to be terrifying and quite daunting, but once you are committed to doing it the adrenaline kicks in –a fantastic feeling which makes you look forward to the next occasion. Lucky for me, I never did have a fear of heights.

Back at the barracks life was still quite good. Again as the CO's driver, I was not involved in duties such as Battalion Orderly Corporal, Company Orderly Sergeant or 2i/c of the Guard. My primary job was keeping my vehicle clean and keeping up to date on radio and voice procedures.

On 16 September 1966, I took my wife, Josephine to the British Military Hospital in Rinteln where she was admitted straight into the maternity ward. A few hours later she was wheeled out to the waiting room in a wheelchair to where I was seated. Initially, I did not even recognise her until she told me that I was the father to a daughter. I think the first thing I said to Josephine was, "What are we going to call her?" After a moment of silence, she replied, "Michelle." I know that before Josephine gave birth, we had discussed many names but at the time we never knew if it was going to be a boy or a girl. The name Michelle was never mentioned before, but at that time the Beatles had come out with their song 'Michelle' which was very popular and it inspired us to choose our daughter's name, Michelle Zawadzka. This brings me back to the question, "What's in a name?"

Becoming a father changed my concept of life as I was now responsible for the lives and safety of both my wife and daughter. Lucky for Josephine and me, we had a large family of friends for support and boy did we need it! Apart from Josephine giving birth, many of the Maltese wives were also giving birth to their babies; I would not like to hazard a guess as to how many gave birth but a couple of dozens at least within a few months of each other. Initially, the times of parties and going to the cinema in the evening were over. Everywhere you looked you saw nappies hanging on washing lines. Pampers and disposable nappies were still a thing of the future. All the wives also had to learn to cope with their babies without the help of their husbands as they were nearly always away on exercise.

Josephine was quite comfortable at home and spent a lot of her time cooking. When I was away, she had her friends around or spent time at their homes but the evenings were another thing. Although we had a black and white television, all the programs were in German. We also had a radio which brought music into the home. I managed to buy a second-hand car from my Signal Platoon Sergeant which allowed me to take my family and friends out during weekends to explore Germany. The car was a dark green Fiat 1500; I've no idea of its year of manufacture. It served me well as I managed to drive it all the way to Malta and back, as well as driving it to the UK.

A short time after the birth of our daughter Michelle, Josephine became pregnant for the second time. It was while I was halfway through a driving course learning how to drive a tracked AFV 432 that my wife went into labour on 26 July 1967 to give birth to our second daughter Alison.

As the main military training season was coming to an end, I decided that I would book my leave for mid-

September to early October to drive to Malta and visit Josephine's family. The journey covered a return distance of over 5,000 kilometres, including four sea crossings. A few of my mates who were married to Maltese girls also decided that they would be making the same trip. I arranged with one of my mates to travel with his wife and one-year-old son with me, Josephine and our daughters Michelle and Alison, who was only six weeks old at the time and to split the cost of the journey.

On making plans for the trip, we decided that we would travel through Switzerland into Italy and make our way to Sicily to catch the ferry to Malta. We never thought about booking the ferry beforehand and took our chances that a space on the ship would be available when we got there, unlike my other mates who did book in advance.

On 12 September, our adventure was to begin. We loaded my car up with all our supplies, mainly nappies and jerry cans of petrol which, being members of the British Army of the Rhine (BAOR), we got at a subsidised price, and all our other requirements.

Then it was a case of four adults and three babies all around one-year-old and younger making ourselves comfortable before we set off.

I can recall setting off on our way towards the St Bernard's Pass in Switzerland to cross over the Pennine Alps into Italy and the feeling of going through the Alps and the stunning scenery. The route we took through Italy was down to Milan – Bologna – Florence and down to Rome where I got slightly lost and ended up driving around the Colosseum twice. We then made our way towards Naples, passing the Famous Monte Cassino on the route. Once having passed Naples, driving became an entirely different ball game. Gone were the toll motorways and dual carriageways as we navigated the coast roads down to Reggio Calabria. The roads on the West coast were narrow and twisting, with steep rises and sudden drops. The scenery was to die for, and on occasions, I think we nearly did. Some roads had sheer drops on one side with no forms of any safety barrier. One mistake and you could easily be a goner.

Again along this coast road you would also come across small villages, and I believe that at the time we were travelling through, it must have been festa season as we came upon bands and people celebrating in the streets. At times it was also near impossible to turn the car around some corners without going backwards and forwards. The drive down to the seaport at Reggio Calabria was a great eye-opener; we had very few problems apart from one puncture and the smell of nappies being changed. It should also be remembered that we did not throw the soiled nappies away; we kept them in a bag in the boot of the car. Although my mate could drive, I did most of the driving as I felt safer with the wheel in my hands as opposed to his. The biggest problem was trying to sleep in the car as it was quite cramped.

On reaching Calabria, it was down to the port to book the ferry across to Sicily, which was no problem and we had a few hours to spare. I was quite surprised that I had not seen hide or hair of my other mates who were making the same journey. The ferry was running late when it docked into Messina which meant that I had to make a quick dash to Syracuse if I was to catch the ferry to Malta – a journey of around 160 kilometres. On arriving at the ferry terminal, I was told that the ship was fully booked and that the next ferry was in a couple of days. We were all deeply disappointed until someone at the booking office came along with the idea that if the Captain agreed, I could have my car, go as deck cargo. It was all agreed, and I drove around to the ferry only to be told that they had one vacant car slot as the customer who had booked the slot had not arrived. I was delighted but even more so when I found out that it was my mate who had not turned up after booking. The journey across to Valletta in Malta was beautiful and smooth, and I am sure I slept all the way.

On arriving in Malta, the Maltese customs gave us a bit of a hard time with questioning on why we had so many empty jerry cans and why we had brought them to Malta. I was more than delighted when he was searching the boot of the car for counter ban cigarettes and he put his hands in the bag with the dirty nappies and started feeling about. He was not a happy customs officer after that little episode although we had warned him what was in the bag beforehand. On leaving the customs building, I dropped off my mate along with his wife and son at his mother in law's home, after having made arrangements to meet up for the return journey.

Our holiday in Malta passed so quickly with meeting the entire family members who were so pleased to meet

Michelle and Alison for the first time. We also took the opportunity to have Alison baptised in the church of St Publius where we got married. I do not think that Josephine wanted to return to Germany but duty was calling, so we had to say our farewells before meeting up with our friends for the return journey.

The return trip was a bit rushed as we had only allowed around 36 hours for the return journey compared to the three days on the initial journey. To speed the journey time we had decided to change the later stages of the trip by going through the Brenner Pass in Austria.

Having passed through the Austrian Customs post, we were stopped by the German Customs Officers and asked for our International Driving Insurance cover. For some reason, I could not find it although I knew I had started the journey with it.

I had my regular German car insurance but for some reason the officer would not accept it. We were then all taken to an office and told that we would have wait until one of their senior officers came along to sort the problem out. At the time I was completely shattered as I had been driving at high speed for the past 15 hours or more, the outside temperature was below minus zero, and it was around 3:00 am. When the senior officer arrived a few hours later, I explained the situation and showed him my German insurance. He then proceeded to give the guy who had stopped us a severe dressing down for not having recognised original German insurance documents before wishing us all a pleasant journey.

On returning home to Minden, I later worked out that my average speed for the return journey was over 100 kilometres per hour. That's 62 miles per hour so I am sure you can imagine what my top speeds were driving down the Italian toll roads and the German Autobahns.

During the month of November 1967, HRH Prince Phillip paid the Regiment a short visit, and it was on this occasion that I was introduced to him for the very first time by the CO. It's an introduction that I will never forget. On being presented the CO said, "This is Lance Corporal Zawadzki, my Driver and Radio Operator. He is usually referred to as 'Z' in the battalion or in my case as Fred." To which the Duke replied, "In that case, I will call him Fred as well." On the many occasions that I met him after this first introduction, he always remembered and called me by the name of Fred.

So yes, just what is in a name?

Well, I believe I can now answer that question. It's your life and destiny. In my case, it had its good points and also its bad points.

During the visit and after meeting members of the Regiment, the Duke of Edinburgh was invited to attend a formal function in the Officers Mess, after which he was to retire for the night in the wooden hut assigned to the living in officers of the battalion. Unknown to many, two young officers dressed in their mess kit made their way outside the hut to the window of the room that he was to use and waited for the Duke to enter. When he opened the door and switched on the light, one of the officers threw a dummy grenade into the room through the window. Seeing the grenade and thinking it was a live grenade, the Duke hurled himself out of the window still dressed in his mess kit. Nobody was hurt in the incident, and it was not long before the news got around the battalion to many howls of laughter. Unfortunately for the two young officers, they received fourteen day extra duties as Battalion Orderly Officer on a day on day off basis until their punishments were completed.

Having served as the CO's Dvr/Op for the best part of two years, it was felt by the powers to be that it was time I was due a change. I was told that I would be attending a Signal Cadre to get my grade one Signaller and to also attend a Regimental Signals Instructors course in Hythe, Kent. This was a course that lasted around six weeks, and as my parents, brothers and sisters had not met my daughters, I thought it would be a good idea to try and build some bridges between Josephine and my family. I arrange for my family to stay with my parents while I was attending the course in Hythe.

Again it was a case of loading up the car with my family and my military uniforms along with bits and pieces that I would require for the course before setting off on the 500 kilometre journey to the seaport in Ostend to Dover. On reaching my parents' home, I found that mother had sorted out a room for us and that they were all pleased to see us. I think that finally after having been married for the best part of three years my mother was finally accepting Josephine into the family.

I found the course quite straightforward but again experienced some prejudice simply because of my name. Most weekends were free, and I used to drive back to Slough and spend my time with the family or studying. The six weeks were soon up, and I was told that I had passed in all subjects, so it was just a case of packing up all my stuff and driving back to Minden. As a thank you to my mother, I agreed to take my brother Julian and my sister Angela back to Germany with us for a holiday. They stayed for quite a few weeks, and I am sure they both enjoyed themselves especially climbing to the Kaiser Wilhelm Memorial in Porta West Falica. I arranged for a friend to drive them back to Slough in his car.

I was promoted to Full Corporal and attached to A Company as the Signal Detachment Commander. My duties took a big change as I was now responsible not only for my detachment and the platoon radio operators, but also for all the radios and communication equipment in the companies, 14 AFV432s, along with the kit and equipment in the company's signals stores. I was also responsible for all radio communications between our two command post vehicles on the Battalion net, including supporting units and company communications to all the section and their vehicles. Within the command post vehicles, you normally had three radios set on different frequencies which would combine onto a No 5 mike and headset resulting in one frequency in your left ear, one in your right ear and the third one in both ears at the same time. You also had an intercom which again came out in both ears while cutting out any radio signal. Pressing the presser switch while on intercom used to blast your ears off and render you deaf for a few minutes. Ouch.

It was not unusual to also have an additional manpack set in operation at the same time. Gone were the comfortable days of driving a Land Rover. It was now a case of travelling in the confined space of a command post in the back of an AFV 432 with the Company Commander or Coy 2i/c and the CSM. On many occasions especially on the big exercises, you were so cramped that you could hardly move. Sleep deprivation was a big thing, but you soon learned to curl up and sleep in the most unusual places. On one occasion just after the completion of a significant exercise in very wet and cold conditions, I had an itch on my right calf that was driving me crazy. I had no idea what it was and did not have time to check out my leg until I got home after the exercise.

While I was being greeted by my daughters, Josephine ran a bath for me which was routine, as I knew I was somewhat dirty and probably stunk after having been in the field for the best part of two weeks. As a matter of routine, I would go to the toilet, drop my combat trousers and relieve myself before stripping off for the bath. On this occasion I had taken my boots and pants off, then I proceeded to remove my long johns, and that was when I noticed that where I had been itching there was a four-inch inflamed burn mark on my calf. I knew that when the exercise had finished the previous night, I had gone on top of the AFV 432, got under the tarpaulin and fallen into a deep sleep. Sometime during the evening, the driver had switched the engine on while not being aware that I was asleep on top. Unfortunately for me, the large exhaust pipe of the engine ran across the top of the vehicle roof and at some stage my leg was resting on top of it. At the time I never heard the engine or felt the heat of the exhaust pipe burning my leg. How long the engine was kept running, I have no idea, but I still have my scar to this day.

Most of the military exercises were hard work and on occasions, I had to leave the comforts of the command post, such as on the occasion when my Company Commander decided to go on a recce accompanied by myself and the CSM, on a freezing and dark winter's evening. On this occasion we had to cross a large open area and while halfway across we were surprised to hear what would have been the sounds of a squadron of tanks starting up their engines around five hundred metres from our position. It looked like they were preparing to advance and we were right in the middle of their advance path. If they had advanced, there was no likelihood of them spotting us and we could have all ended up under their tracks. Panic started to set in as we ran as fast as we could to reach the cover of the woods on the far side of the fields. We all sighed with relief when we made it. After a short period while exploring the woods, we came across an enemy rendezvous point with four Armoured Personnel Carriers (APCs). Nobody appeared to be around, not even a guard, so we thought that it would be appropriate to steal one of the vehicles. The Officer Commanding (OC) jumped into the driver's seat while the CSM took up the vehicle commander's position and I jumped into the back and off we went. There was no pursuit, so we made our way back to our lines with the captured vehicle. I heard that the incident caused a bit of commotion later on during the CO debrief at the end of the exercise.

On another incident, while acting as enemy to the 1st Battalion (Bn) The Gordon Highlander's, my company had advanced so fast that we caught their 'A' Echelon in a compromising location in a small wood. We were stopped by the exercise umpires from advancing any further as the complete exercise would have been put into jeopardy. We had to sit back and wait for the enemy's 'A' Echelon to move out. As they moved out, the first vehicle turned left on exiting the woods, followed by the remaining vehicles of all descriptions at a relatively evenly spaced distance apart. At a guess, there were over 50 odd vehicles within the echelon. Then the big problem arose. The lead vehicle following the track to the left circumnavigated the woods, resulting in the first vehicle meeting up with the rear of the last vehicle and the game of following the leader commenced. The umpires were furious, but I found it quite comical as the officer in charge of the A Echelon was no other than my uncle Bill, who was the RSM when I first became interested in joining the army. He was now a Major and the Quartermaster of the Gordon Highlander's.

Being the Company Signal Corporal was not always the easiest of jobs. On a particular exercise, my company had a squadron of the Royal Scott Grey's tanks attached to them. This resulted in all their tanks being on our company radio's frequency. The only problem was that what appeared to be a stuck pressel switch eliminated the possibility of communicating with everyone.

The only solution to this was for me to find every tank and armoured vehicle on our company net and physically check every radio and microphone. No easy task as the vehicles were spread over a wide area and apart from the climbing up and down into the cupolas of each tank, I never found the cause even after searching for a few hours, as the problem cleared as if by magic.

Being in close proximity to other members of the crew in a command vehicle also meant you had to trust them. On occasions, sometimes may be due to tiredness, trust went out of the window. It was standard procedure that if someone was not on duty, that person would carry out food preparation and make a meal for the complete crew, as well as perform minor tasks to make life easier for all.

We were also responsible for our own weapons and equipment. If ever there was a piece of equipment that was always in your way, it was the 7.62 SLR rifle. Usually, at any given time, there were three of four rifles in the back of the vehicle. I was lucky as my personal weapon was a 9mm SMG which I kept close to me at all times. It was standard practice that every time you left the command post for whatever reason, you took your weapon with you. On many occasions, you took the first rifle that came to hand. At the end of one particular exercise, the rifle belonging to the Company Commander had gone missing or to be blunt about it, lost. Initially the driver was accused of losing it, but I am convinced in my mind that the CSM had taken the weapon, along with a shovel while going to relieve himself. He returned with the shovel but not with the rifle. This event was clearly hushed up at quite a high level with the conclusion being that the company commander had lost his weapon and received a severe reprimand. No action was taken against the CSM that I am aware of, although he was promoted to RSM shortly after the event.

One of the good things that come out of working in the close proximity of the senior officers is gaining a better understanding of the person as opposed to their rank. On many occasions, you were asked your views and opinions of classified or confidential matters, even on personal views of individuals. To some degree, you could classify yourself as being their personal confidant providing you respected their rank. It worked most of the time but not always.

A few weeks before one of the biggest exercises in Germany was to take place, I was working on the exhaust pipe on my private car outside the front door of my house in Bastau Strasse. I had taken both my rear wheels of the car while working on it and while under the car I got a severe pain in my stomach. I manage to stand up, but the pain was getting worse. I told Josephine that I would have to go to the Medical Centre in our barracks to check it out. There was no way that I could walk there so without another thought and working through severe pain, I secured the exhaust pipe back on the car and replaced the wheels before knocking on my next door neighbour's door. I explained my situation and he agreed to take me in my car. On reaching the Medical Centre, I started being sick and was also screaming as I tried to explain the pain in my stomach. An ambulance was called and I was rushed to RMH Rinteln.

After having calmed down due to the administration of a lot of pain relief, the doctors told me that I had suspected gallstones and that I would be admitted to the hospital for observation. After a few days, I was taken off the pain relief and told to drink gallons of water in the hope that I would pass my suspected gallstones. All the water that I passed was strained and tested for gallstone residue, but none was ever found, and my initial condition remained a mystery to this very day.

The day following my release was the start of this big BAOR exercise, and my regiment was moving out. I was told that I would not be going on the exercise as I was entitled to sick leave, which I was looking forward to as I had not seen my wife and children since being admitted into the hospital. To my surprise, when I was discharged two Land Rovers were waiting to take me back to barracks. One was sent by the Military Transport Section (MT Sec) and one sent by my Company Commander. The A Company driver told me that he had been ordered to take me straight to the barracks to see the Company Commander. When I saw him and without him even asking me how I was, he told me that I had to go and check every radio set fitted in the AFV 432 and all the signal equipment as they were due to leave later on that evening by rail to the exercise area with the rest of the company. I explained to him that I had been given sick leave and that I would not be going on the exercise. He exploded and told me that since I had been released from hospital,

I was classified as being fit and that he was cancelling my leave. I went to see the Regimental Medical Officer (RMO) and explained the situation, and he confirmed that I was to go on leave. I then told my Company Commander what the RMO had said, to which he replied that he was going to overrule him and that my leave was still cancelled but, as a concession, I could have the remainder of the day off after I had completed checking over all the radios and vehicles. He also told me that he would send a vehicle to collect me from my home the following day.

Minden was a hard posting and showed everyone what soldiering was all about. We experienced the loss of a few serving members due to some tragic accidents, while also experiencing the joys of becoming fathers for the first time. The route marches with full battle equipment and living in barns with cattle, pigs and chickens and boy, did some of these places stink? Missing out on meals when the Quarter Master had forgotten to order supplies. I mean to say Corn Flakes for a Sunday Lunch? Or the occasions when your CQMS got lost resulting in no food whatsoever. The weather conditions from the hot and dusty plains to the snow-covered fields and frozen rivers. On many occasions, I would be sleeping in my sleeping bag by the side of the road only to wake up to find over a foot of snow covering me. Thank heavens for the extra protective clothing we were given like the white snowsuits, the long johns, and padded liners and we can't forget the Nuclear Biological Suits (NBC) suits. They often came in handy for additional warmth. I would also like to mention the sports that we played. I was not a fantastic sportsman although I did play hockey, football, rugby and cricket on occasions for the Company Teams.

Over the years, I also visited many places as organised by the unit, both to military and civilian establishments. One of these places was a French Army Helicopter Unit which was equipped with the Alouette III helicopters. When we were taken up for a spin in the Alouette, the pilots used to try and put the fear of Shite into us. For some it worked and they came out like shivering wrecks. In my case, I knew they would not put themselves in any danger just to frighten us. It was my first experience of sitting in the front seat of a helicopter which allowed me to appreciate all the controls while watching the pilot in close proximity and I thoroughly enjoyed the flight. I had to pass special clearance to gain entry into their control room and was quite amazed at their set up. Speaking to some of the senior officers ended up with them assessing my potential abilities to becoming a helicopter pilot, and they told me that I should apply to the Army Air Corps to become one. I was most impressed, and I told them that I might take it on board.

While at Minden I managed to get myself on an education course to study and take the ACE II exam in English and Military Calculations and Administration. Two of the subjects were required for the ACE II certificate which I passed the first time. I took the remaining two subjects of World Map Reading and Army and Nations later in the year and having passed all subjects, I was awarded my

ACE II in January of 1969. I was looking forward to taking my ACE I subjects as soon as was possible.

As June 1969 was fast approaching and our tour of Germany was coming to an end, it was a case of getting all our equipment ready for handing over to the next unit. It also involved getting our house ready for handing over which meant packing and boxing all our possessions for transportation to our new address in Catterick, England. We were going to miss our house in Bastau Strasse which had hosted many reunions between Josephine's mother and her aunts along with members of my family and friends that we had made over the years. I managed to sell my old Fiat 1,500 for a few pounds to a chap who served in the unit that was taking over from us. All in all, it was a great tour with many fond memories.

It was also a beautiful day when we flew from Hannover Airport to our new home in Catterick in early June.

Chapter 9
CATTERICK
1969-1971

I n June 1969, I, along with my wife and two daughters moved into a lovely terraced house in Warwick Close in the Catterick Garrison close to Alma Barracks. Our local shopping area was the small town of Richmond.

The battalion role was changed from being an armoured infantry battalion in Germany to an air-portable battalion with a worldwide commitment, meaning we could be put on standby and flown out to any troubled spots within twenty-four hours. I returned to the Signal Platoon although I still held the position of the A Company Signal Detachment Commander. Thankfully my old signal platoon CSgt, who had been promoted to WO2 at the time I was promoted to Corporal, was transferred to A Company as the CSM. I was not very happy about that as it meant that we still had regular contact with each other. It was not long before members of the regiment were on the move with B Company deploying to British Honduras (Belize) in Central America in August 1969 on the start of a five-month tour. Within a week of B Company leaving, A Company was off to Malaysia to spend six weeks at the Jungle Warfare School (JWS) in Johor Bahru, and I was off with them.

MALAYSIA 1969

We flew in an RAF Bristol Britannia from the UK to Bahrain's RAF Muharraq Airfield to refuel and then on to RAF Gan in the Maldives for an overnight stop, before flying onto RAF Changi in Singapore. The journey took approximately 18 hours of flying time. It was quite strange as arriving at Changi Airport I bumped into an old mate of mine who was flying back to the UK. This surprise meeting was the first indicator that I got in my speculation that the world was not as big as I thought it was. We then took transport and crossed the Johor – Singapore Causeway before travelling some 50-odd miles to Kota Tinggi and to the JWS.

We were greeted by mainly Australian and American army instructors who gave us a rundown on what we would be doing. Many of these instructors had first-hand experiences of jungle warfare and survival and had taken an active part in the Vietnam War that was raging on at the time. We learned how to survive in the jungle including what to and what not to eat, the trapping of wildlife and specific safety techniques on how to deal with venomous creatures. We were also given many demonstrations on how the Vietnamese soldier would lay out and build mantraps.

Most of these were very gruesome, and we learned first-hand what the typical American GIs had to put up with. It was a real experience going out into the jungle and not something that I would recommend to the squeamish. Apart from the snakes which appeared everywhere, the area was swarming with beetles and bugs along with flying insects of all shapes and sizes and most notably the many different types of leeches. The sounds emanating from the jungle were also very loud with the noises of monkeys and the screeching of birds along with other larger animals. The colours of the jungle were also something to behold. Never have I seen such beautifully coloured birds of all shapes and sizes. As for the butterflies, they were just unbelievable. The trees, flowers and other plantations were also colourful and spectacular, but thankfully our instructors also pointed out the dangers of some of these plants. Potential hazards were also pointed out before the crossing of rivers and streams. We were also taught how to establish a safe area for the hours of darkness which fell without warning. You had to keep an eye on the time as the transition from daylight to total darkness as night fell was only a few minutes. At night the jungle took on an entirely different outlook. The pitch darkness was broken by the light of glowing, luminous insects and the reflection of lights in the eyes of the night creatures that abound in the trees and plantation. Even the sounds changed as the crickets came alive. We were taught how to raise our beds off the ground, but that did not stop the mice or other creepy crawly insects from crawling all over you. I heard quite a few squeals of alarm coming from the direction of my mates as they tried to sleep.

We experienced fatigue travelling in and through the jungle as apart from the heat and humidity, we normally had to cut a path through the fauna. We had to keep our machete very sharp which meant honing and sharpening them whenever possible.

The time spent in the JWS was not all work and training; we also spent most weekends enjoying the sights and sounds of Singapore. I managed to visit many places in what appeared to be a very environmentally clean and extremely well-populated city. Visiting the Sea Aquarium was perhaps one of the most rewarding experiences of my life. I had always had an interest in the seas of the world and have spent many hours exploring seabeds. It's possible that when I went to the sea aquarium in Singapore and seeing all the variations of life and the wonderful colours on show beneath the sea, this hit me for six. I have always told myself that if I ever had the opportunity to start my life over again, I would become an underwater archaeologist.

I also took the opportunity to visit Changi Prison – the home for many British and Allied prisoners of war (POW) during the war with Japan and other historical sites.

It was standard practice that when you were exploring the hustle and bustling local markets, you would be approached by locals trying to sell you imitation Rolex watches and the like, as well as offering you local women for sexual encounters. As far as I am aware, these were always refused. But on one occasion while I was with a bunch of my mates, we all agreed to go and see some blue movies. This was the start of an adventure that I won't forget. First, we were all bundled into a taxi for what seemed like ages with the cab driver stopping every five minutes or so; he gave us the impression that he was checking to see if he was being followed. He then drove out of the city centre and took a track leading into the jungle. Again he stopped his taxi in an entirely deserted area and waited. My mates and I were getting worried as we did not know what to expect. Then along a narrow track came a man towards us carrying a lit torch and looking like a cinema usher. He opened the car doors and asked us to follow him, again it was a bit scary as it was pitch black and you could only make out the outline of the trees on either side of the path. The path led to a large wooden shed, and when we were shown in, we noticed a number of what appeared to be foreign servicemen and possible tourists sitting on planks and chairs watching a blue movie on a white screen which was no larger than a typical pillowcase. The film was being projected by what looked like a 16mm projector. We all sat down to enjoy the movies, but within five minutes all hell broke loose as the door was kicked in and the projector was sent flying. For some unknown reason, we had been caught in a police raid. The police then lined us all up and then explained to all present that the showing of blue movies in Singapore was illegal. We were then all released and told to make our way back home. That was where our next problem started. We had no idea of where we were apart from some small village in a small part of a jungle and with no means of access to any form of transport, but then again being infantry, we started walking. As we came out of the jungle, we found that we were on relatively high ground and could see the lights of the city in the not too far distance. We eventually made it back to Boogie Street (Bugis Street) in the entertainment centre of Singapore a few hours later and found a table and some seats before ordering our first pints of Tiger Beer, while waiting for the night entertainment to begin.

Boogie Street was one of the hotspots of Singapore which was renowned for its Lady Boys. The centre consisted of many drinking establishments and a large area for dining. During the day it was a busy market street but after ten in the evening, it was a transformed place. It was frequented by servicemen from all over the world. At the time we were there, many American servicemen were taking their leave in Singapore from the Vietnam War which was raging at the time. Both my mates and I spent many hours drinking with the Americans while listening to their Vietnam War stories. I was always thankful of never having been in their shoes.

From late evening you used to start seeing the most attractive and well-dressed women walking down the street giving you the eye and in most cases they were stunning; the only problem was that they were young men. At the time we used to know them as Kyties, but in this modern world, they are now known as Lady Boys.

For dress and looks, they far outshone the local women. I never went with one although I did take the opportunity to chat one up while with my mates. I asked him or her – how much for sex and the reply, in a deep, husky voice was, "Fifty dollars." Knowing that in Singapore it was common knowledge that you had to barter the price, I replied $10 to which the answer was $40; I hit back with $20 and the reply was $30. As it was my turn next, I said $25 to which she agreed.

I then confirmed $25 for my three mates and myself, to which the person replied in the same deep, husky voice, "I will take one or two; I may even take three but four? Never!" She or he then stood up and strutted away while my mates and I almost fell off our chairs with laughter. Time for another Tiger Beer.

On another occasion again sitting with a bunch of mates in Boogie Street enjoying the local passing scenery while drinking our Tiger Beers, we heard a disturbance about 30 meters away. While looking and straining our necks in the direction of the commotion, we saw what was obviously an English man standing in a defensive position surrounded by a large crowd of what appeared to be local men.

It looked like a fight was about to break out as the Englishman yelling at the top of his voice shouted, "I'm a Royal Marine, is there anyone out there to help me?" To which all hell broke out. Tables and chairs were sent flying through the air. Men were being hammered with chairs over their heads and bottles also started to fly. It looked like a brawl you would see in a saloon of an old Wild West Western film. Seeing the devastation and destruction, neither my mates nor I wanted to get involved, so we just picked up our beers and moved to a table away from the immediate area to an area from where we had an unobstructed view. As we sat drinking our beers, it was not long before bodies were being hauled away in front of us for medical attention, followed by the walking wounded.

While at the JWS, some members of the Duke of Wellington's Regiment, typically referred to by members of British military unit as 'The Duke of Boots' had got themselves lost in the jungle close by. All members of A Company, including myself, were detailed to go out on a search party with minimum military equipment apart from water bottles and the medical first aid kit that we all carried. Unfortunately, the radio operators had to take their radios for communication purposes. The manpack radios were not particularly light.

I have mentioned before that one of the things about being in a close-knit group was the 'Buddy – Buddy' system where we all looked after each other regardless of whether you liked the person or not. Unfortunately on this occasion, my company commander detailed me to accompany the CSM to make our way up a steep jungle-covered hill which was quite high and to establish radio communications with all the patrols going out in various directions. Now my CSM was the same person who, as a Sergeant, had shown so much racism and dislike for me from my early Signal Platoon days and although I had very little to do with him, I now discovered that we were going to be together for the next good few hours. He led the way as we made our way to a large clear area on top of the hill. In all, it took a couple of hours to reach the top, and throughout this time, not once did he offer to carry the radio set. He was a big, well-built man standing around 6' 2" compared to my 5' 8". Once on the top, I established communications with my sub-stations during the time the patrols were out looking for the guys who were lost. They were found later in the afternoon, and both the CSM and I were to rendezvous (RV) at the location of our vehicles. Just as we were about to start our trek down the hill, we got a surprise visit from the RAF in the form of a Wessex Helicopter. On seeing the helicopter about to land the first thing my CSM did was to pull out his wristband with his Badge of Rank and place it on his wrist. He must have felt undressed at the time as the RAF Warrant Officer jumped down from the helicopter to ask if we wanted a lift to rejoin our unit. The answer from the CSM was no without even a thank you, and so we made our way down the hill while the helicopter took off. This episode put any respect that I may have had for my CSM into the gutter.

The JWS in Johor Bahru and Singapore was an experience that I learned from and will never forget, but it also taught me not to believe in the Army's Buddy Buddy System and that many senior ranks only consider what is best for them.

I also knew that as long as my CSM remained in the regiment, my chances of promotion were very slim. With this in mind, when I returned to Alma Barracks, I applied for a transfer to the Army Air Corp but was turned down as I did not have the correct education qualifications. I was told that I could re-apply once I had completed and passed my ACE I examination. As A Company was about to move to British Honduras for its six-month tour, I was told that the opportunity to take the exam over there was quite good.

While in Malaysia, the situation in Northern Ireland was fast deteriorating with civil disturbances and rioting increasing to such an extent that the British Army was called in to help stabilise the situation. My regiment was one of the first units to send in their C Company onto the streets of Londonderry in September 1969 to help sort out the mess that was being created by many warring factions. This was the start of a crisis that was to be known internationally as the Northern Ireland Conflict, which lasted until 1998.

One of the joys of returning from an overseas unaccompanied posting or even from short as well as long exercises was returning to your family home to being greeted by first my daughters Michelle and Alison and then by my wife, Josephine. The cuddles, kisses and the looks of joy on their faces along with the sounds of laughter brought a genuine meaning of love to me. We would all then spend time together going through catch-up stories covering the period of my absence before settling back down into normal family life. Did I say normal family life? Being a married man and serving in the British Army could never be classified as normal family life.

No sooner had I got back from Malaysia, than it was a case of preparing for our six months tour in British Honduras (BH). The first and most important thing on my mind at the time was leaving my family behind and what they would do while I was away. I knew that they would be well looked after in my absence through the regiment's Family Services and support groups, but after prolonged discussions with my wife, it was felt that it would be better if she took the kids over to Malta and stayed with her aunt and uncle while I was away. Having reached an agreement all round and as money was still a problem; I applied for an assisted family flight that was organised by the Royal Air Force to fly my wife to Malta.

On being granted seats on an RAF flight flying from RAF Brize Norton to Malta on 12 December 1969, I took a few days leave to travel with my family by train down to my mother's house and stay for a few days before reporting to the RAF airfield and seeing my family board the plane for Malta. I would not be seeing them again until late July the following year.

With B Company in British Honduras and C Company in Northern Ireland, Alma Barracks looked deserted most of the time, but for me, it was still a very busy place. As A Company was carrying out preparations for their move to BH, I was involved in Signal Training cadres to trying to establish direct communications with our signals detachment in BH. This meant trying out all different types of antennas from sloping wire to inverted V-shaped antennas and radio frequencies. We also had to take into account the time difference of nine hours between the two locations and the ionosphere tectonic plates which made a big difference to our radio communications.

This usually meant that we were out from late afternoon to the early hours of the morning. Most of our transmissions were made using Morse although we did manage to get through on voice on some occasions and when that happened, we normally had a queue of wives lining up in the hope that they might get a chance to speak to their husbands. I would also like to point out that the weather conditions in Yorkshire were atrocious on occasions and we were not used to it.

BRITISH HONDURAS

On 29 December 1969, A Company moved down to spend the night at RAF Brize Norton before departing to British Honduras on an RAF C130 Hercules aircraft. It was an 18-hour flight which many were not looking forward to.

The C130 Hercules could carry 92 fully armed troops plus its crew of five and on entering we could see the reason why. The seating consisted of a mesh of ropes secured to metal bars. Possibly the most uncomfortable seats I have ever sat in. Within the centre of the aircraft was an area for our equipment along with other items destined for BH. With a full company packed on the plane, it was going to be a long air journey. I would also like to stress that the sound of the four propeller engines was quite noisy.

Once we had settled down and were up in the air, boredom was quick to set in. Space was at a premium apart from the plane's tail ramp and who would go on that? Boredom was relieved with the constant distribution of tea, coffee and orange drinks accompanied by sandwiches and pastries as we flew across the North Atlantic heading for the Royal Canadian Air Force (RCAF) base of Goose Bay in the area known as Happy Valley in Newfoundland, a journey of over 2,000 miles. The tail ramp started to look more and more inviting and I knew that apart from some major disaster, that was not going to move. With that in mind, I got hold of my sleeping bag, made my way to the ramp and unrolled it before placing it on the ramp and getting in. I received many looks and glances of disbelief as I stretched out and made myself comfortable before falling asleep. When I woke up, I was quite astonished to see that I was surrounded by a large number of men all fast asleep on the ramp.

The landing on the airstrip at Goose Green was quite hair-raising as the runway was coated in a five-inch layer of ice. Thankfully the Hercules was renowned for its stopping distance. On disembarking, we were told that we would spend the night at the base and were ushered off to our accommodation for the evening before going to the canteen for a hot Canadian RCAF meal. Now, that was an excellent meal that put the British Service Catering establishments to shame.

As we had time on our hands, we went out and explored the base and came across a group of Canadian Servicemen playing with their snowmobiles who invited us to try them out. What fun we had only to have it disrupted by a heavy snowfall. As the severe weather conditions had cleared by the following morning, we returned to our plane for the next part of the journey to fly to New York and refuel at J. F. Kennedy International Airport. The distance was around 1,000 miles. I cannot recall disembarking in New York as we were only there for a very short time. So once again we took off for the final part of the journey of just over 1,800 miles to Belize City Airport in British Honduras. Lucky for me I managed to find enough space on the tail ramp for my sleeping bag.

We arrived in British Honduras around midday on 31 December after an air journey of over 5,000 miles and around 18 hours flying time. The airport backed onto the British Garrisons Camp and was called – well I'm sure you would have guessed it – 'Airport Camp'. The change and take over between A and B Companies was quite straightforward and did not take long as the men of B Company were returning back to the UK on the same aircraft that had brought us out that day. I was allocated a small single room next to the room that held the A Company Signal Detachment which consisted of ten men including my Signal Platoon CSgt who was overall in charge of the detachment with me as the 2nd i/c.

It was the first day in an entirely unfamiliar country and to cap it all, it was New Year's Eve. There were no restrictions on going out apart from the fact that Corporals and ranks below had to be back in camp by 02:00 hrs, while Sergeants and above were allowed out until the first parade in the morning. This ruling was to cost me a lot later. My friends and I decided that we would go into the Capital City of British Honduras called Belize City which was just over eight miles away from the camp. A free local bus service ran from the camp gate along Northern Highway which followed the contours of the Belize River into Belize every hour, with the bus trip taking around twenty minutes or so. The road was quite good, but it did suffer from the millions of blue land crabs that used to cross it from the forest to the river. The road was not lit at night but the moon's reflection on the river at night was quite illuminating. I was to learn later that a pilot flying a light aeroplane once mistook the river while bathed in moonlight as the local airport's runway. I can't recall if he got out alive or not.

My first impression of Belize City was no more than a wooden shanty village with a few Victorian and Georgian looking buildings dotted around, which in most cases housed the upper-class citizens of the town. It should be borne in mind that on 31 October 1961 the city was virtually destroyed by 'Hurricane Hattie' when it struck.

The local inhabitants all appeared friendly, and there were young children everywhere. It was not long before they came up to you begging for sweets and money and seeing their faces with their big brown smiling eyes, they were hard to resist. One of the good things the children had in their favour was that most could speak English although Spanish was also spoken by quite a few.

There were not too many bars, restaurants or places of entertainment within the town. After a bit of guidance, we were directed to the Bamboo Bar which was situated close to the Belcan Bridge. The bar itself consisted of a large wooden room built on stilts with part of it jutting out and over Haulovers Creek. The toilets consisted of a couple of small rooms with boxes that you could sit on while relieving yourself. There was no need for flushing as everything went straight into the creek and devoured by the biggest catfish I had ever seen.

The bar area was quite decent with a long bar counter and table and chairs, in fact, it looked like a bar as shown in most black and white western films. Entertainment was normally by small performing groups playing the oil drums or by putting your money into the Juke Box. Drinks were cheap and plentiful, and you also had the local ladies to dance with.

It was not long before me, and my mates got into the swing of thing, talking to the locals and drinking the local drink of Rum and Black (blackcurrant juice). Headaches were to become a common symptom. We celebrated in the New Year in typical army style before trying to find a taxi to take us back to camp. The Bamboo Bar was to become a regular drinking and meeting place in Belize.

My duties within Airport Camp mainly consisted of ensuring the functioning of the Camp's telephone network and radio communication to the Rifle Platoons while deployed to the various locations around the country. The telephone exchange was manned 24 hours a day by one signaller on a 12 hour shift system. He was regularly relieved for meals at the appropriate times. This was seen as quite a good duty as it was the only place that had air-conditioning and a bed. Apart from answering the phone, you spent most of your time reading or writing letters home. Our internal radio communications were run from a building operated by a detachment of the Royal Signals who were responsible for overseas communications, but we only supplied radio operators when we had detachments out. Many of my signallers also accompanied the rifle platoons when they went out generally for a week or two on a particular assignment.

As I spent a lot of time within the camp, I took the opportunity to take my army Administration within the unit exam even though I still needed my maths to complete the ACE I certificate. Unfortunately, my Sig CSgt needed the maths to finish his certificate for his next promotion, and only one of us could be away at the time. He lasted one day and blew it out and told me to take his place but unfortunately, the Royal Army Education Corp (RAEC) officer would not let me take it as I would have missed a day's teaching. All pleading to be allowed to sit fell on deaf ears. My dreams of ever joining the Army Air Corps were finally over as by the time I could find another course, I would be over the age limit. My interest in the army was starting to hit a low point.

As I was well known for my organisational skills, the Company Commander gave me the task of organising a Company Dance, and he also told me that everything was in my hands and to get on with it. Within the confines of the camp was an enormous Nissan Hut built out of corrugated sheets of metal. It usually served as a sports gym and as a cinema in the evening. It must have been a good 30 foot high in the centre if not higher. My job was to convert this into a dance hall. I arranged the bar facilities with the Navy Army & Air Force Institute (NAAFI) manager and then started working on the transformation of the hut into a dance hall. Having an extraordinary imagination, I went to see the officer commanding the Royal Army Ordnance

Corps (RAOC) and asked if he could provide me with around twenty odd camouflage nets and as much foot power as he could let me have. Then it was off to the Royal Signal to see if I could commandeer a sound system and colour light bulbs, followed by a trip to the RAMC doctor to see if he would give me two boxes of Durex, that is a total of 286 Durex.

I consulted with the local Chaplin who had contact with the local civilian churches and was informed that he could get me a steel dance band for the event. He also let it be known within the local churches about the dance and invited any young ladies to attend.

The day before the dance was to be held I was given the best part of 30 odd men to help me transform the hut into a dance hall. I dispatched half of them armed with their machetes and a couple of three-tonne vehicles into some banana plantations and told them not to return without a truck full of Banana plant fronds. Meanwhile, the remainder started to lower the ceiling by suspending the camouflage nets about 20 feet above the floor. When the banana fronds arrived, these were placed all around the walls giving the appearance of being in a banana plantation. The lights were then put in place, and the sound system was installed. As we had no balloons, the Durex were all blown up and placed around the room. The bar was put in place followed by all the tables and chairs around an area designated as the dance floor. The place looked stunning. Up to that time and as I locked the door, not one officer or SNCO had bothered to look into see how thing were coming on.

On the day of the dance, the NAAFI brought in all the drinks, and the band had turned up and were practising on their oil drums while a couple of helpers and I opened all the tins of foot powder and sprinkled it evenly over the dance floor. When the blue neon light bulbs above were switched on, the grey concrete floor was transformed into a brilliant blue looking dance floor. The place had been completely changed, and when the men of the complete Garrison and the local girls turned up, I can honestly say I have never seen such surprised looks. The dance was a roaring success with everyone except the CSM who never even bothered to turn up. I received many thanks from my company commander and everyone who attended, but without the help of all the different services and the men, it would never have happened. It was so successful that I was asked to arrange a second dance before we left British Honduras.

During my spare time, I used to go swimming in the swimming pool close to my bunk on most days and became quite competent at swimming underwater. As dusk started to settle in the early evening, we had to leave the pool because the mosquitoes started making their appearance and bare skin was a great attraction if you wanted to be bitten all over. It was also the time for a chap to come round all the huts with his mosquito smoke repellent generator. I also took up the sport of squash which became very popular. Maybe the reason for that was because the officer in the RAEC was a British Champion in that sport. I never did beat him.

On one occasion I was asked to take one of my signallers and a radio fitted Land Rover, to help the local Honduran Police Force in providing radio communications for them for an unspecified time. I reported to the Police Headquarters in Belize and was told that the police were hunting a man who had used a machete to cut his wife's head off. We were to follow the search team and provide communications back to the police HQ. The search lasted three days during which we travelled all over the country going from one village to another. It was a tiring experience as at times we were stuck in desolated locations and to cap it all we were not even armed. One evening as night had fallen, I was so tired that after stopping the Land Rover, my signaller made himself as comfortable as possible in the front of the vehicle while I found a flat piece of ground to lay out my sleeping bag. When I woke in the morning, I discovered that I had been sleeping on a grave. I never felt scared of the dark after that episode. The man was eventually tracked down, and after receiving lots of thanks for the help that we had provided from the police, we returned back to Airport Camp.

It must have been shortly after this incident that I, along with a few mates, went to the Bamboo Bar in Belize for a night out. For some unknown reason, I became separated from my friend and spent a few hours drinking by myself. It was quite late when I realised what the time was before dashing out to find a taxi to take me back to camp. While looking for a taxi, I bumped into my CSM who was doing a town patrol. He asked me where I was going and if I knew what the time was, I looked at my watch and it was 01:40 am. I told him I was looking for a taxi back to camp. He made no reply and just drove away with his driver.

I got back to camp and booked into the guard room at 01:50 am, a full ten minutes after the official 2:00 am deadline. I made my way to my bunk and no sooner had I got into bed when my CSM banged on the door to see if I was in. On hearing my voice, he told me I was being placed on a charge for being ten minutes late back into camp.

I do not know what went on behind closed doors between my Company Commander and the CSM, but I was marched in and charged with being absent without official leave for ten minutes. I was given a severe reprimand and confined to the barracks for two weeks. For nonmilitary personnel, the meaning of a severe reprimand was the equivalent of serving 28 days in jail and would go down on your service record. I was astounded at the severity of the sentence but was not in a position to do anything about it. In typical situations like this, it would have been dealt with by the CSM and the Cpl with no other person involved. Again this situation should never have arisen as the CSM who was apparently returning to camp after his town patrol could have easily offered me a lift back.

When I returned to Catterick, I learned that both my company commander and CSM had been informed that BHQ had approved my promotion to Sergeant. This promotion was rejected on the pretext of the charge that I had just suffered and was never divulged to me. This was the first time that I had ever been charged and also the first time I had ever been late for a parade. To this day, I do not know why this person held me in such hate. It could only be due to the name Zawadzki. Or possibly, some sort of jealousy?

During my service in British Honduras, I volunteered to go on a 14 day expedition across the Maya Mountains as the radio operator along with another dozen volunteers. It was an expedition that had been previously carried out by the Royal Marines who were also accompanied by donkeys to carry their kit and equipment.

The journey was full of dangers and the unknown, as the Maya Mountain range is mainly undiscovered terrain even to this very day. Initially we gave ourselves two weeks to cross the range, meaning that each and every one of us had to carry food rations and a survival kit to cover the period. Cutting down on excess weight was a big priority, so the first thing that was taken out was our washing and shaving kit. Now that was a first – no shaving? It was unheard of in the British Army except for members of Royal Pioneer Corps. Next to be thrown out was all our spare clothing including socks. As we were going to wear the green jungle boots, one pair of socks should last the journey and no polish or brushes were required.

We were all issued with 14 cans of sardines, 14 large cans of mixed meals along with untold packets of hardtack biscuits, a good few cans of sausages and beans, cans of mixed fruit and rice pudding. We also took with us two metal water bottles filled with plain uncooked rice along with two normal bottles for water. Tea, coffee and lemon powder were also included and not forgetting the sugar sachets. Also, every man was issued with an emergency medical pack which included morphine and syringes. Water filters and purification tablets for the water and the obvious salt tablets. I must not forget to mention that we also carried needles and thread just in case we had to sew someone up. We also took quite a few bottles of insect repellent with us.

Apart from our personal machetes and toggle ropes we also had a rifle and a Greener shotgun with ammunition which we would all take in turns to carry. In all, each man was going to carry a pack weighing around 60 pounds, but in my case, I was also carrying a radio bringing my pack weight up to around 90 odd pounds. At the time there were no radio batteries within the British Army that would last two weeks, so we also had to take a spare battery and a manual hand generator which added a further 18 pounds of weight that had to be distributed among the men. All in all, we were all going to carry quite a bit. Thank heavens that at that time we were all young and fit.

Before the start of the expedition, we were all taken in a three-tonne lorry to Mountain Pine Ridge where we met up with an Australian hunter who gave us a lecture on what to see and expect while crossing the mountain range. Apart from the Jaguars, pumas and cougars we were also warned of various dangerous snakes that were quite common including the coral snakes and boa constrictors. He also mentioned the freshwater crocodiles. As for insects, there were way too many to mention apart from the mosquitoes and leeches. Did I mention the spiders?

We settled down for the night at Pine Ridge to the sounds of the howler monkeys while watching the bats flying through the darkening skies and just before I fell asleep, I think I started dreaming about Tarzan.

The following morning, having had our breakfast, we prepared to move off. The Australian chap came up to me and after seeing my pack and feeling the weight, wished me luck while also saying that I was going to need it with the weight I was going to carry. Shortly after moving off we came across our first barrier in the shape of a relatively fast flowing river and our first casualty. One of our guys was standing by the river bank looking for a crossing point and without noticing he was standing right next to a hornet's nest. Too late, he started to run while being stung and chased by hundreds of hornets. Seeing what was happening everyone else ran until the Hornets stopped chasing and returned to their nest. The chap who initially got attacked was so severely stung on his face and arms, that there was no way that he could continue. Lucky for him, our vehicle was still at our starting point and it was used to evacuate him back to Airport Camp.

We found a place to cross the river and then started our climb up our first mountain. It was a fairly steep climb, but we made it to the top before nightfall. As night was about to fall, it was decided that we would find a place to spend the night. We could not find an area that was flat enough to lie down on, so the only option that was available to us was finding a couple of trees; one to lean your back on while you straddled the other tree with your legs to stop you from sliding down the mountainside. I managed to get off a radio message in Morse to Airport Camp, stating that everything was going to plan, before finding a shallow hole on a narrow footpath that was just large enough for me to lie in. Unfortunately, during the night, the sky opened up with a mighty rainstorm which sent a torrent of rainwater sweeping down the footpath flooding my hole full of water. I had no option but to find a tree and straddle it like the rest of my mates with my ground sheet trying to keep the rain off.

Day two started off with our first can of sardines in tomato sauce and a hot cup of tea. Then it was on with our kit before descending the mountain to our next river. It was not a case of straight up and straight down as that would be too easy. You came across quite a few sheer drops that we were not in a position to negotiate, forcing us to detour and find alternative routes. Normally we would have a couple of chaps trailblazing by cutting a path in the undergrowth with their machetes while a third member would be following them fairly closely with the Greener shotgun. It was not long before this weapon was put to use and quite common to be walking along the path to see large snakes hanging from the branches of trees with their heads blown off.

On reaching the river at the bottom, we found it to be fast flowing and quite wide due to the rain the previous night; it was also quite deep, meaning that we could not wade across it. We had to follow the river for quite some way before finding a crossing point. We found a spot to make the crossing but had to climb an almost sheer cliff face on the opposite side. With the packs we were carrying, it was hard to climb which resulted in one chap climbing with no kit on apart from our toggle ropes all toggled together which he secured somewhere above us. After hauling up his kit, it was our turn to go up. While I was going up with the radio on my back, I somehow slipped and twisted around and dropped a few feet before I made a recovery and got to the top of the climb to the sound of quite a few cheers. We could go no further than a few hundred yards as the side of the mountain was too steep to climb, which left us with no other alternative but to go back down to the river and to follow it along. On occasions, this meant going into the river and at times becoming fully submerged. Once we had found a place to get out of the river we started the uphill struggle to reach the top of the mountain and to find an area to spend the night.

Having determined a safe bivouac area, I proceeded to erect the antenna and set up the radio only to find that the radio had been damaged possibly when I had slipped, breaking a seal on the body resulting in it filling with water. The radio was completely useless and became dead weight, but I could not dump it as I had to return it back to the stores in camp. As we now had no communication, it became a case of whether to return back the way we had come or continue on the expedition. The consequences on the safety factor were quite high. It became a joint decision between everyone that we should continue after weighing all the pros and cons. In the event that someone became seriously injured or ill, we would have no option but to carry them out. The helicopter did not exist in British Honduras at the time and to get a light plane in would mean clearing a makeshift airstrip. Having a working radio would have made no difference in this case apart from giving other people a big headache. That night was one of the best nights of my life. I was completely shattered but lying on top of a mountain with nothing but the stars shining down; it was a truly beautiful sight to behold.

Day three started with our second can of sardines and they were starting to taste good. We had spent a nice peaceful night and recuperated quite a bit of our strength, enabling us to look forward to the trials and tribulations of the day. As we descended into a valley to the sounds of the forest at a steady pace, the sun came out in all its glory and basked us in sunlight and warmth. Warmth? It was hot, very hot, and with an 80 pound pack on your back, you felt the heat. As you trekked along the path, you were required to keep your eyes peeled at all times not only for snakes and the likes but also for the plants and one in particular that we called the 'wait a while plant'. I do not know the exact name of the plant, but our name for it was most appropriate. The plant had small barbs on it, and when you brushed up against it, they would stick into your clothing. Usually, you would not notice or feel anything until you had gone around ten feet past the plant. The tentacles would stretch out behind you until they could stretch no more and being unyielding, they would pull you up with a big jolt. They could quite easily rip your clothing and even trip you up which was quite common.

A few hours before sunset we reached yet another river and as we had had a somewhat gruelling day it was decided that we would spend the night on the riverbed as the sides of the river embankment were too steep to climb. Lucky for us the water was only a few inches deep with a very fine sandy bottom. We managed to cook our evening meals which normally consisted of boiled rice or powdered potatoes and a can of stewed steak or the likes, followed by a dessert of fruit salad or creamed rice. We managed to find various spots for our kit and equipment but not so many places where you could lie down, so after a chat and a couple of cigarettes, you just laid down on the sandy river bed and went to sleep, always praying that there would not be a rainstorm in the night.

Day four, yes you guessed it, the third can of sardines before heading down the river to find an exit point. Walking on riverbeds can be very tiring as you have to watch your footing. A broken foot or a twisted ankle would not go down well with anyone especially if they had to carry you. Sometimes we would follow the rivers for hours and our strength would rapidly drain away. When this happened, we took additional rest breaks until we found an area from where we could start the ascent to the next mountaintop. I think it was on day four that our man with the Greener shotgun got the opportunity to shoot a couple of birds that looked and appeared to be large turkeys. These were taken with us to our next overnight location and roasted on an open fire and shared between us all. They did in fact taste great and my only complaint was the number of steel ball bearings that you had to spit out.

Day five saw the fourth tin of sardines consumed before we started making our way down to the next river that we had to cross. As I was walking along, I did notice that my pack was getting lighter. I should also mention that my pack with the radio in it was carried and shared around by everyone. Again we got to the next river and had to follow it downstream. The river bed was very sandy, and the water was not flowing and only a foot or so deep. At the time I was carrying the radio and taking into consideration the weight on my back and the sandy bottom, I was finding it quite hard to keep up. On seeing my predicament, the Lieutenant who was in charge of the expedition stopped everyone and waited for me to catch up, also suggesting that I lead the way. Initially it was not a problem until we came to a bend in the river with sheer cliffs on either side of the river. The water was getting waist deep when I spotted the water going from a light blue to a very dark blue. I told our leader that the water that we had to cross was going to be very deep to which he replied that I should be okay. I took a few steps forward only to step on a very steep underwater bank of sand. With the weight of my kit and radio, I just slid down this bank and went completely underwater. I think that it was only due to my underwater swimming experience that I managed to get my hand above the water level, where somebody grabbed it and I was pulled to safety. This was an experience that I will never forget as it was 29 May 1970, my 26th birthday and possibly the day I was reborn.

This deep water proved to be quite an obstacle being on a bend of the river as we did not know what was beyond. It was a case of going back to find an alternative route or to build some sort of raft to carry our kit and equipment. We settled for the second option and made some floats out of a few tree trunks tied together with our toggle sticks. When these were loaded up with our kit and equipment, they were pushed out and with the lads holding and swimming alongside; we made our way around the bend to a point where we could get back onto dry land.

As we had spent a lot of time going down the river and building the rafts, we never made too much progress going up the next mountain, but we did find a place to rest for the night which we were all desperately in need of.

The next few days were basically the same, climbing, trekking, descending and crossing riverbeds. We often heard the roars and screeches from the wild animals but very seldom saw any apart from the monkeys in the trees. Spotting the different birds was a beautiful sight to see. How many different varieties we actually saw was too many to even commutate. I think the birds I liked best were the hummingbirds, again many different types and all the colours under the sun. They often flew within feet of you. We also came across a couple of huge boa constrictors and saw many other different types of snakes.

On one particular day while trekking through the forest, the skies opened up, and the rain just poured down in a typical tropical storm. Being soaking wet was quite normal but trying to see through the rain was quite difficult. Luckily we stumbled into a typical deserted Indian village which consisted of half a dozen or more huts made from bamboo. The roofs were also covered in the leaves of the bamboo plant which made them somewhat waterproof. This was an ideal place to stop for a break until the rain stopped. We also took the opportunity to light some fires to start cooking our midday meal on. As we sat around our fires which took some time to light due to the wood being quite wet, which also created a lot of smoke that drifted up and into the roof structure, there came a mighty scream from one of the men who yelled out, "Quick! Get the fuck out of here! Scorpions are falling from the roof!" As I was sitting next to him, I replied, "I know as there is one crawling down my arm." He looked at me and saw the biggest black scorpion that I had ever seen crawling down my bare arm. He yelled back, "What shall I do? What shall I do?" For some unknown reason, I was feeling very calm and told him, "Take your machete out and just flick it off my arm." Seeing him taking out his machete, I could see that he was in panic mode, but he did manage to flick the scorpion off. I then rushed out to join the other lads who were all double checking that they had no scorpions on themselves. Looking back into the hut I could see hundreds of scorpions falling from the roof. Thankfully this happened in daylight and not at night. The consequences would have been too scary even to think of.

I would like to reiterate that most of the Maya Mountain range was completely undiscovered and in most cases we were travelling over virgin land. This was highlighted by the number of mahogany trees that we came across and what beautiful looking trees they were! Many of them may have been over two hundred years old as they can live up to the age of 350 years and grow up to 200 feet high. British Honduras became a British Colony in the early 19th century mainly for its mahogany resources.

The Maya Indians used to roam the mountains and built many cities which have become world famous for their Mayan Temples and even today new places that were once inhabited by the Maya Indians are being discovered. During our trek across the mountains we came across many interesting artefacts but as time was against us, we could not stop to explore.

On the tenth day of the trek, we had cleared all our mountaintops and started the slow descent towards the town of Punta Gorda and the Caribbean Sea, a trek that was to last for two days and possibly the hardest days of the whole adventure. As we descended we started to lose the cover of the trees. We entered into a large area of bamboo trees and scrubland. With the sun shining down overhead, the temperature started to soar over 100°. Water became a problem as most of the old river beds that we followed were now completely dry. Our only water source was what we found in small pools, and that had to be strained and purified before we could quench our thirst.

Our two plastic water bottles had now been supplemented by one of the metal water bottles that we had carried rice in, but it still took a long time to fill all the bottles before we could continue on our journey. We also had to ration our water intake.

On the 11th day, we could see our final destination point where we had to rendezvous with our truck, but that was still many hours away. As we travelled to our RV point we ran out of water, and the sun started to play havoc on our senses. With heat and dehydration setting in, I started hallucinating for the first time in my life. I can see it now, me stumbling along a dry river bed still carrying my radio and seeing bottles of Coke, Fanta and Tango orange floating in the air in front of my eyes. Strange that I never ever saw any beer or water.

It was by pure luck that one of the guys came across a small pool of water. When I say a small pool of water, it held about a gallon of the most polluted water you ever saw. The water was a dark yellowish brown and full of mosquito larva along with other floating and swimming insects. We manage to scoop all the water out and strained it before adding the purification tablets. Normally you had to leave around an hour for the tablets to work but due to the state of us all, we only left it for about five minutes before we drank it. The water still looked a dirty yellow/brown, but it was the best-tasting water that I have ever drunk.

As we carried on walking, it was not long before the dehydration started to settle in again. This was soon forgotten as in the near distance we spotted a cloud of dust heading towards us and after a short time, we realised that it was our truck. A short while later we met up with the truck to great big cheers and shouts of delight which soon turned into moaning when we discovered that there was no water on the vehicle. The driver looked at all of us and from his face, you could see that he was slightly shocked which was quite understandable as none of us had washed, shaved or even changed our clothing in the past 12 days. We had also lost quite a bit of weight. When he was helping me get on the back of the truck, he picked up my pack and was surprised at its weight.

This was the first day that the driver had driven to the RV point and he told us that we were not expected for at least another day. As we were being driven along this dusty track towards Punta Gorda, it started to rain which resulted in everyone holding out our plastic mugs in the hope of catching some rain.

On reaching Punta Gorda, we were greeted by our CQMS and a couple of cooks who were as surprised as we were on seeing each other. The cooks got down to preparing a meal while the CQMS opened an Auxillary box (A box) filled with ice and bottles of beer. I knew I should have drunk some water first, but the beer was so tempting which resulted in me being able to claim that I got drunk on one bottle of beer and that's God's honest truth. After a good, hearty meal, we all got to sleep on proper sleeping camp beds.

We were all in a state of enthusiasm the following morning as we took the long drive home to Airport Camp. We had knocked off two days from the previous record of 14 days as held by the Royal Marines but what many may find surprising is we only covered a distance of 22 miles, but that's as the crow flies from start to finishing point.

That evening when getting back to camp, I washed but did not shave, changed and went to town to the Bamboo Bar to let my hair down. I was woken the following morning from my sleep by the Company Commander who came to personally congratulate me on my achievement. When I recount this experience, I always say it was the hardest and one of the most rewarding experiences of my life.

When I reflect on my tour in British Honduras I recall plenty of incidents both good and bad, and one of the stories that I like to tell is about the time a group of us went on a weekend break to a place called Gales Point, which is a small fishing village some 25 miles south of Belize City. The journey took two or three hours in the back of a three-tonner. The village is situated on a long narrow peninsula in the Southern Lagoon. Apart from the church, schoolhouse, one or two shops and a bar it mainly consisted of wooden huts that housed the local fishermen and farmers.

We arrived late afternoon on a Friday and were accommodated in a relatively large cabin where we set up our camp beds. After an evening meal prepared by one of our cooks, it was then off to the bar to meet up with the locals and to learn more about the place. On that first night, most of us retired to bed quite early and were looking forward to the following day. On Saturday we went exploring around the area and to see the colony of Manatee sea cows on the point of the peninsula. At one stage I was approached by a group of fishermen wheeling a trolley barrel with the biggest and most beautiful rainbow parrot fish I had ever seen. They wanted to sell it to me but that was a strict no-no.

Later on in the day, we held a football match against the local youngsters which went down well with everyone. We were also seen as a centre of attraction by all the children who, as always, were after sweets and maybe some coins. The owner of the local bar, who was Canadian, had arranged for a small steel band to play in the bar in the evening to which we were all invited.

During the night we met a lot of really nice people including the local school teacher who gave us a complete local rundown on the village and its inhabitants. Apart from the talking we also participated in the dancing although the locals did not know too much about reggae or doing the twist. As the drinks were flowing the time was also flying past.

In the early hours of the morning the door of the bar was slammed open and a man carrying a knife ran towards our table and grabbed a woman who was sitting on one of the chairs near us and slapped her across the face before dragging her out. As we were about to get involved, we were told by the locals that the woman was the man's wife and to steer clear of the argument.

At the time of the incident, the man had shown no interest in either my friends or me but we were not taking any chances of walking to our accommodation in the dark. So it was a case of 'whose round is it'. We slept in the bar and were awakened by the Canadian who asked my mate and me if we would like to go for a ride on his speedboat, an offer that we could not decline. He told us to go and put our swimming trunks on, to which I replied, "I've got mine on already," as I dropped my shorts and took off my shirt. It was then that I realised that I needed to go to the toilet which was no more than a small shed at the end of a small pier out on the Caribbean. As I left the bar, I stepped onto the street to be greeted by a bunch of children all dressed in their Sunday best on their way to Church. They surrounded me and while talking they were all laughing and giggling which I found very amusing until I got to the hut and was about to take it out to relieve myself only to discover that I was already out. I just jumped into the sea after that to hide my embarrassment and to wait for the children to disappear.

A few minutes later the Canadian turned up with his big red speedboat and what a boat it was, with two great big marine engines on the back. Me and my mate got in, and I'm sure we must have had a look of awe on our faces as we looked at the white leather seat and the steering wheel. As we started to move, we spotted the English teacher and one of his friends sailing towards us in a sailing boat. After greetings had been exchanged, they were also invited onto the speedboat.

Just as we were about to get underway I spotted one of the most spectacular sights of my life; a massive sailfish had sailed out of the sea before gliding back out of sight. It only lasted seconds, but I can still see it today.

Then we were off to explore the Keys. On one key that we passed all we saw were hundreds of thousands of conch shells rotting in the sun among the palm trees. We also saw the wrecks of a few boats and looked at the clear waters covering the coral reefs. After a while, my stomach was starting to play me up, and I wanted to be sick. The boat was stopped and I jumped overboard. After having cleared my stomach, I went for a little swim. After a short time I started to feel a bit tired, so after spotting where the boat was, I turned over on my back with the intention of slowly paddling my way back. After some time I was feeling a bit surprised that I had not bumped my head on the side of the boat so I turned over, only to spot the boat quite a distance from me. I never realised that the tide at the time was taking me further and further from the boat. Panic started to settle in as I knew that the area I was swimming in was infested by barracuda, which would attack anything. I think that at the time it was the fastest that I had ever swum.

On getting back onto the speedboat, I was asked if I would like to drive it back. What an experience! At times I'm sure half the boat was out of the water. It was not long before we got back and after thanking everyone both me and my mate jumped into the water to wade back to the shore. The water was only around two feet deep so you can imagine my surprise when my friend, who was walking right next to me, suddenly disappeared. My mate was over six foot tall.

As I looked down, I could only see the top of my friends head and an outstretched arm under the water which was still only two foot deep at most. I grabbed his arm and head by the neck and pulled him up, and while he was still gasping for air, I looked at the hole that he had fallen into. It was no more than two foot in diameter, and I was told by my mate later that he could not feel the bottom. It possibly led into an underwater cave and if it were not for the fact that he had one arm out when he entered the hole, his days would have surely been numbered. We still meet up quite regularly, and this story always comes up, and he always tells me, "That was the day you saved my life."

Apart from visiting most of the military points of interest, I also took the opportunity to spend a weekend in Chetumal, a small town just across the border in Mexico, with a friend. There is not too much that I can say about the town apart from seeing real brick built houses and quite a few shops. The thing that I most remember about this trip was the journey from Belize City to the Mexican border checkpoint. Initially, I was told that I would be taking a bus for the trip from Belize but on turning up at the transport location, all I could see were trucks with their canvas tops rolled halfway up the sides. Looking inside the back of the truck, I could see wooden planks crossing from one side to the other and spaced about three to four feet apart, and that was it. Passengers were then helped up into the back where they sat on the wooden plank and tried to make themselves as comfortable as possible. Comfort? Forget it, and it got worse. The journey took hours and the road was no more than a dirt road which meant the truck and passengers were bouncing all over. In the back of the truck, it was also very dusty. Luckily we were warned to take a couple of bottles of water with us. The only nice part of the journey was meeting and talking to the local Belizeans who in some cases were accompanied by goats, sheep, and chickens. To them the journey was typical, but to my mate and myself, it was a nightmare and this was further compounded with the thoughts that we also had to do a return journey in two days' time.

I have mentioned the people that I met while in British Honduras but not their ethnicity. The true Belizean are the descendants of the Maya Indians while the majority of Creole Belizeans are the descendants of the African slaves that were brought to the colony by the British in the early 18th century. The majority of Belizeans are the Latino of Spanish descent who arrived and settled in the mid 16th century. The most recent arrivals and settlers in British Honduras are the Mennonites who turned up in the 1950s from Mexico but with roots to the Russian Empire in the 18th century. These were, in my opinion, one of the strangest kinds of people I have ever met. They appeared to live in the past and rejected anything considered modern from cars to bicycles and from radios to electrical appliances. Thank heavens they did appreciate the wheel. Their only means of transport was horse and cart or other animals that could carry a load or pull a barrow. They were very religious and believed in inter-family marriage. They mainly lived in communities away from the most populated areas.

I enjoyed my tour of six and a half months in British Honduras with the sights that I was privileged to encounter, the people I met and my personal trial that I underwent. The only thing that marred the tour was my CSM.

On 14 July 1970, I boarded a British Caledonian plane for the long return journey back to the UK where our first stop was Miami International Airport. As we landed, I noticed that there were aircraft landing on either side of our plane. This was surely the biggest airport that I had ever landed on, and as we were going to be grounded for around four hours, I knew that there was going to be a lot of exploring going on. A good mate of mine and I decided to go into Miami, but on walking out of the airport's main entrance, we found that it was so windy that we decided to return to one of the bar lounges for a few drinks. While sitting at the bar, we met an American who was by himself, and it was not long before we started an acquaintance with him. Once he had found out that we were British Army, he began buying us drinks one after another. He refused to let us buy him any drinks and explained that he could afford it as he was the Rolls Royce representative in America. Some hours later, a very attractive young lady came and joined the American and us. In a half-drunken stupor, the American introduced her to us as 'his broad' - in English, meaning his wife. We spent all our time in that bar with the American and his wife and were a little tipsy when we re-boarded our plane for the next part of the journey to Gander International Airfield in Newfoundland, before taking the flight to the UK. Due to our excursion to the bar in Miami, the remaining flight details are slightly baffling. All I am sure of was that we landed back in the UK on 15 July 1970 and returned to Alma Barracks, before I went home to a lonely house.

On returning to the UK, the entire company was sent on three weeks disembarkation leave which allowed me time to make arrangements for the return of Josephine and my two daughters back from Malta. I had not seen them for seven months and was looking forward to seeing them all again, and I did not have to wait too long. I managed to get them a flight from Malta to RAF Brize Norton on 23 July. A few days before they were due I took the opportunity to visit my parents in Slough and to spend some free time with my brothers and sisters. My father drove me down to Brize Norton to collect Josephine and my daughters who I hardly recognised as they had grown up so much since I last saw them. After spending a further couple of days with my family, we then got the train to return to Catterick. Being home again with my family was like being in heaven. The only problem we had was that Josephine spotted that I had lost a lot of weight and it was her ambition to see me put it back on.

No sooner had I, along with the rest of my signals detachment and A Company returned from leave, that the rest of my battalion was sent on two weeks leave. Before going on leave, my signals officers told me that I was to take charge of all the remaining signallers and to work out a training programme to cover the two weeks; this also included a two nights out of camp training period. This was quite easy as most of the equipment that we had returned with from British Honduras had to be cleaned and in some cases repaired. As for the two nights out, I arranged a small exercise with the aim of getting my signallers used to our radios and driving on the UK roads again. Our task was to drive to John O'Groats in Scotland before returning home on a 900 mile journey. On paper, it looked quite simple, but I also had to look at locations for the two overnights stops plus arranging refuelling stops at military locations, radio frequency allocations and not forgetting the 24 hour ration packs. I had to put all these details down on paper and submit them to the A Company Commander who was acting CO for his approval which was given with no problems. I do wish that I had kept a copy of this exercise but then again, who would have thought that I would be writing a book 46 years later?

The exercise was quite straightforward and having set up four ¼ tonne Land Rovers with radios and other items of equipment, along with our sleeping bags and other items of kit, we were off. Our first overnight destination was Kingussie some 300 miles away. On the way and as our route was relatively close to Dundee, I decided to go on a diversion and take the opportunity to meet up with my granny Rita for a cup of tea and to say hello. The guys in the remaining vehicle were told to go to a location just past Kingussie and on reaching it to set up an overnight camp and that I would catch up with them later. Lucky for my driver and me, Rita was in when we knocked on her front door, and she looked a bit shocked when she saw us. Well, it's no wonder as she had not seen me for over eight years. We stayed a short while drinking tea and eating cakes while chatting and then it was time to hit the road again as we had some catching up to do. When we reached our RV point in the early evening, I found all my men there and the vehicles all parked and the two command post tents set up which was to be our overnight accommodation. They were also preparing the evening meal. As it was still relatively early in the evening after the meal, a few of us decided to walk down to a local bar that was not too far away.

When we entered the bar, we were greeted by silence and maybe a little shock for although the bar was quite crowded, nobody had ever seen soldiers dress like us. Initially, they thought they had been invaded by the Russians and that we were Russian soldiers. Once we had established we were British, the drinks and banter started flowing again. The reason behind this episode was that the British Army was changing the conventional olive green combat suit to the disrupted patterned brown, black and green combat suit that we were wearing, but they had not reached or been issued in Scotland at that time.

While having conversations with some of the local lads we were asked if we were going to the dance that evening up at the castle. I replied that we knew nothing about the dance. The chap then produced a couple of tickets for the dance and asked us if we would like to go as he could not attend. I told him that two tickets were of no use to us as there was quite a few of us. He then yelled out for any spare tickets to the dance, and we were given another four. He then gave us directions to the castle. We went back to our campsite and asked if anyone was interested in going to the dance but only three of us were interested, so we got one of the Land Rovers and set off for the castle.

I do not know the name of the castle, but the dance was a very posh occasion as all the men we saw entering were wearing evening suits and bow ties while the women were all wearing long dresses. It looked like it was all film stars and the likes and there was us all dressed up in our DP combat suits. As we approached the doormen came up to us and told us that it was a private dance and that we could not enter without a ticket. They looked a bit shocked as we produced our tickets and gave way to us so that we could enter. On walking in, we were all given a glass of champagne and after the initial strange looks were made most welcome. Yes, they were a posh upper-class lot, and not many had ever had a conversation with a common British soldier. The women loved the uniform and were queuing up for a dance. We never paid a penny for any drinks or canapés that kept being passed around. It was a most enjoyable evening, and it was a shame that we had to get back to the rest of the men.

The following day as we were driving up to Inverness I could see that the lads were getting a bit bored with all the driving, so I decided to deviate from my program and instead of heading for John O'Groats we changed direction and went to Loch Ness in the hope of seeing the Loch Ness monster. The scenery was absolutely stunning, and we had no problems finding a spot for our overnight stay. In the morning after breakfast, we loaded up the vehicles and made our way back to Catterick with no major incidents. All in all the exercise achieved its aims even if we never made it to John O'Groats and at the same time it was enjoyable for the lads who had never been to Scotland before.

Life within the Battalion was starting to get back to normal until we were all told that the Regiment was going on a six-week exercise to Canada the following month.

CANADA

In mid-September 1970, A and B Companies plus elements of HQ Company made their way down to RAF Brize Norton and boarded RAF Britannia planes to fly to Edmonton International Airport in Alberta, Canada, via Gander. This was my second visit to this airport within a few months and I now considered myself a seasoned air traveller. On reaching Edmonton, we were bundled into coaches and driven one hundred and twenty odd miles to the Canadian Forces Base known as Camp Wainwright. It was an enormous camp spread over quite a few miles. It had been considerably modernised after having served as a POW camp for German officers, men and civilians of WWII in 1945-1946. It is recorded that only two German POWs escaped from the camp, but both were recaptured just over a month later in Gary, Indiana in the USA.

The Duke of Edinburgh's Royal Regiment (Berkshire &Wiltshire) were the first British Infantry Regiment to make use of these new training areas in Canada. With the Bn HQ located in the camp, the other companies rotated between training areas near Hinton in the Jasper National Park and the Rocky Mountains and Calgary.

At one stage I was attached with two signallers and an MT driver to provide radio back up to a platoon of B Company who were about to undertake a winter survival course run by the RCAF. The course was being held in an area of thick forest near a relatively fast flowing river in the foothills of the Rocky Mountains and although it was only late September the weather had taken a turn for the worse with snow and ice on the ground and zero temperatures. Although not directly involved in the course, we had to remain with the platoon at all times, but we did attend all the lectures and demonstration and got involved where possible. The big difference between us and the platoon was that we had a 1-tonne signals truck which we used to carry all our additional supplies including 24 hour ration packs and a few crates of beer. Before the course started, all members of the rifle platoon were searched for any items of food including matches and lighters which were strictly forbidden. Over the next three days, the only food they would eat was what they caught.

I well remember the first lecture and demonstration. It was all about laying traps and snares for the smaller wild animals like squirrels rabbits and birds, plus a demonstration on how to find and use common items to make them. This also included tips on how to make a fishing line and hooks plus the typical spear for fishing. This was followed by a demonstration on how to start and light a fire using granite stones to strike a spark and making feather stick out of dead wood to help start the fire, followed by a demonstration on how to cook the animals caught. This was absorbing as they had some dead squirrels which they had skinned and cleaned before showing us how to roast them, followed by a dead hedgehog which, after cleaning its insides out, showed us how to encase it into a ball made of mud before placing it into the embers of the fire to roast. They also showed us how to cook snakes. When everything had been cooked, a small taster was given to all in attendance but, not wishing to upset the pangs of hunger that were now beginning to settle in the bellies of the men, all the leftovers were given to my two men and me along with our driver. Well, to be fair we were not part of the course. Was it enjoyable? Yes, it was.

The men were also shown how to make shelters which was quite easy as we were surrounded by fallen trees, and in the making of fire pits not only for cooking purposes but also for heating.

With the night time temperatures dropping well below freezing these became an essential part to surviving. Wild fruit and berries, along with unknown edible foods were also covered, along with items deemed as being poisonous.

After these initial demonstrations and lectures, all the men were split up into groups of two or three men and told to get on with setting up their own shelters and setting out their traps and snares.

Along with my two signallers and driver, I set up and found a location relatively close to our vehicle and commenced with building our shelter between two trees roughly eight foot apart. We made a lean too, with the back constructed out of branches and covered in leaves, while leaving the front open and facing the open fire pit which was slightly longer than the shelter and about five or six foot away, as we did not want sparks to fly into the shelter while we were asleep. We were told later by the instructors that it was the best-constructed shelter of all they had seen. I would like to point out that we had the time to construct as unlike the others we did not have to go hunting for our food.

As night fell, everyone was rewarded by seeing one of the most magnificent displays of the Aurora Borealis light. I can now appreciate why this site is on so many people's bucket lists.

As the first day was coming to a close and as we had eaten quite well, my driver and one of the signallers went and got their heads down in our shelter while me and my mate went to the waggon to have a quiet beer and a chat. We had to keep the doors closed as we did not want to upset any of the other lads just in case they spotted us drinking beer. One beer led to another and another and as we listened to the noises of the night which at times were interrupted by howls and possible grunts, the talk turned to the wild animals outside including the grizzly bear. We began to get a bit anguished with the thoughts that there could be one outside the door. Drinking more beer did not alleviate our fears and when it was suggested that one of us should go outside to check, we decided to have another beer and to toss a coin to see who would open the door and go outside. My mate lost the bet, and as he opened the door, I jumped up onto the table and tried to hide behind the radio set with the result that my friend slammed the door shut and burst into uncontrollable laughter. For some unknown reason I also joined in. There were no grizzly bears or any other wild animals, but it was an unforgettable night.

Over the next few days, we participated in the course and went out scouring the forest for food, ending up with a catch of a few trout and a salmon from the river. All in all, it was a great experience, and I learned a lot from it.

I was involved in quite a few military scenarios over the six weeks in Canada but also enjoyed some free time going into the town of Wainwright and meeting the local Canadians who were very amicable and a real pleasure to know, unlike the French Canadians who I was to meet in Calgary later on.

While in Canada we were granted two days leave in the City of Calgary. The only stipulation was that we had to wear No 2 Dress uniform for going out – a case of flying the British flag. We were resident in a hotel of which I do not recall too many details, but I do remember that on my first day out with a few mates we visited the local shopping malls that looked as if they had jumped out of an American movie. They were massive. I bought my wife a silver ring watch with a blue face surrounded with tiny diamonds. It cost me a fortune, plus presents for my daughters.

I then paid a visit to the Husky Tower at 627ft high, the tallest structure in Calgary at that time and later to be renamed The Calgary Tower, to see the superb views from the viewing platform. Later I was to meet up at a bar with some mates to sample the local nightlife. It was here that I was to encounter a few French Canadians while relieving myself in the toilets.

They had taken exception to the British Army uniform I was wearing and started slating me off and condemning anything British. I had mentioned before that I was somewhat quite tempered, but these men were starting to make my blood boil and had it not been for the intervention of a friendly Canadian; I would have exploded. I spent quite a bit of time in that toilet calming down, and when I went to rejoin my colleagues, I found that they had all disappeared.

The chap who came to my rescue in the toilets saw me and seeing the despair in my face came over and asked if he could help. After explaining my situation he offered me a lift back to my hotel. He took me to his car and what a car it was; it was a great big cream coloured Cadillac with cream leather seats. I felt like the 'King of the Road'. I would like to point out at this stage that the chap was or appeared to be in his twenties and as straight as you could find; he just had a thing about the British Army. While in conversation with him he asked me if I would like to go to a point that overlooked the city of Calgary from the Rocky Mountains to which I replied that I would be delighted to go with him.

As we drove out of the city, I must confess that I was getting a bit worried as we drove out into the darkness. Heading towards the mountains, but my worries were all for nothing as we drove into an area high in the Banff National Park overlooking the city of Calgary with all its lights glowing in the dark. There were other cars parked in the area, and I was later told that it was a popular lovers spot. It was also a place that you could view the Northern Light from.

While sitting there admiring the views and chatting away I was asked if I would like a drink. Looking around me, I responded, "And where do you get a drink around here?" To which he replied, "Follow me." I followed him round to the boot of the car which he opened to reveal a case of Malt Whisky and, believe it or not, white plastic cups. Suffice to say we opened a bottle and wished each other good health in all the languages we knew. While I was sitting in the front seat of the car, I started feeling a bit woozy and sick, so I opened the door, bowed my head out and brought up all the food and drink that I had had that day. The chap I was with got a bit worried and asked if there was anything he could do. I replied, "Pour me another drink." He was amazed, and he told me so, as he was pouring my drink saying that he had never in his life come across anyone who had been sick from drinking having a drink so soon after. I replied, "Typical British Army." A short while later we left and he took me back to my hotel. We parted the best of company even as we remained total strangers.

Canada was a fantastic experience and an adventure that I was lucky enough to go on. The sights of the Northern Lights, the Rocky Mountains, and the people will always be with me. The downside was the long roads with a maximum speed limit of fifty miles an hour and the dust in the flatlands of Alberta. I went through many places of historical importance including the famous town of Medicine Hat and home to the Blackfoot Indian tribe. Having read so many westerns about the Blackfoot Indians through my life, it was like being home.

I was happy that on 27 October 1970, I was returning home to my family back in Catterick.

Shortly after returning to Alma Barracks I was informed that I was being transferred to A Company on a permanent basis as a section commander. I was not particularly happy, as I was back with my old CSM. I was posted to 1 Platoon and took over No 1 Section. Now that was a bit strange. Me, Zawadzki, the chap who was always last in the pay queue, always last to have his name called out on a roll call, being given the Command of the 1st Section in the 1st Platoon in the 1st Company in the 1st Bn The Duke of Edinburgh's Royal Regiment (Berkshire & Wiltshire). Who would have thought it and just,what is in a name?

In December of 1970, my old nemesis, namely my CSM, was promoted to Regimental Sergeant Major which meant that I would not have to spend half my time looking over my shoulder, apart from when I had to report to him while carrying out regimental duties. Things were starting to go my way.

Over the next five months, I settled into my new position within the company and got used to my lads as they got used to me. I now had a regular supply of babysitters if ever I wanted to go out with Josephine in the evening to the local cinema or to meet up with family friends. I was also pleased that I would no longer have to carry any radio sets – I had a man to do that for me.

It was a big change for me as my responsibilities had changed from communication and equipment to the actual lives of my men. Trust had to be earned and shown both ways along with knowledge of the individual habits and mannerisms of all your men. This became very apparent as the situation in Northern Ireland started to deteriorate yet again.

During this time, I also had the opportunity to sit my Military Calculation and Accounting exam which I passed. I was awarded my Army Certificate of Education 1st Class. This was the highest education certificate awarded in the British Army, meaning that future promotions to the most senior ranks were not going to be hindered by educational standards.

NORTHERN IRELAND

On 22 April 1971, I started my first tour with the battalion being tasked to police the whole of Northern Ireland for the next six weeks, less the big cities of Londonderry and Belfast. It proved to be a relevant peaceful time, and although we were caught up in quite a few incidents, we suffered no losses.

While being billeted in an old mill in the small village of Sion Mills, the rifle platoons were tasked with patrolling parts of the border including overnight standing patrols. We also carried out searches of houses and outbuildings, especially of farms. It was surprising what you came across and the lifestyles of some of the people. I recall taking my section to search an old farmhouse owned by two brothers who lived together but had not spoken to each other for many years. I was told that they were both quite wealthy, but while carrying out the search of their home, I had never seen such a mess. It was evident that they ate out of tins and when they were empty, they were just thrown on the floor.

The kitchen was alive with rats and the filth was everywhere to be seen. I guess they used to have a clean-up every now and again as all the empty cans and rubbish were deposited into a large room. My chaps were not very happy searching that room as apart from the stink they had no idea of what they might find. Their toilet facilities were also non-existent. We never found anything, but we did carry the smell around with us for hours.

I recall one evening while overseeing the Strabane border crossing stopping a Volkswagen Camper in the early hours of the morning with a rowdy pop group that had just finished a session across the border. There was no way that I would let them carry on without a thorough search of their vehicle which caused an even greater outrage. I was told that the girl in the group was Philomena Begley, who was a young singer of some prominence at that time and that they belonged to a band called The County Flavour. I did not believe them and got them to prove themselves by playing and singing her latest record release. She was good, but I still had her van checked out. We were all quite amicable when they left over an hour later.

I used to enjoy doing the checkpoint at the Strabane Border crossing which at times was quite busy. It also came under fire from the IRA on some occasions from across the border. At times while my men were carrying out searches of vehicles, we would get a tailback of cars trying to cross. We tried to check vehicles as fast as possible but civilian drivers were not particularly patient and would press their horns and create a mighty din. My solution to this was to march out to the front of the queue and just stand there while folding my arms. They soon got the message. I used to deal with a lot of irate people, but they always lost out as I was the man in charge of the crossing and nobody could cross without my saying so.

It was strange in Northern Ireland at that time; the local people were very friendly and used to come out offering you cups of tea and sandwiches with good humour and chatter. We knew that there was a danger of threat, but it was so difficult to spot any signs of imminent danger. When not on duty, we were allowed to go into Londonderry (Derry) and sample the nightlife but were always warned to be on the alert as even in civilian clothing there was no mistaking that we were army. I only went out on a couple of occasions and that was to the 'Irish Kitchen' – a popular bar known for its Irish stew and good Irish entertainment. I think it must have been the first time that I had ever seen live Irish dancing and I have loved it ever since.

There are many stories that I could tell like when I was out with my men on a night patrol and I spotted two cars parked in a suspicious location. Creeping up, we checked the first car, and there was nobody in it, so we crept up to the second car which was rocking gently backwards, and forewords and all the windows were steamed up. It was easy to guess what was going on. I gently tapped on the window; there was a great big yelp of surprise and the window was wound down with the guy poking his head out, saying, "Check the car behind first." We never bothered checking the cars; we could see they were both deeply embarrassed as they drove away in separate cars.

Or the occasion when the complete platoon was in a night hide on top of the Mourne Mountains carrying out night observations. Having completed our task, we were preparing to move out in the morning when we were disturbed by a group of woodcutters. Having passed the morning pleasantries with them, we were just about to move out when there was a yell of alarm as one of the men spotted a fire breaking out among some trees. As the area was covered in pine trees and it was quite warm and dry, it was not long before it turned into a raging fire. We did our best to help put it out but were not equipped for the task. As more and more men and firefighters turned up, we had to call it a day and return to our unit. It was still raging even a few hours later. I always wondered just what the cause of the fire was and I always come up with the same conclusion that it was deliberately started by one of the woodcutters so that they could claim insurance and possibly blame the British Army. In my mind, I know that none of my men would have started the fire, not even by accident.

I returned back to Catterick on Josephine's birthday on 28 May 1971, but there was very little time left to celebrate as we only had a few weeks to go before our next battalion posting to Berlin in Germany.

Chapter 10
BERLIN
1971-1972

On 6 July 1971, Josephine and I, along with our daughters Michelle and Alison, flew into Tempelhof Airport in Berlin, before being taken to our new flat in Schimidt – Knobelsdorf Strasse, which was only a short distance from Brooke Barracks, our new Regimental home.

Our flat was located on the second floor of one of four blocks of flats built around a large opened grassed area which also included a children's play area with swings and a sandpit. The apartment was very well laid out with good quality furniture and fittings as well as having three bedrooms and central heating. Josephine was quite pleased with it. The school that Michelle and Alison would be attending was quite close and Josephine's friends were all relatively close by. The family settled in quite well, and it was not long before we started to benefit from additional incentives that were only available within the confines of the Berlin Garrison, like items sold being duty-free in the NAAFI and the Family Ration Issue Supplement (FRIS).

This was a scheme that used to sell items that were nearing their best before date from food stocks held in Berlin against the possibilities of a future blockade, such as whole tinned chicken or tins of ham among other such items, all sold to married families at substantially reduced prices.

One of the things that we were not too familiar with, both by the soldiers and wives, was the BAFVs also known as British Armed Forces Vouchers. This was a form of currency issued in Berlin with values equal to the pound sterling and which were issued along with German Deutsche Marks on pay parades. BAFVs were only accepted in British-run organisations such as the NAAFI. This used to lead to a bit of confusion especially when the wives went shopping in German shops. One of the other benefits that the wives found most welcoming was being entitled to a maid who used to come two or three times a week for a few hours to help out with the housework. As ours was a middle-aged German lady who could speak English, we were able to learn a lot about Berlin and its cultures. She also told us about her experiences living in Berlin during WWII. The only downside I saw in her was when I had a day off and she was due to arrive for her chores. No lie in for me – Josephine made sure I was out of bed.

Brooke Barracks was originally built in 1935-6 and named von Seekt Kaserne for the Reickswehr. It was taken over by the German Wehrmacht during the period 1939-45 and was the home of the 218 Infantry Replacement Regiment. It was later taken over by the British and became a part of the British Berlin Garrison. Over the years it was modernised and regarded by all as a fairly decent and well set out barracks. It was also close to Spandau Prison which at the time housed WWII German official Rudolf von Hess.

The posting to Berlin was an entirely different experience from our previous role as an Air Portable Battalion to a Garrison role. Our primary purpose was the defence of Berlin, and I should point out that at the time Berlin was located in Eastern Germany and surrounded by the armed forces of Soviet Russia and the East German Army. Berlin was also split in half with the East sector controlled by the Soviet Union and the West sector controlled by the British, French and USA governments.

In carrying out our duties, we were all on a constant two-hour standby for whatever reason. We had what was called a 'Rocking Horse' – a codename that was given at any time of day or night which meant that we had a two hour period to return to camp and to be ready and fully equipped to move to any given location and ready for action. Practice call-outs were held quite regularly and could never be predicted. They mostly commenced at very early morning hours like 2:00 am and would last for about 12 to 36 hours.

Between our regiment and the other serving infantry regiments in Berlin, we used to take it in turns to be the duty battalion and were given various tasks that we were responsible for. One of these tasks was to provide a standby platoon which reported to GHQ and was accommodated in a building for 24 hours in case of an immediate emergency.

We were also tasked with providing the guard at Spandau Prison which again lasted for 24 hours over a set number of days, as well as the Berlin – Braunschweig Express train guard. I would also like to point out that on top of this we also had to provide our own Barracks Guard, the Fire Piquet (a number of individuals responsible for the control of any fire that may break out within the barrack area for what ever reason) and Cookhouse Fatigues (a group of individuals tasked with helping the cooks in the cookhouse mainly in keeping the standards of hygiene up to scratch).

My duties were further compounded as on 1 August 1971, I was promoted to Sergeant, meaning that my duties would change with more responsibilities coming my way. On the day of my promotion, I bumped into my nemesis the RSM who simply told me to go to the WOs & Sgts' Mess and get myself a cup of tea and a slice of toast. At no time were any congratulations given to me on my promotion to the rank of sergeant.

It was not all duties and due to the fact that we were limited to a very small training area in the Grunewald, most training was restricted within the barracks area.

Sports was a great past time, and as I was into hockey, I decided to apply for a Hockey Umpire Course which I passed and had the unique Army Umpire's registration number of 'Z1'. It just goes to show that there is something in a name.

On my promotion I was posted from 1 Platoon to 2 Platoon as the Pl Sgt under the command of a young 2nd Lieutenant, a great guy even if a little naive at the time. One day the alarms went off in the early hours of the morning for a Rocking Horse call out. I rushed into camp and prepared my platoon, checking all the equipment and the men before getting them mounted on their vehicles and moving off to the Grunewald Area. On reaching the area that my company was deployed to, my Pl Comd told me that we had to dig in and site the locations of the platoon's slit trenches.

Everything was going fine. The trenches had been dug and were occupied by the men when my Pl Comd came up to me and said, "Sgt Z, we have a problem. We have no batteries for the A40 radios and have no communications between the trenches. The Coy Comd is coming round checking on communications, and he is furious, as the other two platoons have no communications either." Leaving without the batteries was entirely my fault and responsibility, so I turned round to my Pl Comd and said, "Don't worry, Sir, I will sort it out." He looked at me and then made his way to where the Company Commander was with the CSM. I immediately got onto my Pl radio operator and told him that when I tell him to do an 'all stations radio check' he would answer, "All stations OK Out." He replied, "But Sgt, I don't have a battery in the set." I told him I knew that, but to follow my orders still.

When the Company Commander came along to my position with the CSM and my Pl Comd, who was not looking too happy, he said everything was looking good but asked if I had radio communications with the other three sections. I turned to the radio operator and asked him to do a radio check. He picked up his mike and spoke into it saying, "Hello all, station 12 this is 12 Radio Check over." After pausing for a few moments he again spoke into the mike and said, "All stations this is 12 OK out". The Company Commander was overjoyed as he said, "Well done, you're the only platoon to have full communication in the company." As he was walking away, my CSM uttered a "well done" before joining my Pl Comd, who was receiving heaps of praise from the OC.

When we returned to camp later that day, I apologised to my Pl Comd and told him that it would not happen again. He was not in any real position to do anything about it after all the praise that he had received that day, but he never forgot.

During the early seventies, the British Army was feeling the pinch in manpower shortages with many former National servicemen who had signed up for an additional nine years' service coming to an end without wanting to extend their service commitment. This also resulted in a decrease in the number of officers being posted to regiments. After a short period of time, my Pl Comd was promoted and posted to another position with the result that a senior sergeant was posted to my platoon to take over the position of Pl Comd. I had known this particular Sgt for years as we had both been on the 1st JNCO Cadre in Malta together.

We both got on together, but there was a big difference between having a Sgt as your Pl Comd and having a Commissioned Officer as your Pl Comd. In my case, I ended up doing both jobs, and he received all the praise. This was not to last very long as he was posted to the anti-tank platoon. I was then promoted to the position of Pl Comd and assigned a junior sergeant as my Pl Sgt.

It is worth pointing out that when my promotion to Sgt was rejected while in British Honduras, a large number of junior corporals were promoted to the acting rank of sergeant. Lucky for me none were made substantive until after I was promoted to sergeant. So when the substantive ranks were published a couple of weeks later and being a senior substantive corporal, I became quite a senior sergeant jumping all who had been promoted before me in the previous year. It was also a bit strange to find out that quite a few older sergeants with many years in the rank, never made substantive rank. I was later to find out that in most cases this was due to the fact that they had never completed and passed their ACE II. This was compounded even more when attending my first WOs & Sgts' Mess Dinner Night.

Dinner nights were very formal occasions which included a table layout with the top table occupied by the RSM and any especially invited guests sitting by his side and other senior warrant officers. The remaining tables would then be occupied in strict seniority of ranks from the top down to the most junior sergeant. The actual seating plan was always made out by the mess steward who also made sure that a name tag was placed on the table so nobody would get upset by sitting in the wrong place.

I was very surprised to find myself sitting above a dozen or more sergeants who had been in that same rank for years. This caused quite a bit of resentment towards me, and it is entirely understandable; for years in some cases they had been my seniors. Now I had become their senior and in the British Army, seniority mattered.

Once a year the officers of the battalion were invited into the WO and Sgts' Mess, and this was reciprocated by them inviting us into their Officer's Mess for drinks. This invitation normally lasted about one hour, but during that time we would drink as much as we could as the cost of the drinks were paid for equally by all the officers on their next Mess Bill.

The officers always complained when receiving their Mess Bill after this event and could never understand how it was possible for the Sgts' Mess members to consume so much spirits in such a short time. There was a simple answer to that, one which fortunately for us the officers never spotted. For every drink that was consumed by the WOs and Sgts, an additional drink was discreetly emptied onto the carpet.

I have mentioned that my posting to Berlin was so different to all my previous posting and this was normally due to the various tasks that we had to undertake. One of these tasks was the security and guarding of Rudolf Hess in Spandau Prison.

Rudolf Hess was the last of seven high-profile German officials of WWII who was condemned by the Nuremberg Trials of 1946 to serve a prison sentence in Spandau Prison. He was sentenced to life imprisonment for "crimes against peace and conspiracy with other German leaders to commit crimes." He arrived in Spandau Prison on 18 July 1947 and remained there until his death on 17 August 1987. Many attempts were made to formulate his release, but all were thwarted by the Soviet Union.

The guarding of Hess was taken by an agreement set up between the four Governmental bodies of Great Britain, France, USA and the Soviet Union in which they all conceded that they would each take a period of three months a year in guarding him.

Many stories and rumours have come out of Spandau Prison ranging from how the four different national guards carried out their duties and the number of suicides committed by serving soldiers while being on guard duty. At times Hess used to scream out during the night which was quite unnerving for the soldiers in the sentry towers and especially for the Russian soldier who used to spend a whole week within the confines of the prison.

Hess was given a lot of freedom within the prison gardens although he was always accompanied by his own personal assistant, but this did not stop him from making a nuisance of himself. He often used to stand under a watchtower and try to get into a conversation with the tower sentries who were all forbidden to speak to him. He would then try to bum cigarettes from the guards; an item that the guards were forbidden to take or carry to their watchtower, but dare I say that cigarettes did get past the search before they took up their positions in the watchtowers. The only problem was that if you did speak or give him a cigarette, he would report you.

One of my duties while carrying out my duties within the compound was the changing of the sentries within the six watchtowers every two hours. Before going into the courtyard, all the men would be checked for any illegal items such as weapons, cigarettes and yes even books and newspapers. Their jobs were simply to man the towers and to watch and observe the prison compound and surrounding area. Nobody, apart from the officer in charge of the guard and I, were armed. The officer, normally a junior officer and I were both armed with a fully loaded 9mm Browning pistol.

On some occasions, while marching the guard in single file along a pathway between the towers, Hess used to take great delight in heading towards us on the same path at a relatively fast pace with the intention of forcing my guard off the path. I always instructed my guard that regardless of the outcome, they were not to step off the path even if it meant that they would trample Hess to the ground. It never happened as Hess soon got to know that we were not going to move off the path for him although we had some very close encounters within a few feet.

It was on one of these occasions with Hess being only a few feet away from me that I thought to myself, "I could go down in history and make my name world famous, especially in the eyes of the Polish war veterans. At the same time I would be taking away the Soviet Union's excuse to enter West Berlin. All I had to do was to take my pistol out and shoot Rudolf Hess." Well, I'm still alive. So it could only have been a passing thought.

Spandau Prison was built in 1876 and was completely demolished shortly after the death of Hess in 1987 to prevent it from becoming a Neo-Nazi shrine. It has served as a main military prison with a capacity of 600 inmates. It was also used during the war period as a collection point for Jews before the establishment of the Nazi concentration camps.

While carrying out my duties within the prison, my CSM who was a small guy who had transfer to the Regiment from the Royal Welsh Fusiliers and who was also my next door neighbour in our married quarters, paid a visit to the prison and decided that we should both go and explore the parts of the prison that were out of bounds. This was a great experience as no physical repairs or building works had ever been undertaken apart from minor repairs to the parts of the prison that were occupied. We visited the underground cellars and saw the hooks fixed on ceilings and walls, where they used to hang human beings. We also entered some cells which had small slits as windows, along with what must have been a medical section with tiled mortuary tables where bodies were operated on. This was a big eye-opener and it was not long before the imagination started playing havoc with one's mind. Spandau Prison was not a place that anyone wanted to be a guest of. The death and suffering that must have gone on in that place is too great even to contemplate.

Another of the duties that I used to enjoy was the Berlin Express train guard commander. The train, frequently referred to as The Berliner, was put into service after an agreement was reached with the Soviet Union to allow daily passage from West Berlin to West Germany. If memory serves me well, the only day it was exempted from operating was on Christmas Day. It was always feared that if the train failed to run on any other day, the concession would be stopped by the Soviet Union. The military train service started in 1945 and ran every day except for Christmas Days until 1990.

The train guard consisted of a Sgt and four men, although an officer accompanied by a WO was designated as the Train Commander. The train used to set off from Charlottenburg to Potsdam, where the engine would be changed for an East German engine. All doors would be secured before the train crossed into East Germany and made its way down to Marienborn where the train would stop again, and all documentation would be taken by the train commander and WO for checking by the Russian Military. This would be quite a challenging time as while the documentation was being checked, both Russian and East German soldiers would be checking the train carriages on the outside with their dogs. They were not allowed to board the train in any way. Once checked, the train would then move to Helmstedt where the East German engine would be changed yet again to a West German engine before departing for its final destination of Braunschweig in West Germany. The complete train journey used to take a little over four hours to cover around 145 miles. The return trip used to be the exact opposite and usually arriving back in Berlin just after 6:00 pm.

The above reads like a nice pleasant duty but it did not finish there, as basically you took over the role of an official military spy. The Cold War was still going on and military information on just what was happening in East Germany was highly sought after. The train journey through the East German territories involved moving through areas close to military sites and camps where it was possible to check on the activity within these locations. If you saw military tanks being washed down, it was easy to see that they had been on exercises. If you never saw any military tanks where you would expect to see them, you knew they were out. Seeing tanks with their engines being dismantled, gave you a good insight into their maintenance programs. We also used to check on train cargos. I used to make notes on all that I had observed during the train journey and would hand these notes into the Intelligence Section on my return to the barrack where they would also interrogate me on various aspects of my report.

On a few occasions, I had the opportunity to go out on patrol with the British Frontier Service (BFS) who were responsible for the patrolling of the East/West Berlin border. They also had unlimited access to the Eastern part of Berlin. The BFS was staffed by mainly ex-British Royal Navy, Air Force and Army personnel who had an excellent knowledge of the history of Berlin. We frequently drove through the famous Check Point Charlie and visited places of interest while at the same time being given a brief history of the places. I recall going to a location that was a known Stasi (East Germany Secret Police) location and before getting there, being told that we were going to stop our vehicle in the entrance to the building and to watch the cellar window just to the left of the main door. I was also told to watch it open and note the large camera lens that would be poked out as the Stasi started taking photos of the occupants of the vehicle. Everything happened just as he said and I can confirm that somewhere, there is a photo of me on the records held by the Stasi.

Another location that we went to was near a Soviet Military Camp where we stopped our vehicle and just watched. It was not long before we were spotted by a group of Soviet soldiers and one started making his way towards us from a distance of a few hundred meters. As the soldier marched towards us and got closer, we soon realised that it was a female soldier and she must have been the most beautiful Soviet soldier that I had ever seen. As she got within 50 meters of us and recognised us as British Soldiers, she changed her marching step into the Russian Military Goose Step. It was a sight to see, but we could not hang about and started up the vehicle engine and moved out before she got to us and yes, I was disappointed. This is a memory that I will never forget and it is easily compounded every time I hear Elton John singing his hit song, Nikita.

I learned a lot on these BFS patrols apart from seeing close-ups of the watchtowers, the electrical fencing and the mined no-go areas, which were the spots where Berliners were killed while trying to cross the no man's land. I also learned a lot about the standard Soviet soldier and their everyday environment.

Apart from all the duties, pomp and ceremony that go into making up the life of a serviceman, attention also has to be made towards his family. With both my daughters now going to school, Josephine availed herself of the opportunity to take up a part-time job with the NAAFI and to become a little bit more independent.

When I had free time on my hand, I used to take the family out on trips to places like the Berlin Tiergarten Zoo or the Grunewald Forest. I also took Josephine into East Berlin on a few occasions. That was an entirely different experience for her, as it was like stepping back in time. East Berlin was still full of cobbled streets, and it was quite easy to see the damage that had been done to the city during WWII. Even the large stores were twenty to thirty years behind the modern shops of West Berlin. The good thing about it was the pottery, ceramic figurines and the Dresden china which Josephine took a fondness to. Lucky for me the prices were the cheapest that I have ever seen. I still have a few items left even after all these years of moving backwards and forwards, and will one day get them valued.

During the evenings I would on occasions take Josephine and a few close friends out to explore the Berlin nightlife in the Red Light District of Kurfurstendamm and Charlottenburg which was famous for its live sex shows. Usually, we would just go for a pizza and a few drinks and savour the passing nightlife. On one of these occasion, while waiting for a bus to take us back home, both Josephine and her friend were standing too close to the kerb, and it was not long before cars were stopping with the occupants trying to pick them up. Initially, they did not know what was happening until I told them that the driver thought they were both prostitutes. Apart from the screams and howls of laughter coming from them, they both wet themselves. As for the seat in the bus when we reached our destination?

Josephine also got used to attending Dinners and Dances in the WOs & Sgts' Mess and became quite popular among the members. It was not unusual on these occasions to have members of the US Forces being invited. We both got friendly with a few of them who were also invited to our home parties as we were invited to their function on the American bases.

One of my greatest times in Berlin was when I got the opportunity to go to the Egyptian Museum and seeing the bust of Nefertiti. I think this was one of my life greatest achievements after having spent so much time in my youth reading about her and the Egyptian Dynasty.

All in all, life was pretty good although I still had problems with my RSM or to be more correct, he still had a serious issue with me. I would keep out of his way but on occasions that was completely impossible like the time when he was taking a battalion drill parade practice for a major ceremonial parade. On this occasion, I was the right-hand marker of a line-up of four companies. At one stage during the drill practice, all four companies were lined up and standing to attention in three ranks facing the RSM, when he gave the order, "Dressing, Right Dress". On receiving this command, the complete parade would take one step forwards while turning their heads to the right before shuffling into a straight line. While this was happening, I would have turned to my right, marched off three paces, halted and then done an about turn to face the parade and to shout instructions to get them into line. Once I was happy that they were all in a straight line, I would shout out the order, "Battalion Eyes Front," before marching back to my position. On hearing this command, the whole of the parade would whip their head around and face the front. On this occasion, the RSM was not happy with my command of 'Battalion Eyes Front' and took the opportunity to belittle me in front of the whole Battalion, while at the same time threatening to lock me up in the guard room, before ordering me to do it again and stressing that I was to "shout louder". I knew that I had done nothing wrong at the time and I had always prided myself in having one of the loudest drill commands in the regiment.

This was later confirmed in the Sgts' Mess when other senior ranks asked me what I had done so wrong to upset the RSM; they also confirmed that they could hear my words of command with no difficulties whatsoever.

On 4 May 1972, I was detailed for duty on the Berlin Express which meant that I was to parade outside our guard room at 6:00 am with the rest of my guard, before moving off to Charlottenburg railway station. For the first time in my life, I was late for a military parade by arriving a few minutes late with the result that my guard had already left for the station. I took immediate steps to try and catch up my detachment by ordering the duty MT driver to take me to the station. I arrived at the station a short while later but the WO had already contacted the Sgt on the Standby Platoon to take my place with the names on the documentation having already been changed, and he was in no mood to change it back again. I had no other option but to return to barrack and report the situation to the RSM.

I knew that this was going to make his day, but I also accepted that I was completely at fault and to make matters even worse was that the sergeant that took my place was from another unit.

I reported to the RSM, and he gave me a right going over before telling me to go away while he thought it over. I did not have to wait too long as I was called over to BHQ and marched into the CO office by the RSM, where a charge of 'Absent without Leave and Failing to attend a Duty' was read out. After explaining the situation, the CO found me guilty and awarded me a "Severe Reprimand and confined to barracks for 14 days."

This was a bit strange, as this was the second time that I had been awarded a Severe Reprimand which I could understand, but the awarding of the confinement to camp for the second time? I knew that the RSM was behind it. Many years later, I managed to get my military records and on my conduct sheets both awards of the Severe Reprimand are documented, but no records of the awarding of the confinement to barracks are mentioned.

I was allowed to go and see my wife and to explain to her and my children that I was being confined to barrack, which she was not very pleased with, while collecting all my military clothing and washing kit before moving into the Sgts' Mess.

I believe the RSM was euphoric with the outcome as over the next two weeks I was put on constant duty, which included a couple of extra train guards, Bn Orderly Sgt every other day and anything else he could throw at me.

While carrying out one of these extra duties as the Bn Ord Sgt, I noticed that the cookhouse was in the process of being broken into, with the result that I managed to apprehend two soldiers. They had stolen some extra rations from the stores, which were going to be given to members of Support Company, who were due out on an exercise the following day. I had both chaps locked up in the cells in the guard room and put on CO Orders that day, and each was awarded 28 days in jail.

This put me back into the good books of the Commanding Officer, and he mentions it on a number of occasions as "A big well done". When this praise happened in front of the RSM, I could see it on his face that he wished it was anybody but me involved in the incident.

During the following days, while carrying out more Bn Ord Sgt duties, I was required to visit all prisoners held in the guard room in the evening just to check that everything was fine with them. On meeting the two chaps that I had locked up, they told me that if it had not been for me, they would have both been "out of the Army". Apparently, on the day that I caught them, they were both being discharged from the Army having served their time. Thanks to me they had to serve an extra 28 days. I must say that they showed no animosity towards me and accepted that it was a fair cop. The reason they carried out the robbery was a farewell gesture to help their mates out.

On the last night of my confinement to barrack, I was duty-free. It was also a Regimental Dinner Night which meant dressing up to the nines in our mess kit. Our mess kit consisted of a Scarlett mess jacket trimmed in gold, dress trousers, a dark blue waist bib, white shirt, and cummerbund. A very smart outfit even if I have to say it myself. The dinner used to be served in a significant number of courses and lasted around four hours during which time you were not allowed to leave the table. This was a problem for the first timers, who generally went and had a few pints at the bar before the meal. Not a very good move as we also had a lot of wine with our courses.

Even the older experienced members used to suffer, but from past experiences, they knew how to fill a bottle under the table with urine. If a bottle was not available, the Regimental Silverware was put to good use.

After the meal, my Pl Sgt mentioned that as I have not been out of camp for the past two weeks, how would I like to go down to the Kuefurstendamm in our Mess Kit for a few hours and have a quiet drink away from the Mess. I agreed, and after having had a few quiet drinks, I returned to the barracks at around 6:00 am only to be greeted by one of the most disliked WOs in the Battalion who was on duty as the Bn Ord Officer.

He yelled out to me, after seeing that I was still in my Mess Kit and asked me where I had been. I told him, and he replied that he was going to report me to the RSM for breaking my confinement to camp conditions. I told him to go ahead and report me, but my confinement to camp expired at midnight last night.

In July of 1972, my company was sent to La Courtine, which is a small village in central France to carry out a variety of military training programs. The countryside was well wooded and was an ideal training area. On the whole, we spent a great couple of weeks getting to know the area and meeting the local French civilians. The only real problem that my platoon encountered was our daily rations. On occasions, we were left without food supplies, which was not a real problem if we were in or close to a village, as we could go and buy some food but if we were in an isolated position it was a case of living off the land. On one such occasion, while bedding down for the night in a barn with no food, two of my men had noticed a chicken farm not too far from our location and volunteered to go and try to smuggle some eggs out. I agreed and off they went. They returned sometime later laden with eggs and on seeing the eggs all the men got their stoves and mess tins out and started to make preparations to cook the eggs. Everyone was over the moon. Food at last! The euphoria did not last long, however, as the first man tried to crack his egg only to find that it would not crack. He tried another one and still, it would not crack, and that was when we discovered that all the eggs were china eggs. We never ate that night.

Returning to Berlin, It was back to normal routine, and it was shortly after our return that I was called to the RSM office. At the time, I knew I had done nothing wrong and felt quite worried. On reporting to him in his office, he was smiling when he saw me and that was when he told me that I was being posted back to the UK to take up the position of the Signal's PSI (Permanent Staff Instructor) in 1 Wessex (RV) stationed in Trowbridge in Wiltshire.

Josephine was not particularly happy when I told her, as it meant that our children would have to leave their school and go to a new one in England while she would be away from all her friends and have to give up her job with the NAAFI (Navy, Army and Air Force Institute)

It was now a case of packing all our goods and possessions into boxes and getting the flat ready for handover on 10 October 1972.

When I sit back and reflect on my posting in Berlin, I recall the many places that I visited with a few of them standing out, like the times I ran around the track of the Berlin Olympic Stadium which held the Olympic Games of 1936 and was opened by the then-Chancellor Adolf Hitler. I even participated in some swimming races in the Olympic pool.

I also met with members of the US Armed forces on the ranges and firing their weapons and having shooting competitions. Many war veterans and people I met had been castrated in Nazi concentration camps.

I also recall the number of times that we took off from RAF Gatow to fly down to West Germany to carry out various exercises and range days.

One of my last achievements in Berlin was the 'Battalion Platoon Indoor .22 Shooting Competition' which I am proud to say, we won.

On 10 October 1972 after having handed my married quarters over, my family and I were driven to a hotel to spend the night before flying off to the UK the following day.

Chapter 11
TROWBRIDGE
1972–1974

On 11 October 1972, we flew to Heathrow from Berlin where I was intercepted by a Customs and Excise Officer, who very politely asked me if I had anything to declare, before asking me to open my suitcases. I told him that I had two bottles of spirits and four bottles of wine which, at that time, was the customary allowance for both Josephine and me. I also told him that I had a dozen or more open bottles of spirits in my suitcases. This led him to raise his eyebrows, so I explained that I was in the army and was being posted to Trowbridge at fairly short notice, which left me with the option of either throwing all my bottles of spirits away or packing them in a suitcase in the hope that they would be allowed through. If they were not allowed through and were confiscated, I was not losing anything, but if they were allowed to go through, I would be gaining plenty.

On further searching of my cases, he came across regular everyday kitchen items like salt, pepper, tea bags and other everyday condiments, but it was the sealed 1lb box of Tate & Lyle Icing Sugar that he paid most attention to. Again I explained that it was a case of throwing it away or putting it in the suitcase. Initially, he would not accept my explanation which resulted in him opening the packet, and you could see his eyes rise as he saw the smooth white powder content in the package. I'm sure that initially, he had thought to himself that he had made a drugs bust with a 1lb box of pure cocaine. As he looked at me, I said, "Taste it, it's only icing sugar." After he had tasted it, we all had a good laugh, and I was waved through with all my opened bottles of spirits and all.

My father picked us up from the airport and took us home to Slough to spend the night before moving down to Trowbridge in Wiltshire, where we moved into our army married quarters at No 20, Arras Close.

After a short period to settle in and get my two daughters enrolled into St John's RC School, I reported to 1 Wessex (RV) Battalion Headquarter Company which at the time was located in Trowbridge. The Training Major at the time was one of my old company commanders and also the officer who was in charge of the first JNCO Cadre that I went on in Malta. We both knew each other very well, and in my opinion, he was one of the best officers that I have ever served under. He explained how the regiment worked and my actual role within the Signal Platoon which was an advisory role. I was also informed that HQ Company would be moving its headquarters to Le Marchant Barracks in Devizes in early 1973.

1 Wessex was a NATO rolled Reserve Battalion that was headquartered in Trowbridge with A. Company in Gloucester, plus a platoon in Bristol. B. Company in Winchester with a platoon on the Isle of Wight and two platoons in Southampton. C. Company in Dorchester with a platoon in Poole and D. Company in Reading with a platoon in Swindon. As can be seen, the Battalion was spread all over the South West of England and one of my responsibilities was to visit all the Company Headquarters and various locations where I had Regimental Signallers on a regular basis. I also learned that as many of the places were so distanced from each other, I could claim for an overnight stop in a local bed and breakfast Guest Houses. Also, if I used my private car for these and any other military journeys, I could claim mileage allowance.

It was not long before I bought myself a secondhand Austin Cambridge which came in handy both for my military work and my own private domestic use.

The Territorial Army (TA) soldier was, in most cases, an entirely different type of guy from the regular soldiers. Some were very highly educated and held such jobs as school teachers and businessmen, and from young entrepreneurs to the chaps that held mundane or boring types of jobs such as road sweepers. What they all had in common was a sense of duty and a keenness that was hard to rival.

In most cases, they would meet up once a week on a Drill Night for two hours training followed with weekend training at least once a month. They were also required to attend an Annual Training Camp for two weeks during the course of a year.

On my initial meeting with the Signal Platoon members, they greeted and made me feel welcome to their Platoon but also showed their despair at the current situation within the Platoon. They told me that many members had left in the past couple of years mainly due to the previous Signal PSI not showing any interest and paying very little attention to their needs. They also stated that unless a significant improvement was made, most of them would also be leaving.

I spoke to my Training Major (Trg Maj), and he asked me to come up with a plan and a training program to stimulate the interest of the Signal Platoon members. I came up with a scheme that also included seeking the collaboration of the platoon members and including additional weekend training and a recruiting drive. Members of the platoon were also encouraged to seek out their previous mates and to try and get them to re-enlist. The Trg Maj was delighted with my plans and gave me the full go ahead.

It was not long before members of the platoon noted the change around in attitudes, including the fact that the Signal Platoon Commander was also attending most Drill Nights and weekend training. I also ensured that the top overall structure was being put into place with the promotion of a Signals WO, Csgt, and Sgt. It was not long before I organised a Signal Cadre and taught them how to use the A13 Radio set which was a newly issued radio for the TA.

Apart from getting the Signal Platoon sorted out, I was also tasked with sorting out the Battalions communications

Standing Operation Procedures (SOPs). Although I received a pat on the back when I had completed this major work, no real credit was ever given to me, considering the hours of research that I had to carry out along with the laying out of the regulations. I would have thought that unlike the Regular Army, the TA would be different but no, they are both the same. You do the hard work, while your officers and senior ranks take the credit.

It should be pointed out that the majority of Officers and other ranks are usually out of their comfort zones when it comes to radio communications and the organisation behind it. Their understanding is rudimentary and can be summarised into a concept of 'headphones and mike.' The regular staffing levels within our headquarters were very small, numbering around ten men on most days of the week apart from the regular Tuesday 'Drill Nights' and weekend training events. The majority were seniors to me and each one concerned with his own workload and agenda. I was left to my own devices and only came in contact with the other as and when required.

Shortly after taking up my position with 1 Wessex, I managed to get on a TA Signals Cadre at the Signal Wing in Warminster to revise on my Signalling skills and to check out the TA signaller's requirements. As the location was relatively close to my home, I was not required to be accommodated at the base with the result that I commuted from home on a daily basis.

Meanwhile at home, Josephine and the kids had settled in. The MFO boxes with our everyday possessions had arrived from Berlin and we had also managed to buy a new television. Both Michelle and Alison soon settled into their first real RC English school which was run by nuns. They both enjoyed meeting new friends even though they were both called Germans. It was also the time when they both showed concern over their surname. I well remember the day they both came home from school and quizzed me, "How come we have such a funny name?" After my explanation of their names, they never mentioned it again although they would both tell us if they were being called names.

As the kids were growing fast, they needed more and more everyday items, and money was still at a premium, so Josephine took up a part-time job at the famous Bowyers Factory in Trowbridge town centre. If anyone used to mention Bowyers, the first thing that came to mind was pork pies and sausage rolls. She enjoyed her job and made many friends, and apart from the wages that she was bringing home every week, she was also allowed to buy Bowyers products at a staff discount. I think this is one of the reasons that I started putting on weight.

Family life was good and much of our spare time was taken up by going out in the car and exploring the surrounding areas like Stonehenge. At that time, the area was not subject to any fencing which meant you could go up and touch the stones and even have a picnic on them. We also travelled up to my mother's house in Slough and paid her short visits. At times we were also inundated with visits from my family members and Josephine's family and friends from Malta. On many occasions, both Josephine and I had to give up our beds and sleep on the living room floor.

In early 1973, BHQ 1 Wessex along with HQ Company were moved to Le Marchant Barracks in Devizes. This was a great move as the available accommodation and storage facilities were vastly superior to what we had in Trowbridge. On the downside, the UK was going through a period of unsustainable work practices with the then Prime Minister Edward Heath having imposed a 3-day work order due to miners' strikes and power shortages. On taking over the Signal Platoon office and stores, I was also obliged to take over a large mobile electricity generator and the best part of a hundred large 12-volt wet batteries. All these batteries were connected in such a way that when there was a power cut, I could supply additional electric power for essential use by starting up the generator.

When I took over the Signal stores, there was very limited shelving, and nobody was in a position to tell me how to get additional shelving. I was told to get it sorted out, but nobody had the faintest idea of how to go about it.

As the responsibility fell on me, I recalled the help that I used to get from the RAOC in British Honduras and made plans to go to the RAOC Depot in Bicester, Oxfordshire. On reporting to the guardroom of the RAOC, I asked to speak to the man in charge of stores and was directed to see an elderly Major. After explaining my position in the TA and the fact that we had moved locations with minimum resources, he promised to give me everything I needed and more. He took me to a large warehouse and showed me enough second-hand furniture and shelving to fit out half a dozen barracks. He told me to look around and make a list out with one of his workers and to arrange a date and time to pick it up. He then shook my hand, gave me a cheerful wave and said goodbye. Initially, I had only come to see if I could get some shelving, which I got, and most of it was like new. I also got some cupboards, bookcases, office tables and chairs; in fact, I got so much that I could not use it all, but I knew the additional furniture and fittings would be very handy in the other offices of the BHQ.

A few days later I sent a couple of trucks up to the RAOC Depot to collect the items, and not one single piece of paper required signing. This was totally unheard of in the British Army as without signatures the army would collapse. The Signals CSgt was delighted with his new shelves and security cupboards as was the orderly room with its new tables and chairs along with the bookcases, and the CO was also happy with his new office table and chair along with his new carpet. Most of my seniors were absolutely amazed at the amount of furniture I had managed to scrounge and kept asking me how I had managed it.

Over the next few months, I got to know the training areas of Salisbury Plains, Thetford, Sennybridge and Knook Camp plus a few others where we carried out Battalion as well as Company exercises. The Signal Platoon also held its own exercises where we would go to a more exotic location like Alderney in the Channel Isles. This was made possible with the collaboration of the Royal Navy who transported us there on an RN Frigate from Portsmouth. As the Frigate could not dock in Alderney, we had to go over the sides down rope netting onto small boats and taken to a suitable landing site.

The exercise on Alderney was a small 'Manpack Exercise' which mainly involved map reading and radio communication procedures. It included most of the signallers from the Battalion who all had to make their way to an RV point from all over the SW Regions of England. On the start of the exercise, the men were divided into pairs and given a map grid reference in code which they had to decipher before moving off to their first location. On reaching their destination, they would inform the controlling station which, in return, would ask a question referring to their actual location. Once the control had received the correct answer, they were given a new grid reference to go to.

I recall that the day of the actual exercise which was called 'Exercise Tempus Fugit' was a warm and sunny day which made the exercise very pleasant. Going around the various location of Alderney, also brought to mind the history of the place especially during its occupation by the Germans in WWII.

The Channel Islands which included Jersey, Guernsey, Alderney, Sark and some smaller island were occupied by German Forces from 30 June 1940 until 16 May 1945 with Alderney being the last to be liberated. The majority of its civilian inhabitants had been evacuated before the German invasion. During the occupation period, it was mainly used as a camp for Russian and Polish POW. It also housed scores of slave labourers who were forced to build many military constructions which remain to this day, especially the pillboxes, or gun emplacements.

On returning to the Frigate the next day for our return journey back to Portsmouth, the weather had taken a change for the worse with a Force 8 Gale being predicted. As the men were scrambling up the nets on the side of the Frigate, one of them dropped an A41 Radio and its pack into the sea which sunk to the bottom due to its weight. After a bit of persuasion by my Signals Officer, the Captain agreed to send a frogman down to the seabed to recover the set. Once the set had been recovered, I made my way down to the Petty Officers' Mess and was served up with a glass of rum. As the ship was making headway, the Force 8 Gale started to take hold with the motion of the ship beginning to take off in earnest. As I was sitting in the PO's Mess drinking my rum, I noticed that the POs with us were starting to feel the pitching of the ship, and it was not too long before they had to rush off to be sick in the John's. I along with my other SNCOs were not affected, so we just carried on drinking until we got back to port.

All in all, it was a great weekend exercise which I am sure will be well remembered by all who participated.

The 1973 Annual Training Camp was to be held in Knook Camp, Heytesbury in June with the highlight being the Presentation of Colours to the 1st Battalion, The Wessex Regiment (RV) on 16 June 1973 by General Sir Basil Eugster. I personally only played a small part in this ceremony although it was of significant importance as without my input and setting up of the speaker system nobody would have heard a thing.

I was also involved in overseeing the running of a cadre for company signallers while at the same time taking any possible opportunities to drive back home to spend time with my family.

In July 1973 my battalion, 1 DERR, was posted from Berlin to Abercorn Barrack, Ballykinler in Northern Ireland to start a two-year family accompanied posting.

In August of that year, the Signal Platoon was involved with providing a Radio Safety Net for the Cowes Week Fastnet Yacht Races. This meant that a team of signallers with a number of Land Rovers fully kitted out with radios would take up strategic positions on the Isle of Wight overlooking the Solent. Our main task was to simply inform the Race Control Centre if we saw any yachts in any sort of difficulties. The primary concern was a Yacht called Yeoman XIX which was crewed by Prince Phillip and his 13 year old son Prince Andrew who was participating in the race for the very first time.

I finished what I must say was an absorbing and productive year by organising a Company Dinner and Dance for the Christmas Celebrations which was very well attended.

It was also the year that saw my battalion's first casualties in Northern Ireland with two members who I knew being killed. One was killed in a tragic accident and the other one by a bomb placed by the IRA.

On 23 March 1974 a good mate of mine was killed along with two others. Another was seriously injured in what became known as 'The Honey Trap Incident'. The incident revolved around four plain-clothed soldiers who were out enjoying a drink in Belfast. They were all invited to a party by two young girls. They were taken to a house in Antrim Road where they met a third girl. One of the girls then went out with the excuse of getting some more girls for the party, only to return with two gunmen armed with a pistol and an automatic machine gun.

They were all forced to lie on a bed and subsequently shot in the back. All but one were killed instantly while the fourth one, although seriously injured, managed to get out of the house and called for help.

As my mate was from Newbury, his body was flown home after the investigation. Both I and my RSM attended his funeral and the wake which was held at the Robin Hood Pub in Newbury. It was well attended and at the same time very harrowing, seeing the looks on the faces of his family and friends. The realities of the troubles in Northern Ireland were starting to settle in.

With the introduction of HF radio sets, I got the signallers involved in trying to communicate between the various company locations on drill nights. It was no easy matter as drill nights were held on different evenings. I overcame this problem by arranging for additional training nights to be allowed for this purpose. As with all frequencies, these had to be allocated down from Brigade level, which was not a real problem. Our problem was that the frequencies issued were not compatible with the times and distances that we were to work over. To put it into context, as the evening approaches, the ionosphere contracts and squeezes high frequency (HF) signals together, resulting in a lot of static signals and interference from other frequencies. It also relied on the radio mast and the antenna being used. We experimented with sloping wire antennas, dipoles, T-shaped antennas and inverted V antennas, in most cases, with no results. This was carried out over a few months and I finally cancelled the experiment when it was plain to see that we were not going to achieve our goals. We did, however, improve our knowledge of HF Antennas and working closer together.

A few months after this internal exercise, I was called into the Training Majors (Trg Maj) office for my Annual Confidential Report to be read out. The Trg Maj, who was new to the unit, had written my report and downgraded my assessment due to the facts that I had not achieved my aims on the HF initiative. I was flabbergasted and asked if I could speak to him on an equal standing with no rank difference being involved. It was now his turn to exhibit surprise, but he agreed. I then tore into him and described the situation at the time I had taken over and what I had done to turn the Signal Platoon around. He was completely oblivious of all the procedures I had undertaken in this endeavour and took note of what I had said, agreeing to amend my report where it was possible. However, he could not change the assessment for promotion as stated by the CO. On switching back to Military mode, I saluted the Major and marched out of the office. I should point out that after this episode the Trj

Maj treated me in an altogether different light and with the respect that I deserved every time we met.

Would I say that any racism was directed at me by my Regular and Non-Regular Officers during my time with 1 Wessex? Possibly, yes. My Commanding Officer was a Headmaster with a TA commission who was always consorting with people of high standings. Very seldom would he speak to the lower ranks unless he had to. I would classify the Trg Maj as an old soldier who came up through the ranks before getting his regular commission. There was no racism shown by the majority of TA Officers who in most cases just wanted to learn from your experiences.

One of my favourite stories of Le Marchant Barracks was the time I drove into the barracks and having parked up my car, I was walking towards my office when I bumped into a Brigadier. As he failed to return my salute, I wondered, "Who the hell is this?" I had never seen such a scruffy looking Brigadier in all my life. He stopped in front of me and smiled before saying that he was not a real Brigadier and that his name was Nicholas Courtney who played the Brigadier in Dr Who.

The crew was using the barracks to film one of their episodes. After a bit of chatter, I left him to go up to my office where I bumped into Elisabeth Sladen who played Sarah Jane Smith in the series, looking for the female toilet with one of her female actress. At that time we had no female toilets in the block, but I did take them both to the gents' toilets and having checked that they were empty, I told them they could both go in and that I would stand guard at the main doorway. I'm sure one and all can imagine the giggling that went on after that.

I also met up with Jon Pertwee who played Dr Who during the period 1970–1974 along with Sgt Benton, played by John Levene plus other members of the cast. The most memorable part of the day was Elisabeth Sladen and sitting in Dr Who's car, Bessie, more commonly known as WHO 1.

As my two year posting to 1 Wessex was nearing its end, I can reflect although initially I never wanted to go to a TA Battalion, it was a venture that I was incredibly grateful to have experienced. The majority of my time I was my own boss and had very little interference from my superiors. In most cases, I was given a free hand. I travelled all over England and Wales including having the privilege of working with RAF and RN personnel.

On the family side of life, both my daughters were both doing very well at school and were extremely popular, but maybe that was due to me picking them up from school while dressed in army uniform and driving a military Land Rover. Their entire group of friends used to love clambering on the Land Rover and playing with the fitted radios, and if I had an SMG or SLR weapon with me at the time, which I allowed them to handle, they were over the moon. The kids also got quite jealous seeing me drive away with my daughters sitting in the front of the Land Rover.

Both my daughters also received the Blessed Eucharist for the first time at St John's Church in Trowbridge on 22 June 1974.

I had also upgraded my car to a beautiful Vauxhall Victor Estate after having found out that my Battalion would be moving to Shoeburyness in Essex on completion of their Northern Ireland tour in January 1975.

Josephine and the kids had settled in well, while at Trowbridge and on more than one occasion I was asked to leave the army and to settle down somewhere with a civilian job.

Chapter 12

NORTHERN IRELAND

oving to rejoin my Battalion in Abercorn Barrack, Ballykinler in Northern Ireland was not going to be so straightforward. When I went to collect my travel documents, I was told to report to Westbury railway station on 15 October 1974 dressed in full No2 Dress and to meet up with the Royal Military Police (RMP). I also had to take all my military and civilian clothing with me, which meant a fully loaded suitcase and kit bag.

At Westbury station, I met up with the RMP who quickly handcuffed a prisoner to my left wrist and gave me the key before wishing me a safe journey. The prisoner, whose name I cannot recall, told me that he had been caught by the RMPs after having been reported as being AWOL or 'Absent Without Official Leave'. He knew that he was re-joining the Battalion and that he was expecting 28 days in jail. He also promised not to put up any resistance towards me. Lucky for me, he had no baggage which meant that he could carry one of my bits of luggage.

The rail trip from Westbury to Liverpool via Waterloo and Euston caused quite a bit of excitement especially among the children, when they saw me dressed in army uniform with a guy in civilian clothing handcuffed to me. Many comments were made, some being quite comical while others were very hostile. I was glad to reach and board the late ferry to Belfast in the evening. My prisoner had no money with him, and as I needed my food and drink, I also paid for his, which he was thankful for. Once the ferry was moving out of port, I removed the handcuffs, and we both settled in a small bunk for the night.

In the morning as we arrived in Belfast I replaced the cuffs on my prisoner, disembarked shortly after and set out on the task of looking for our transport. That did not take too long as our Regimental Police Sergeant quickly spotted me and came up to me to relieve me of my prisoner. As we walked down to his Land Rover, he pointed out a second Land Rover and told me that that was my transport back to camp. I could not understand why they sent out two Land Rovers when one would have been quite sufficient.

On reaching the barracks, I was taken straight to the Sgts' Mess and given a room in one of the wings on the ground floor. I did not recognise anyone initially, but maybe that was because there was nobody around from the Regiment; just a few strangers and a few senior NCOs from the Women's Royal Army Corps (WRAC). I found it a bit strange at the time as I had never been billeted in a WOs & Sgts' Mess which had female members.

I later found out that while I was travelling on the ferry, an uprising had begun in the Long Kesh Maze Prison which held an estimated 1,500 convicted prisoners and internees.

Fires were started as the prisoners rebelled against the prison wardens and the army was called in to help quell the uprising. The majority of available men of my battalion were deployed to the 'Kesh' to help subdue the inmates. In many cases hand to hand conflicts took place, and the use of a very potent Dibenzoxazepine Gas (CR Gas) was used for the first time on the prisoners.

Many buildings were burned down including almost all of the inmates' accommodation before the situation was brought back and under the control of the authorities involved. It was late evening when members of the battalion started to return to barracks after having spent the majority of the past 24 hours at the prison.

At around 9:30 pm, I went into the bar of the Sgt's Mess which was empty apart from the barman and ordered myself a pint. I was a bit worried as I had not packed a civilian jacket in my luggage which I knew was part of the dress code of the mess, so I wore a cardigan and tie and hoped nobody would notice.

As the night drew on, the place was still deserted. Then a few SNCOs started to stumble in and when I say stumbled in, I mean stumbled in. They were still dressed in their combat uniform and wearing their webbing, carrying their weapons and batons and sporting bandages, scars and black eyes. They looked a sorry sight. All they wanted at that particular time was a pint of beer before retiring to their room for a well-earned rest. A few comments were directed towards me which was entirely understandable seeing that I was well dressed and showing no signs of having been in any conflict while at the same time welcoming me back to the Battalion.

The RSM, who was my old Pl Sgt from my days in Malta, entered the bar just before it was due to close and spotted that I was inappropriately dressed. I ended up having to buy everyone in the mess a pint of beer. Lucky for me there was less than half a dozen in the mess at the time, so it did not cost me a fortune.

Initially, nobody appeared to have any idea on what position I would fill within the Regiment apart from the fact that I had to attend a Northern Ireland induction course which would last approximately two weeks. This course was held just outside the barracks in a complex that was staffed by members of the armed forces from all three services. It was an engaging course covering the history of the Northern Ireland conflict, search and hold techniques, weapons used by the IRA including their constructions of pipe mortars and the making of petrol bombs. Names of prominent members and photos of wanted IRA personnel were also included.

To conclude the course, I was attached to a Royal Green Jacket's patrol in Belfast headed by one of their Corporals. When he saw me as a Sergeant being attached to his patrol, he was a bit unnerved until I told him to treat me as a private as his experience was far greater than mine. The main aim of this particular patrol was the gathering of information, which I found very interesting.

I would like to remind any readers of this book that the year was 1974. The days of mobile phones and everyday computers and laptops were a thing of the distant future. Access to information was severely limited. The checking of a person's identity was also severely curtailed although human rights were not a big issue at the time.

Unlike most countries, ID or Identity Cards are not a regular part of everyday life. Although there have been calls in the UK to make such documents compulsory, governments have always stated that it would be too expensive to implicate and enforce and at the same time would impeach the citizens' right to privacy.

To combat this ridiculous situation in Northern Ireland, the British Army came up with the 'P' Check or the personnel audit. This involved members of army patrols visiting every house in every street within a given area. After knocking on a door, they would ask the occupant if they could enter their home in order to establish who actually lived in the house. While one person was taking the details of the residents, another would be noting and taking particulars of the house decor from the colour of the living room walls, the make of the TV, down even to the colour of the settee. In fact, they would take note of anything within the house that only the persons living in the house would know. All this data would then be handed over to the local Intelligence Section who would then store the information in a relatively restricted, but accessible place for future use.

This information was then later used when a person or persons were seen to be acting suspiciously. They would be stopped and asked for their name and home address. Once they had given us their name and address, this would be radioed back to our base for confirmation that the name given was a resident of that address. If the reply to our radio conversation came back either positive or negative, they would also be asked if they had anything that could confirm their name and address. If this was not available or further suspicions were aroused, we would ask them a question that had been given to us by our radio operator on their house. For instance, what is the make of your TV? If they answered correctly, they were allowed to continue on their way, but if they answered negatively, they were held over and sent back to our camp for further interrogation. It was a simple but effective means of certifying the identity of a person but at the same time, many man-hours were spent in its instrumentation.

At the end of the day, I thanked the Corporal for all that he had taught me, knowing that the knowledge that I had gained from his experiences would put me in good stead.

That same evening while eating my evening meal in the Sgts' Mess, I was informed that I was being posted to D Company and would be moving to Crossmaglen as the Admin Sgt.

The following day was my last day of the induction course which finished just after midday. When making my way back to the Barracks, I would walk past Sandes Home which was the equivalent to an NAAFI and used by all the servicemen and their accompanying families. I had contemplated going in for a drink but decided against it and made my way back to my room in the Mess. I had just reached my room when I heard a massive explosion followed by many sirens going off. I went outside to see many men and women running all over the place while at the same time seeing a pall of smoke floating over the area of Sandes Home. It became blatantly obvious that a massive bomb had just gone off. I went to see if I could help but had to step back as I saw everything was being taken in hand and I would only end up being a nuisance.

I was quite surprised at my calmness and returned to my room and laid on my bed. Possibly an hour later, I was startled by a lot of shouting and banging on my door and told to get out of my room as a suspect package was seen outside next to my room. Apparently, after the bombing of Sandes Home, search parties were sent to search the entire barracks to confirm that no other explosive charges had been laid to go off at a later time. During one of these searches, a large box was seen against the outside wall of the Sgts' Mess under the window of the room that I occupied. The Sgts' Mess was completely vacated, and the Bomb Disposal Team was brought in. Nobody approached the box, but a small Bomb Disposal Robot was sent in which fired a shot into the box. Nothing happened. On closer examination, the box was found to be empty; it was agreed by all in attendance that the wind had blown the box to its present position from a nearby rubbish point. But due to the current situation at that time, nothing could be overlooked.

As the facts about the bombing started to emerge, it became clear that the bomb of approximately 300 lbs of explosives was packed into a white van parked close to Sandes Home and timed to go off for maximum impact. Two of our soldiers were killed in the explosion with a further 31 servicemen and two civilians suffering injuries. Many suffered severe injuries, including a close friend of mine.

Some later suggested that the bombing of Sandes Home was directed against my Regiment in retaliation for their role in suppressing the Long Kesh Maze Prison uprising.

I was posted to D Company the following day, which was a composite company formed by members of the Corp of Drums and members of both the Mortar and Anti-Tank Platoons, acting in a normal Rifle Company roll. I was told that I would be moving to Crossmaglen with the Company 2 i/c along with the two Platoon and the Section Commanders. I was also told that I would take over and become responsible for all the stores and equipment from the Royal Marine Commandos (RM) who were located within the Police station in Crossmaglen. A few hours later we all boarded a Wessex Helicopter and moved to our new location.

We were greeted by the Officer Commanding the RM Detachment and given a brief history of the events around the Police Station and Crossmaglen before being shown around the building. While walking around the outside of the building, we were shown a spot where two RPG 7 rockets had hit the building on either side of a window which had been filled in. It later transpired that the window belonged to the room that I was going to occupy. We were also told that the building and compound often came under fire from small arms and pipe mortars.

The complex was also staffed by members of the Royal Ulster Constabulary (RUC).

Over the next few day I took over all the stores and was also shown how to marshal all the helicopter comings and goings as everything coming into the base was airlifted in or out of the camp, including all our rubbish. I was also shown how to manage underslung loads especially the large gas canisters that we used for cooking and heating.

Every time a helicopter came in, I had to ensure that there was an armed guard present and that a machine gun was also manned in the tower overlooking the landing zone which was outside the walls of the compound. It was well known that the IRA was always looking for an opportunity to shoot a helicopter down and that they were most vulnerable while either landing and taking off. My job also included ensuring the helicopter was on the ground for the minimum time possible.

While I was getting on with my work, the section NCOs were being taken out on the RM patrols to get used to the routes and techniques employed by the RMs. I was told and also discovered that many members of the RM showed an avant-garde attitude towards the local civilians and treated them with contempt. When out on patrol, they would do things to aggravate people, like snap off car radio aerials and scratch the cars' paintwork, shootout or smash light bulbs and kill dogs. When confronted on the light bulbs and dogs, they would say it was to make them less visible at night, as the dogs used to give warning of when they approached certain locations. Although I understood the implications, I could never condone this situation. While accompanying these patrols all our men had to wear the Green Beret of the RM as they never wanted the locals to know that they were due to handover to another unit. It later became known that they had leaked out a leaving date although not the correct date.

On the day of the handover, no patrols went out as our men were taking over their accommodation and being briefed about the area, while at the same time the RM were all helicoptered out.

The following day our first patrol set off with disastrous consequences after walking into an IRA ambush.

The sounds of heavy gunfire could be heard from a few hundred meters away in the town centre. The standby section was put on immediate alert, boarding a Saracen armoured car and heading towards the sound of the gunfire. Five minutes later, it returned with three of our soldiers who had been shot in the ambush. All three soldiers were put on stretchers and taken to the back of the compound to await the arrival of a helicopter. It was soon noted that the Section Commander was in a critical condition and unconscious although there were no visible signs of any injuries. Both my Coy 2i/c and I did our best to help him with my 2i/c even performing mouth to mouth resuscitation while I held him, it did not work, and without regaining consciousness, he died in my arms.

It became apparent that he had been shot in his left side just below his heart with the bullet passing between the space that separated the front and back of his flak jacket.

While all this was going on, an elderly Sgt from the Royal Army Medical Corps (RAMC) approached me and on seeing the injured soldiers started flapping his hands and in an extremely agitated state asked me what was going on. I was not stressed out at the time but I was extremely angry, so I shouted out the first thing that came into my head which was, "We are coming under a gas attack, go and put your respirator on!" He then disappeared.

One of the other soldiers was also unconscious; although he was breathing regularly his chances of survival looked very slim. The remaining soldier was fully conscious and was in a position to relate exactly what had happened. He was also one of the soldiers that had returned fire. Unfortunately, he turned out to be the second soldier to die from his wounds. Once the three had been airlifted out, some sort of order descended on the camp although the RAMC Sgt was seen still wearing his respirator half an hour later. I reported his actions to my 2i/c, and he was sent back to his unit on the very next available helicopter out.

I would like to mention and show respect to my 2i/c for the valiant attempt that he showed in trying to save the life of a soldier.

I was later entrusted to go through the personal effects of the deceased men and to remove any items that I thought were inappropriate to release to their families.

It was later found out that the ambush was set to catch out the RM on the actual day of the handover but as no patrols were sent out that day, they came back in the hope of catching them on their last day. The ambush must be seen as a success on their side but not the success that they wanted as they were targeting the RM and not our unit. Unfortunately, my 2i/c and the OC RM agreed to keep up the pretence that the RM were moving out on the day of the ambush by instructing the members of our patrol to wear the Green Berets of the RM.

A few days after the incident, a suspect who was believed to have been involved in the ambush was picked up and escorted back in one of our helicopters for interrogation back at our barracks. We knew that without hard evidence he would be released. In fact, we all knew he would be released which resulted in one of his armed escorts asking me what he should do with him. I replied, "When you are relatively high up in the helicopter, ask him to jump." On the escorts' return they told me that the RAF Warrant Officer would not move away from the open door of the helicopter, so it was a waste of time asking him to jump.

Having lived with this incident for the past forty years, I frequently thought about the wife and children of the chap that died in my arms. Although I knew him quite well, I was never one of his close mates and as far as I'm aware never met his wife, although the chances are that she would have known me by name. I always wanted to tell her exactly what happened especially that he was not the target and the fact that he was wearing an RM beret when he died. Forty years on, while living in Malta, I managed to track her down and was given her home phone number. I had also found out that she had remarried and changed her surname. I was now in a quandary – should I or should I not phone her?

Would I be awakening old wounds? Do I have the right to call her? Finally, I plucked up enough courage and phoned her but no one answered. I tried the following day and got through. After mentioning who I was, I explained why I had called her. She was delighted and mentioned that one of her sons was in the process of researching his father's history and that he would be over the moon with the details that I had given her of which she was completely unaware.

After this main incident, I got myself into a routine, checking the main water supply for any sort of contamination on a daily basis, along with the rations and anything that would keep the complex running. I also took turns in the Operations Room, manning the radio communications. So basically I had things relatively easy; a fact that was not going unnoticed by all within the compound. So one night when I was fast asleep in my room, someone came in and grabbed the Wellington boots that I always wore. They were returned before I had woken up, but the colour had changed from the standard grey to gold. I was never a person that went out of my way to distress people, so I wore them with pride. The James Bond film 'The Man with the Golden Gun' had just been released, but I was 'The Man with the Golden Boots'. I never found out who sprayed them but they did create quite a few laughs.

At times I managed to go out on patrols around the town with one of the sections which I not only found to be exciting but I could also feel the hate that emanated from the town itself. At times I used to think that you could cut it with a knife. It's the only place in this world that I have ever experienced such a feeling of hate.

One night I managed to go out with a patrol to an overnight observation location. It was a patrol that required a lot of stealthy movement to get into position without being seen. Once in position, we settled to command a 360° view of the surrounding area and started observing. We noted the local farmers in their fields as well as people going about their daily chores. As night fell and it got darker and darker we took it in turns using night vision goggles while at the same time as keeping radio contact with our control room. Before coming out on this patrol, I was briefed that there would be no friendly forces operating in our area that evening. By friendly forces, I mean no other units including the Special Air Service (SAS), the Royal Ulster Constabulary (RUC), or the Ulster Defence Forces (UDR).

It came as a bit of a shock when it was noted that a somewhat large, fully armed patrol was spotted moving toward us along a hedgerow. I reported back to our control room who clearly stated that there were no friendly forces in the area. It was hard to distinguish who these people were, were they friendly forces or was it an IRA patrol? I was in a situation where although we had the element of surprise on our side, the moment I opened my mouth to challenge them I would be giving my position away. If it was an IRA patrol, they would open fire in an instant while I had to wait for a reply to my challenge. If that was the case, I could see casualties on both sides. I came to the conclusion that we would remain silent and concealed, letting them walk by and taking no action.

On returning to our operations room, I submitted my report including the details of what we had observed and the unidentified patrol. A lot of interest was shown in this patrol, but no information ever surfaced as to who it was. I can only conclude that my initial assumption that it was an IRA patrol was correct.

Over the years, I have always asked myself, "Did I make the right decision?"

On one occasion I was asked by our Drum Major who was acting as a Platoon Commander and who also held the rank of WO2, if I would like to go out on a helicopter patrol around the area. I was up for it and went to grab my SLR and change my boots before meeting up with him and a radio operator, as well as a Warrant Officer of the Australian Army who came along to study our tactics. We then took off in a Bell helicopter flown by the Army Air Corp (AAC).

A short time after flying around we spotted a car on a relatively long, narrow road and thought we should land to do a vehicle spot check on it. The pilot had to find a suitable landing spot for the helicopter ahead of the car, but both sides of the road were covered in woodland apart from a small triangular piece of land by the side of the road which appeared just about large enough to land on. As the pilot lowered his craft, he was made aware of the telephone lines running along the side of the road. It was going to be a tight squeeze, but he got down and just hovered over the ground which was my cue to jump out while at the same time being handed the radio by the operator and then it happened. I started sinking into what was a bog.

Seeing my predicament, the other two remained in the helicopter. The radio operator managed to grab the radio back from me. In the meantime, the helicopter was drifting forwards and away from me. The pilot then found himself in a real situation. As he drifted forwards, his main rotors were now under the tree branches which meant he could not raise the helicopter while I was behind him in line with the tail rotor and at the same time very close to it, which meant he could not go back. He only had one option, and that was to drift towards the road and go under the telephone wire, which he did and landed on the road just in front of the car that we wanted to stop. The pilot demonstrated an outstanding flying manoeuvre along with his piloting skills. He later told me that he was, to put it bluntly, shitting himself while carrying out that manoeuvre. I managed to extract myself from the bog with a bit of help while at the same time congratulating myself for having the forethought to change my golden wellingtons for my Boots Direct Moulded Soles (DMS). Can you imagine going into a bog with wellingtons on? The car which had stopped was checked over before we reboarded the helicopter and flew back to Crossmaglen. It was an exciting episode which brought howls of laughter when the story was told back at our base.

On some occasions while walking along the top passageway in the building I would come across members of the RUC crawling along the floor. I would ask them what they were up to and they would reply that the building was under fire. I would always laugh and carry on my way. I'm sure that they thought I was a bit mad.

It was a fairly well-known fact that Crossmaglen was an IRA stronghold with many local supporters, but trying to get intelligence from the community was like looking for a pin in a haystack. So it was no real surprise when members of the Army Intelligence Corps descended on the Police Station with a twenty-foot container filled with surveillance equipment.

They had located a house that they believed was used by members of the IRA and it was deemed desirable to get a microphone into the house to listen into their conversations. To make this possible, they concocted a plan to place an explosive device within the confines of the garden of the house before warning the occupants that they had been informed by an informant that an explosive device had been placed near the house and that they would have to evacuate all in the house before they could proceed with the search. One of the occupants was bedridden within her room on the top floor which entailed calling in the local Fire Brigade who managed to stretcher her out. Once all the occupants were out, a thorough search was made of the place. The explosive device was found and dealt with before the all clear was given. The house occupiers were very thankful to all that the rescuers had done, and I believe a few bottles of Whisky also changed hands.

I was not privileged to know of any information that may have been gleaned from this incursion, but I do know that the Intelligent Corp members were always cocooned in their 20ft container.

I suppose one of the biggest memories I have of Crossmaglen was the number of times I had to return to Abercorn Barracks to deliver or even collect the mail. Travelling in the front seat of a Scout or Gazelle helicopter with only the pilot was quite an experience. All the pilots were Army Air Corps (AAC), and they got a buzz out of flying at very low levels, they got an even bigger buzz if they thought they could frighten their passengers. It never bothered me as I knew that they would not put their lives in danger and I did appreciate their flying skills. It also reminded me of what could have been, if I had passed my education earlier on in life.

Unlike the RAF pilots of the Wessex and Puma helicopters who brought in supplies, some of these pilots were quite stubborn and used to waste time while at the same time putting their lives as well as the people on the ground at risk, such as when I had an underslung load of a dozen or more 6ft gas cylinders which were empty and needed to be returned for refilling. The RAF Load Master, who was a Flight Sergeant, was not happy with the load and asked me to rearrange it. As this would take a few minutes, he returned to his Wessex Helicopter, which took off and then landed in the centre of the field a few hundred yards away from my location, making themselves an easy target for the IRA. After re-assembling the gas cylinders, I waved towards the helicopter and motioned that I was ready to attach the under-slung load. The pilot never paid any attention to me and remained where he was. After a few minutes, I stormed around to our control room and explained the situation to the officer on watch, who contacted the pilot with a few unsavoury words while I went back to the landing spot. I finally got the pilot to hover just over the load and went under the helicopter to attach the strop to its underbelly, when for some unknown reason the helicopter dropped a couple of feet, almost squashing my head against the helicopter's underbelly and the gas cylinders. After the strap was attached, I scrambled out and gave the pilot the all clear to take the load away. He was one pilot I was glad to see the back of.

Crossmaglen was always regarded as one of the worst, if not the worst troubled regions within the Northern Ireland conflict, and I am sure that many stories of the place and its occupiers will never rise to the surface. To some degree, I can still feel the hate of the place, even today.

On returning to Ballykinler, the OC D Company told me that I was being assigned as the Platoon Sgt to a Platoon which was commanded by a Junior Sgt to myself. The Major knew by rights that I should have taken the position as the Platoon Commander due to my seniority, but he stressed that this Sgt had more experience than me of Northern Ireland.

The battalion's tour of Northern Ireland was coming to a close, and I was not particularly bothered as to whether I was a Pl Sgt or a Pl Comd, although I did stress to my Junior Sgt that he could remain as the Platoon Commander. But he would also be responsible for the signing of all stores. It later transpired that this Sgt was seen as a blue-eyed boy as he was responsible for two large weapons finds, but I later found out that during the first discovery, he had discreetly removed some items from the cache and hidden them. These items were then placed in another location that he was searching with his platoon and claimed as another find to his credit.

The remaining period was spent on searches and roadside vehicle checks until it was time to move back to the UK to our new posting in Shoeburyness in Essex.

OPERATION BANNER was the name given to the Northern Ireland conflict that ran from August 1969 to July 2007. It is also called The Forgotten War. During the conflict, 1441 British Servicemen died, of which 722 died at the hands of paramilitary attacks. Thousands of members of the Armed Forces were injured; many of them suffering severe disability with loss of limbs. These soldiers are seldom mentioned. Today it's as if the conflict never happened. Many injustices were never put right, and many people who were involved against the British Servicemen are now in high positions within the Northern Ireland government and community.

I always chuckle to myself when I recall being told how members of the armed services always found a way to bring justice to men who are known to have participated in crimes against our members of the military. It was quite simple and completely justifiable. It happened thus. A person who was known to have committed a crime against us, but to which we had no supportive evidence to have him arrested would be called down to a local police station. When he got to the police station, he would be placed in a room by himself for a good few hours. At no time would he be questioned. Sometime later he would be released. As he walked out of the police station, a stranger would walk towards him and hand over some money. This would have been discreetly photographed with the photos being passed on to unknown persons.

His mates would have known about his visit to the police station, and suspicions would soon arise when questioned about his visit and why had he accepted payment. With no answers forthcoming, he would be classified as an informant, which frequently resulted in a kneecapping or even an unfortunate accident.

I have no proven knowledge of this being true or not and leave it entirely up to the reader of this book to make up his own mind.

Chapter 13
SHOEBURYNESS

My Battalion departed Northern Ireland on 10 January 1975, and I went straight on leave before reporting back for duty on 3 February 1975 at Horseshoe Barracks in Shoeburyness.

Although I had only been away from my wife and daughters for three months, it had seemed like a lifetime and I had really missed them. My daughters were now eight and seven years old, and in the three months I was away they appeared to have both grown by at least a foot. On top of that, both were turning into very intelligent and beautiful young ladies. I think Josephine was also pleased to see me as she was tired of having to keep my car clean, which had been standing outside the house while I was away.

Josephine was well and truly upset when I informed her that at present we had not been allocated a married quarter in Shoeburyness and that I was also due to go to Cyprus on a six months unaccompanied posting later on in the year. At present we were still living in our married quarters in Trowbridge, and I knew that the local housing office was trying to get us to vacate the house as soon as possible. The possibilities of leaving the army were brought up during discussions but at the time no decisions were being made.

On rejoining my battalion, significant changes were being made with the Regiment taking on the role of Spearhead Battalion This meant that we could be deployed anywhere in the world at minimum notice. The battalion again reformed into three rifle companies, a support company and a HQ company along with BHQ. D Company was disbanded which resulted in me taking up the position of the Signal Platoon Sergeant. Many overall changes were being made at all levels. My Coy Comd from A Company and British Honduras had been promoted to Lt Col and had taken over as the CO, while one of my Platoon Commanders from Berlin had been promoted and taken over as the Regimental Signal Office (RSO).

I well remember reporting to him in his office for the first time. It was the first time I had seen him since he left my platoon in Berlin. He was in the office with the Signal Platoon Sergeant Major, who used to be a full corporal when I first joined the platoon way back in 1963. I marched into the office and halted and gave him a salute and was told to stand at ease. He then welcomed me to the platoon and without stopping warned me not to forget any batteries. This led to us both bursting out in laughter while the Sgt Maj stood and looked on in disbelief.

I was soon involved in a Signals Cadre and my duties ranged from teaching procedures to writing radio exercises. The name of one of my exercises stuck in my head for the past forty-odd years; it was the second exercise that I called 'Exercise Tempus Fugit'. The exercise was based on a radio manpack activity around Horseshoe Barracks. Apart from practising communication procedures and decrypting codes and map reading, it was also designed to familiarise everyone involved on the layout of the barracks and surrounding area.

The barracks, which were in a dilapidated state, were built around 1859-1862 and was formally the home to the RA (Royal Artillery) School of Gunnery. It covered a large area and was situated at the mouth of the Thames Estuary. The Signal Platoons' office, lecture rooms, and stores were some distance from the main barrack accommodation which required me to march the platoon from one location to another on most days. The platoon had also grown in size to around 40 men. On one occasion while marching the men back to their accommodation, I noticed an officer walking towards us. I soon recognised him as my old nemesis from the days when he was the Sig Sgt in Malta and recalled the rollicking I got from him when I returned a salute to him on behalf of the CO who was driving my Land Rover in Minden. Bearing this in mind, I just marched the platoon past him without giving him an 'Eyes Left' from my platoon or a salute. As my platoon marched past him (I know that they were expecting my words of command) I allowed them to keep marching. He was furious with me and yelled me over and gave me yet another bollocking. I knew I had done wrong but under my breath, I was laughing my head off.

While I was at Shoeburyness, I was accommodated in the WOs & Sgts' Mess and had a tendency of remaining within the barrack confines when not on duty, spending the majority of my time either in my room or in the Mess bar. On most free weekends I would jump in my car and return to my family in Trowbridge. This was getting both Josephine and me down.

I do not know why I had not received a married quarter in the Shoeburyness area when qualifications were first assessed as apart from being a senior Sgt at the time, I had also been separated from my family for over three months while still occupying a service married quarter in Trowbridge that I had to vacate. Typically this would have been regarded and given a priority status, but again I think it came down to my name or maybe even my nemesis being involved in the housing allocation. Eventually in March, I was allocated a married quarter in the centre of Southend. It was fine for me, it was okay, but for Josephine, it was like being isolated at the centre of a desert. Josephine had been away from her army friends for the best part of two and a half years and was placed in a position where she had no friends or any support in everyday life including getting our children into a new school. On top of that, I was due to move to Cyprus in a few months.

I took my wife down to see the quarters in Southend with my children where she broke down and started crying and after a few arguments, I drove her straight back to Trowbridge. The following day I reported to the Family Officer and told him that I did not want the married quarter and asked him if he had anything else available to which he replied, "No."

In March, I was starting to feel depressed with the current situation, and although I had been told that I had been named on a very short list for promotion, I decided that it was time for me to leave the Army.

Without discussing the situation with Josephine, I went and saw my Pl Comd and told him that I would like to buy myself out of the army in the shortest possible time. He was most surprised and tried his best to talk me out of it, but I was having nothing of it. I was later told to see the CO who also tried to talk me out of it and for the second time in my service life, I asked if I could speak to him on an equal footing which he agreed to.

All the anger that I had kept pent up within me started to come out with the unjustifiable discrimination and bias that had been shown towards me by senior officers and other ranks. After calming me down, he told me that he understood what I had been saying and also told me that he would correct the situation as much as he could. He tried quite hard to get me to change my mind and even went into the current employment situation which was being experienced in Civvy Street at the time. I told him not to worry about me and even told him that when he left the army, he could look me up and maybe I would give him a job. He finally accepted my application for a discharge and told me I could start handing my kit and equipment in and that I should be ready for release on 1 April 1975. We both shook hands and departed in an amicable and friendly manner.

My discharge by purchase cost me a total of £50.00.

It was not long before the rumour that I was buying myself out started to circulate the battalion lines, with many being taken by surprise when I confirmed that it was true. Many friends along with their family members rallied around me offering support and help if required for which I felt grateful. In fact one of my mates from the Royal Army Pay Corps (RAPC) contacted me. He told me to try and delay my discharge by one week as the Ministry of Defence was in the process of approving a service pension to all members of the armed forces who had completed twelve years or more of service, and who would be discharged from the military after 3 April 1975.

I managed to have my release date changed to 7 April 1975 and qualified for a service pension from the age of 60. My mate and those two days have made a big difference in my present-day life.

Just before my discharge, one other Mess member and I were dined out by the WOs & Sgts' Mess, during which the customary 'Presentation Silver Mug' was made to me by the RSM and all the members of the Mess. On reading the inscription on my tankard, I noticed that even on this occasion they could not get the spelling of my name right.

As I have mentioned, I never discussed leaving the army with Josephine or anybody else; it was my decision and mine alone. Over the years, I have made a few similar decisions which have been followed by years of reflections on whether I had made the correct decision at the time. When I reflect on my army decision and look back on my service career, I also look at the service careers of my many mates who were in the same age group as me with similar qualifications.

The British Army was going through many changes mainly due to the shortage of suitable candidates for officers, which meant an ever-growing number of shortages of commissioned officers within units. Platoons were now commanded by sergeants while warrant officers were being seen to run organisation which were normally headed by an officer. To alleviate this problem, suitable SNCOs and WOs were earmarked for commissions which included many of my old friends who rose to the ranks of Captains, Majors, Lt Colonels and yes, even to full Colonel.

Racism was also being tackled. In the 60s you rarely, if ever, saw a black RSM, never mind a black sergeant in a traditional British Army unit. The same applied to the tightly knit family of commissioned officers. This was all to change in the 70s with anything that smelled of racism being severely dealt with. In my opinion, many played this racism to their advantage while others went along with it purely for the sake of being seen as anti-racist.

Seeing how many of my friends had been commissioned, I have always said to myself that if I had remained, I could have or would have made it to Brigadier simply because of my name. Do I regret it? Yes and no, but I made my bed and was prepared to lie in it.

At the same time that racism was being dealt with, human rights were also coming into the picture especially on the gay rights issue. In the army, being gay was frowned upon. Any gay person would be dishonourably discharged from the military at the earliest opportunity if discovered. At the same time, it was common knowledge that this was going on, even in my Regiment and in some cases, among the other ranks and the commissioned officers. Again many played this knowledge to their own personal advantage.

Again, I quite often reflect on the men that I met during my service career, some quite brilliant, and two or three who I would follow where ever they led me. One of them was my last Platoon Commander who rose to the rank of Brigadier at a very young age and whose service career was cut short when he was brutally murdered in a drive-by shooting in Athens, Greece on 2 June 2000. It later transpired that he was shot in a case of mistaken identity by two gunmen belonging to the terrorist group known as the 'Revolutionary Organisation 17 November'. At the time of his death he was the British Military Attaché in Athens.

Many, including officers and some SNCOs, were a complete waste of time in my opinion, while others were brilliant in their military knowledge and leadership but had been denied promotion due to not having reached the required educational standards.

I also reflect on the mishaps of many of my old colleagues, who were brilliant mates as well as soldiers. Mates who would go way out of their way to help anybody, not only me. Mates who died in tragic accidents while on or off duty. Mates who were murdered while carrying out their duties as servants to the Crown and their country. Mates who died in the most depressing ways possible. Mates who died of injuries and diseases like cancer. My heart goes out to them and their families.

When I think of them, I typically see the person as I last saw him during our times of service together. I see them as being young, fit, robust and healthy; in many cases younger than myself.

I also think of what went wrong in many cases when hearing stories about men I had close contact with, such as the chap who I met in 1 Wessex Signal Platoon who ended up in Broadmoor Hospital; a high-security psychiatric hospital in Crowthorne. He was a likeable older soldier who had an extremely good looking German wife of whom he was extremely jealous. On one occasion his jealousy overwhelmed him and he ended up killing her and cutting her body into pieces. He also killed his Alsatian Dog. I never saw him after I left Trowbridge but I do believe I was responsible for delivering a meal to him many years later in Broadmoor.

A short time after handing in my application for discharge, I went home to Trowbridge and told Josephine what I had done. At first she did not believe me, and then reality hit home not only for her but also for me. My world came crashing down to my feet. I had not thought of where we would live, never mind not having a job and at that time the UK unemployment was at a record high. Money was also a problem as I can't say we had much in the bank at the time.

The only option I had was to go and see my mother who was now separated from my father and see if she could put us up for a period of time. Josephine was not happy with this arrangement for although her relationship with my mother had significantly improved, the thought of living in my mother's home, albeit temporarily, was not very comforting. Lucky for us, she agreed to let us have a room on the understanding that I would seek work on my discharge. It was also a case of finding a place to store all our household goods.

After packing and handing my quarters over in Trowbridge, the army then transported all my household goods to Slough for me, for which I will always be grateful. I then returned to Horseshoe Barracks for my final days and saying goodbye to all my friends and their families before driving out of the main gate for the last time after having completed 12 years and 175 days of Reckonable Army Service.

Sometime after leaving the army, I received my Certificate of Service which is a short record of service which includes an assessment of military conduct and character, which describes me as follows:

Military Conduct: EXEMPLARY
Testimonial:

I have known Sergeant Zawadski for several years and have found him to be an intelligent man who readily accepts responsibility. He can be left alone to organise and instruct without any supervision. He is loyal and hardworking and very adaptable. He is always polite and truthful and works well with everyone. He has been in the army for over twelve years during which time he has either been employed in the Signal Platoon or detached to the TAVR as a Signals instructor.

This was signed by my Commanding Officer on 3 April 1975.

Although this testimonial is quite acceptable, and bearing in mind that this is the same officer who had sentenced me to a Severe Reprimand and confined me to camp for fourteen days as punishment for being ten minutes late into camp, while not being on any kind of duty at the time, no knowledge or recognition is shown to me for my service within a Rifle Platoon or even being a Platoon Commander. As for knowing me for several years, he actually knew me for 12 years from the time he was the Adjutant in Malta in 1963.

Having passed through the barrack gates for the last time, I made my way back to Slough as a civilian. My thoughts were now centred on finding a job and getting my own home.

Chapter 14
SLOUGH TO BRACKNELL

Back to being a civilian was not going to be an easy task. It was a case of standing on my own two feet and becoming not only accountable to myself, but also to my family and friends. Moving into my mother's home was not such a bad thing although it did feel overcrowded at times and as for privacy, well that just went out of the window. My sisters Sandra and Basha, along with my brothers Leonard and Ryszard had all got married and flown the coop.

My first priority was to try and get a house and the only thing I could think of at the time was to apply for a local council house or flat. Going to the Slough Council, I was told that there was a large waiting list, at the same time I was also told that Bracknell had been designated as a new town and it might prove to be quicker by applying there.

I went to the local Bracknell Council who at first gave the impression that they did not even want to entertain me in my efforts of seeking a council house within the locality. Again, I believe my surname had something to do with this. They came up with the excuse that the housing had been reserved for people who were residents of London and were seeking a job in Bracknell, with the intent to move to Bracknell. I explained I had just left the local county regiment and also the fact that I had been a resident of London in my early years. It appeared to work as after a change of heart, I was given the name of a company that allocated council houses. I was told that if I managed to get a job there, I might manage to get one of their allotted houses.

At the time, I was not sure as to what kind of job I was after although I did make a few tentative inquiries about joining the local Thames Valley Police Force. Josephine was all for it, but my mother told me that if I applied for the local police force, I would have to move out of the house straight away. This all stemmed from the problems that my younger brothers had with the police, and the family name was well known on their records. She also thought that it would cause conflict between my brothers and me.

I was left with no alternative than to seek employment with the company whose name I had been given by the Bracknell Council. What the job entailed, I had no idea. I made an appointment with the employment manager at Waitrose Headquarters on the Southern Industrial Estate in Bracknell. I had been told by my mother that Waitrose was a large supermarket chain but she had no idea what they did in Bracknell. I was soon to find out.

When I met the person who was responsible for staff recruitment, I still had no idea of what type of jobs were on offer, so I came clean about my situation, my background in the army and also the fact that I was hoping to get one of their allocated council houses. The only jobs that were on offer at the time was working in their extremely modern computer run and fully automated warehouse in a manual lifting capacity. The job was also on a shift basis with an early shift starting at 6:00 am and finishing at 2:30 pm and the alternative shift that changed weekly starting at 2:30 pm and ending at 11:00 pm. Additional overtime could also be worked on Saturdays. I was told that if I accepted the job, completed a satisfactory three-month trial and if all were in agreement, I would be placed on the register for one of their allocated houses. After being given a tour of the warehouse and shown exactly what I would be doing, I agreed to their terms and conditions and was told to report the following Monday to start my first shift.

When I returned home later that day, I could not conceal my excitement, I had been given a full-time job, and I had only been out of the Army a couple of days, with the possibilities of getting my first council home in the very near future.

It was also important to get Michelle and Alison into the local Claycots Junior School which luckily was just down the road from us on the Britwell Estate. It was also the school that most of my brothers and sisters attended and yes, they were still being asked if they were Germans.

My first shift at Waitrose started at 6:00 am which meant that I would have to leave home at around 5:15 am. The distance between the Britwell Estate and Bracknell is approximately 15 miles and took about half an hour travelling time in a car. I reported to the shift manager and was introduced to members of the workforce which totalled no more than twenty men in their 20s and 40s. I was teamed up with one of them and shown my workstation. It consisted of a two-man platform looking onto an area which can only be described as a goods yard with hundreds of wired cages mounted on wheels that were placed on a numbered mobile base connected to tram lines. All in all, there was six two men platforms in a straight line, each having its own large oval shaped tram lines which also included an 'On and Off' spur to the main branch line. Two of these wired cages would come and stop automatically where you were standing with an open side facing you. At the back there was the biggest warehouse that I have ever seen, with racks upon racks stacked with every commodity you could think of. I cannot recall the length or height of the storage areas shelving or how many pallets were held, although I do know that it ran into the thousands. Everything within the storage area was completely computerised, and nobody ventured into that area unless they were engineers carrying out maintenance work.

Each workstation had its own hydraulic automated pallet lifter which would be directed from our computerised control room to collect a pallet of goods from a specific location and bring it to our station, where it would be put onto rollers and moved to a position just behind us where it would stop. I would then look just above my partner's head at a display that would show a number and pick the indicated number of boxes or packages from the pallet to place them in the cage next to me. On completion, I would press a button which informed the computer that the commodity was in the cage. While I was filling my cage, my partner would be doing the same with his cage. Once both cages were done, they would move off automatically and go around the tram line circuit until they were required to be filled with more items.

No brain work was actually needed, but you did need strength and stamina especially from the waist upwards. Your feet hardly moved, but you were twisting from left to right to left continuously. With the speed that we were working at, everyone had a staggered fifteen minutes break during each hour. At 10:00 am, we would all stop for half an hour and head towards the canteen for breakfast. If you were lucky, you sometimes caught your fifteen-minute break at 9:45 am or at 10:30 am which meant that you took a complete 45 minutes break.

The afternoon or evening shift was the same as the morning shift but with one significant advantage. At the canteen there was also a bar that opened at 6:00 am which served Carlsberg Hof beer on draft at a reduced market price. This used to result in me having a pint every hour from 6:00 pm onwards until the shift had finished. Lucky for me the bar closed at 11:00 pm. And yes, I did get tipsy at times.

Initially, the job was an eye-opener and downright boring, but it had its perks. Saturday overtime was nearly always available and apart from our discount cards that we could use in all the Waitrose and John Lewis Partnership outlets, we also got the opportunity to buy products that were slightly damaged or nearing their best by sales date at vastly reduced rates.

As the department's workforce was quite small, we all got to know each other quite well which led to lots of banter and some stupid stunts. It was common practice to challenge your partner on who was the fastest picker, resulting in many races in which we ended up picking over a thousand units within one hour. That's when you really started to sweat.

Opportunities for any form of improving your standing within the company never really materialised as most of the managers were quite young, and nobody appeared to be in the retiring mode. But at that time I was not particularly worried as all I was doing was concentrating on getting a house allocated to me in the not too distant future.

After having worked at Waitrose for a few months, my brother Ronnie applied for and was given a job there within a different department but on the same shift pattern as myself. My mother was pleased as Ronnie had a bad habit of not getting out of bed in the mornings. It was now up to me to get him up, and he had to get up if he wanted a lift to work.

Meanwhile back at 72, Doddsfield Road (it used to be 56, but additional houses had been built in my absence while in the army, on the area that I used to play around in my younger days), tensions in the house were also rising. Annetta, who was always the most dominant member of the family, was having more and more conflicts with Josephine and my two daughters. With Josephine, it was more about who would do the cooking as she liked Maltese cuisine, while Annetta loved to be seen as the cook in the house as well as being in charge. Both Michelle and Alison also were at that age where they had a mind of their own and were always running about and getting into mischief. I well recall the day my mother was running late for getting to work that she dashed out of the house only to run back in when she realised that she didn't have her false teeth in. More eruptions followed as she could not find them which meant she had to go to work with no teeth. It later transpired that Michelle and Alison had found them in a glass and were so taken aback by them that they decided to take them into the garden and play with them. After a while, they got bored with them and just threw them away. I think we may have told my mother about it many years later.

With all the altercation with Annetta, Josephine decided that she would apply for a part-time catering job with Bestobel on the Slough Trading Estate. She got the job and soon made friends with the kitchen staff and enjoyed doing the work, or maybe it was the joys of being away from Annetta for a few hours each day. Whatever it was, she was happy while at the same time bringing in a little extra money which was always in demand with the girls growing so fast.

Soon after my trial period at Waitrose had passed and I was accepted as being permanent, I was offered the choice of waiting for a newly built Council house on the Birch Hill Estate or a vacant older house. The new house would be ready in around three months' time, or I could opt for one of three vacant houses. I was all for waiting the three months, but when I mentioned it to Josephine and my mother, my mother said to take the first one possible. It looked like I had no option but to take the first one possible.

A few days later I was given a list of the three houses to visit in Bracknell with Josephine which included a house in Harmanswater, one in Wild Ridings and the one we chose at 98 Appledore in Great Hollands. The house was a three bedroomed end of terrace house with a garage which backed onto the back garden. It was also the last house in an enclosed area. Apart from the three bedrooms, it had a separate bathroom and two separate toilets, a dining room, kitchen and a large sitting room. The back garden was also of a reasonable size. All in all, it was a great modern house; all we had to do was to furnish it. We moved in a few weeks later, and that was when the fun started.

Less than six months had passed from the time that I had surprised everyone with my declaration of leaving the army to finding a full-time job and getting a council house. Now I could relax to some degree and savour the delights of being a civilian.

Relax? Who was it that ever came up with this word?

Moving into 98, Appledore was quite easy, for although I had been married for the best part of ten years, being in the services restricted you to buying minimum items for your home as all army married quarters came complete with all standard housing requirements. From the pots and pans, crockery, knives forks and spoons to beds, linen and blankets and all the other furnishing that goes to making a comfortable home.

In our case, it was like starting from scratch. Although the house needed minimum maintenance, it did require a lot of wallpapering and painting. Initially, a lot of hard work was put into the decorating and furnishing to bring it up to scratch and turning it into a comfortable home.

Michelle and Alison soon settled at Great Hollands Junior School which could not have been too easy for them as it was the third school that they had attended in the past year. It was not long before they started bringing their new found friends home with them. They were also getting into pets, having had pet rabbits and a tortoise in the past, which was quite understandable as they had always been surrounded by pets in my mother's house. It was not too long before we had our first cat called Jasper.

I continued my work at Waitrose, and although I knew I had no future there, I was thankful for being in full-time employment with plenty of opportunities to do overtime. I was also aware that every March a yearly bonus was paid out to all members of the John Lewis Partnership based on the companies' profits. It was also based on one's annual wages including overtime.

With my full-time job and the never-ending jobs within the house, I had very little time for going out to restaurants and pubs. Not only did I not have the time, I did not even have any spare money as that was going towards furnishing the house and everyday requirements. All my spare time was spent in gardening which I had truly missed over the past twelve years or so, and reading.

Reading was a great passion of mine, and I was now in a position to get back into it. It was not so long before I started visiting the library in Bracknell Town Centre. I recall my first visit there, meeting an elderly grey-haired woman who was all smiles and helpfulness explaining the library and how it worked before giving me a registration card to fill in. Having filled in the card and giving it back to her, the expression on her face did a great about turn as she tried to read the surname, before expressing, in a hostile voice, "What name is that? It's not English." I replied, "I know, it's Zawadzki, which is Smith in Polish." She was taken aback by my quick response while at the same time she really believed that Zawadzki was Smith in Polish. She apologised for her attitude as she could see that she had offended me, but we did leave on good terms.

I used to go to the library every month and take out half a dozen books at a time covering all subjects especially books on UFOs, ghosts and apparitions, Egyptology as well as gardening.

Our first Christmas as a civilian had come and gone in a flash although we had many visits from family members and Josephine was starting to get into my mother's good books, in fact, they were starting to become good friends. My father used to come and stay for a few days at a time which was a good excuse for me to go with him and have a pint in the local pub.

Josephine got herself a job at Apex and soon settled into her first full-time job involving air fresheners. The house always smelt nice after that.

As we went into 1976, things were starting to look up which allowed us time to go out in the car on weekends and explore the surrounding area. Places like Virginia Waters, Windsor Safari Park, Windsor Castle and not forgetting Blackbush Sunday Market.

Almost a year to the day after leaving the army, I answered a knock on the door to be confronted by the chap who was my best man at my wedding in Malta. He was dressed in military uniform with the rank of Colour Sergeant. I was really surprised to see him and invited him in. We started chatting, and he told me that he had just been posted to D Company, 1 Wessex (RV) at Brock Barracks in Reading as a Permanent Staff Instructor (PSI). He also told me that they had a vacancy for a rifle platoon Sergeant and asked me if I would be interested in joining up as they could do with someone of my experience. Initially, I told him that I had no interest, but I also said that I would think about it.

Over the next few weeks, I discussed joining the TAVR (Territorial Army Volunteer Reserve) with Josephine and what it would imply if I joined. She encouraged me to go to Brock Barracks to meet up with my old mate and to check out the situation. This resulted in me meeting up on a Tuesday Drill Night with the CSM of D Company, who was also my CSM in HQ Company in Malta and the chap who I initially had to ask for permission to marry Josephine.

I also met up with quite a few old mates from my time as the Signals PSI in Devizes. To a certain effect, it was like meeting up with long-lost family. I was also introduced to the JNCOs and men of the platoon who, if I were to join, would become my men. They looked a reasonable bunch of men from initial appearances.

After spending a couple of hours viewing and meeting the officers and men of D Company, I went into the Dragon Club and sat back and drank a few pints and that's when I realised that I was missing this in my present-day circumstances.

I told my mate that I would join and asked him to make all the arrangements for a medical and interview. I knew that this was only a formality, but even I had to go through with it before I could be enlisted.

I finally enlisted on 19 May 1976 into D Company, 1st Bn the Wessex Regiment (RV) and started getting back into the swing of being a platoon sergeant once again.

As 1976 was drawing to a close, it was quite easy to reflect on my first full year of being a civilian again and what the future might hold for me. It was a busy year with the continuing work within the home and garden. There was also the shift work and extra overtime worked at Waitrose which was becoming quite boring with no prospects in sight. My first six months back in uniform with the TAVR also included my first Annual Camp that lasted 14 days plus a dozen or so training weekends and the customary Tuesday evening drill night.

It was also the year that I managed to take my family on a two week holiday in Cornwall, accompanied by my sister

Sandra and her husband Fred and their children Andrew and Sahra Jane. This was a great vacation spent at St Ives Holiday Village with exploration trips to the many places of interest within the surrounding area. One of my best memories of the occasion was when my sister's husband Fred and I went into a bookie to place bets on some horse races. At that time I was not a gambling man and knew nothing about horse betting, but Fred was a real professional and showed me how to go about putting a bet on. Again as I knew nothing about horses or jockeys, I listened to what Fred had to say about individual jockeys and horses.

Fred mentioned a horse and rider to me that he thought was quite good, so I decided to place a £10 win bet on this horse. Now £10 to me was quite a bit of money at the time, and I was a bit worried as the race went off. If I lost, how was I going to explain to Josephine that I had lost £10 on a bet? I never told Fred that I had placed a bet on that horse, as far as he was concerned I was only a spectator. This was soon to change as the horse stomped home and won the race at odds of 12/1.

Fred was too busy selecting his next horse in the next race to notice me going up to the teller to collect my winnings of £120 plus my £10 stake. I was over the moon as I walked over to Fred and asked him how much he had won on the same horse as I had done, only to be told that he had changed his mind and done another horse that failed to finish. I think everyone can imagine what he said when I told him that I had bet on the horse and how much I had won. He never placed any more bets that day, but we did have a good few pints of beer later that day even though I had to pay for them.

My first six months in the TA was quite busy for me as I got back into the rhythm of being in uniform once again, getting to know the men of my platoon and company along with the officers. Very few members had seen any regular army service which resulted in a somewhat relaxed attitude to military discipline. This was all going to change as I was a firm believer in the rank structure. No longer were private soldiers going to call their senior ranks by their first names while in uniform.

This was quite strange as quite a few lower ranks in the TA were employees of some of their senior ranks in Civvy Street. But then again what they called each other in Civvy Street was up to them.

One of the things that I found to be quite surprising was the keenness shown by these so-called part-time soldiers. The harder the challenge, the more effort they would exert in the task, although they did have a tendency to sleep on evening sentry duty.

As an ex regular soldier, I always appeared to be given additional tasks or being asked for advice on military subjects especially from the officers who at times seemed to be complete idiots, although in a friendly sort of way.

Training weekends in most cases were looked forward to, especially when spent at the military shooting ranges, practising weapon handling and shooting skills. On other occasions, we would spend time on field craft and practice section and platoon attacks, as well as the dreaded route marches with full kit on. In most cases, the men's physical fitness was quite good, but there were quite a few who had office bound and driving jobs which involved a lot of sitting down in their civilian occupation. This restricted their ability to carry out the necessary physical exercises to keep them fit. In fact, in most cases, the only physical exercise they got was while training with the TA.

The two weeks Annual Camp was a period when the whole of 1 Wessex (RV) could train together, and when you take into consideration that the battalion was spread all over the South of England, it was also a chance for all members to meet up with friends from other companies. It also gave the RSM the opportunity to take the battalion on Drill Parades and practice the art of marching as a battalion. Competitions were also organised on an intercompany basis, be it shooting, tactics or even sporting events. In most cases, it was hard graft but very rewarding at the end. In my case, I now had a fairly well-trained rifle platoon that I could pit against any regular army infantry platoon.

As the Christmas period approached, once again I got involved in helping to organise a children's party for the children of the company members and a Christmas dance for the wives and guests within Brock Barracks. Both events were very well attended.

As I moved on into the year 1977, I started to get the feeling that I was starting to miss out on an exciting full-time job. The lack of challenge became boring and I started looking for another job. It was also a period of retrospection, as I started to blame my parents and my upbringing for my inadequate education in my earlier years. I had no real qualification or experiences in civilian jobs and at the age of 33, life appeared to be leaving me behind. Thankfully I had my part-time job within the TA which put my boredom in check for periods at a time. I also took the opportunity to check out the Open University sites but was put off as all correspondence courses were by post, unlike today with the online web services which would have been a win-win situation all around.

In early July, I heard that there was a vacancy for a Staff Car Driver at the RAF Staff College in Bracknell which appealed to me through my love of driving and my military connections. I applied for the job, which was seen as a Government Civil Service job. The pay was less than my present job with Waitrose, but it came with a few perks including a pension and other forms of monetary claims. Initially, I thought I would be employed driving members of the RAF, but I was told that I would be working for the Met Office, which is the Meteorological Office Headquarter Building near the Bracknell Town Centre. At that time, it came under the RAF as the UK National Weather Service.

A point to note is that at the time, the Director General (DG) of the Met Office held the equivalent rank of Air Marshal of the RAF with a service staff car and civilian driver.

I was offered the job which I accepted. I handed my notice into Waitrose and having worked my notice, I left after completing my last shift on 22 July. On the weekend of 23/24 July, I was off on a TA weekend and the following Monday 25 July, I started my driving job as a Civil Servant at the RAF Staff College, Bracknell. Whoever said you only work five days a week as a civilian was crazy.

I reported to the Motor Transport Section (MT) within the RAF Staff College and was made welcome by the RAF Flight Sergeant (F/Sgt) who ran the section. The section was teamed by an RAF Cpl who was the Commandant's staff car driver, plus an RAF Senior Air Craftsman (SAC) driver. There were also an additional nine civilian drivers who were split into two groups of five. One group worked on the RAF side and the remaining group of five, including myself worked on the Met Office side. The drivers on the RAF side were all quite old and retired ex-servicemen while the Met Office drivers were all in my age group.

I later found out that three of the RAF drivers served in the Royal Berkshire Regiment during WWII, which was the forerunner of my regiment, resulting in quite a close bond between us. Also, one of the Met drivers attended the same school and at the same time as me when I was living in the White City in London. The chances are that we were in the same class together as we were the same age but his name never rang any bells with me. It's a small world, and you can never tell where and when you will bump into a person with a common link to yourself.

When you tell people that you were once a staff car driver or even a chauffeur, they tend to look down their noses towards you as if you are a complete nobody. To me, it was one of the finest times of my life. At the mention of the Met Office, all people see is the weather forecast or rain. When you see the weather forecast on television or read it in the papers, you only see the end game, the only part that interests you. If you were to mention food and the Met Office together, very few people would see the connection. If you think of it, however, without the weather, there would be no food and no human race.

Over the next few years, I was to drive Met Office personnel thousands upon thousands of miles around the UK visiting hundreds of places. The majority of these people were professors, doctors, scientists and engineers – all within the Met Office with their own agendas and, in most cases, the only denominator being the weather. Although I was only the driver getting them from location A to location B and maybe to location C, D, E and back again, I took an interest in what they were doing and at times became involved at their invitation. On many occasions, I would take someone out to the remotest of locations to collect weather readings. At other times we went to meet up with farmers to discuss weather conditions spanning many years to deem if a location was suitable for growing grapes for the wine industry or even to build a cowshed or barn. In the mid-70s, there were very few vineyards and these were mainly in the Southern parts of England. At that time the UK was never seen as a wine producing nation. It was always left up to the Spanish, French and Italians to supply our wine. That has now changed with the UK producing some of the finest wines in the world from the many hundreds of British vineyards that are now dotted all over the country.

One of my constant recurring memories of working with the Met Office is when I see the Post Office Tower in

London. I always comment, "I've been to the very top of that tower on the outside," and not many people can say that. The building of the tower commenced in June 1961 and became the tallest building in the UK at 581ft high or 627ft high if you included the aerials on top. It remained the tallest building in the UK up to 1980. The rotating restaurant was closed in 1980 and access by the general public was stopped in 1981 for security reasons.

The occasion arose when I had to take some Met engineers to the location, who had been assigned to carry out some maintenance work on the satellite dishes and antennas on top of the tower. As it was going to take some time I was asked if I would like to join them. Now, who would not want to join them? The initial part of getting to the top was quite easy as we took the lift to the rotating restaurant near the top, from there into the kitchen area before going up some stairs and through a trap door and onto the top outside floor. I was greeted by the most magnificent views of London that I had ever seen. It was also possible to see and feel just how much the tower actually sways in the wind. It was also nice to see helicopters flying below to the various private helipads that abound in London, although you would not know it from the ground. I was given the opportunity to climb the steel ladder to the topmost rung between the satellite dishes and the aerials which really set my adrenaline into full flow.

I mentioned that when I took this job, that the pay was less than what I was receiving at Waitrose. But I soon made up the difference as every job that involved being out on a driving detail of five hours or more entitled you to an additional bonus which was further increased if you exceeded ten hours, In addition, you were also paid an additional rate for every mile that you drove. At that time I estimate that I was driving an absolute minimum of 1,000 miles per week.

I remained working on the Met Office side for approximately two years when our civilian charge hand who drove on the RAF side asked me if I would like to join their team. The main difference between the two sides was that the Met drivers worked a straight forward 40 hour week with overtime, starting at 8:00 am and finishing at 5:00 pm Monday to Friday. The RAF's drivers covered 24 hours a day, seven days a week.

In all, it involved a relatively complex shift system with a shift up to twelve hours long, but it sounds worse than it actually was. You were also entitled to a pay rise and a shift bonus. It's also worth mentioning that you were allowed to sleep during the evening shifts in a room that even had a bed provided, along with your own cooker and fridge. The reason I was asked, and this came out of the blue, was because one of the older drivers who was on the night shift that day was found dead in the morning by one of the drivers who came in early to carry out his morning duties. He was sitting in his armchair and initially was thought to be sleeping. It was only when he tried to awaken him that he realised that he was dead. It was learned later that he had died of natural causes.

I accepted without hesitation as I had driven a few RAF Officers at times when there was a shortage of drivers on the RAF side which I rather enjoyed.

When I accepted the driving on the RAF side, I had also been promoted to WO II and CSM of D Company in the TAVR which to some degree our F/Sgt was not too keen on, as in theory I now outranked him, and a certain amount of prejudice started to creep in.

Over the next six years I drove thousands of miles, chauffeuring many dignitaries from all walks of life including great WWII heroes along with many unsung heroes. I was also involved in many situations that to a certain extent are quite unbelievable but at the same time true. Was I involved in any key government situations? I will let you decide on that.

The following chapter is all about incidents that I recall but not in a date order. Some are funny, some are sad, some may be seen as taking the complete mickey out of the system. All in all, it's a reminder of what incredible things I got up to while being a driver.

Chapter 15
RAF STAFF COLLEGE – BRACKNELL

As I have mentioned in the previous chapter, only five civilian drivers were working on the RAF Staff College side. Between them they covered 24 hours a day, seven days a week, driving details through the year. The shifts were quite complicated, and you generally did not see more than three drivers in the restroom at any one time. The night shift driver started at 8:00 pm and finished at 8:00 am. A standby driver came in at 8:00 am and remained until 8:00 pm with a further daytime driver coming on at 8:00 am until 5:00 pm.

This left one remaining driver who was referred to as the coach driver, coming in at 6:30 am until 6:30 pm. His primary job was the collection of married servicemen from their married quarters which were mainly in the village of White Waltham and bringing them into work at the College and returning them home in the evening. He was also responsible for collecting all the school children from the officer's quarters within the College area and taking them to school and collecting them for the return journey in the afternoon.

It is quite obvious that the fifth driver was having a well deserved day off. As can be seen, most shifts were of twelve hours, but it was not unusual to work additional hours as overtime.

When not on a driving detail, we spent most of our time cleaning and maintaining our staff cars to quite a high standard, taking into consideration who we may be chauffeuring around the country. Apart from the staff cars we also had a couple of 3-tonne Lorries, a 39-seater coach, a couple of combi vans and a military ambulance. If I remember correctly we also had a couple of bicycles.

Lucky for me I had taken my Heavy Goods Vehicle (HGV) driving test in 1973, but I was required to take some coach driving lessons although exempt from taking any form of a test, as I was covered by my normal driving license due to it being a service vehicle.

Over the past years when meeting up with friends and new acquaintances, I have often been asked if I have ever been in a prison. I honestly do not know why they ask me these types of questions. Maybe it's because I look guilty of some unknown crime? I don't know, but they do look startled when I say yes. They then ask me which one and are even more surprised when I mention HM Prisons Ashford, Brixton, Chelmsford, Feltham, Holloway (yes, I know that's a women's prison) Wandsworth and Wormwood Scrubs. (Never thought I would ever enter that prison when I was a young lad.) After mentioning all these prisons and looking at the expressions on their face, you would think I was a master criminal. It was only later that I would mention that these prisons were responsible for doing the RAF Staff College's laundry which would be delivered and collect on a weekly basis. Why the prisons changed so much over the years was possibly due to contracts and strikes. I used to drive one of the combi vans when delivering or collecting the laundry into the prison yard or near to the prison laundry, where the prisoners used to load and unload the van. I always had a prison warden with me, but I was also allowed to talk to the inmates in an open and friendly manner.

Before leaving it was quite normal for the prison warden to say something to me, along the lines of, "Do you know who you were talking to back there?" To which I frequently replied no and he would reply with something like, "That was … who is in for murder for having killed …" I think the wardens used to get a rise out of telling you these little bits of information just to see what your reaction would be.

HM Ashford and Feltham were not really prisons but remand centres or Borstals. Going behind the wall of these establishments was a bit of an eye-opener, especially seeing the youngsters working in the laundry rooms and on the garden patch. They never appeared to smile and always looked depressed.

The wardens used to tell me about the old buildings and the sites of the many unmarked graves. To me, these were utterly depressing places, and I know that if the walls could speak, they would tell a story that would make a great horror film.

The RAF Staff College mainly dealt in the teaching of British and foreign Air Force officers destined to be promoted to higher ranks. The Commandant of the College held the rank of Air Vice Marshal which was a very senior rank and typically a person such as me in the military would very seldom, if ever, speak to someone holding this rank. I made my first real connection with a new Commandant when I was detailed to collect him from Heathrow Airport and deliver him to his new residence called Brookham House, which was set adjacent to the Staff College.

At Heathrow, I had no problem parking outside the main terminal as no policeman or traffic warden was going to move an RAF staff car displaying two stars. The AVM dressed in civilian clothing saw the car which I was standing next to and introduced himself to me. In return, I welcomed him while opening the car door. As I was driving back to the college he started chatting to me and asked me my name. I told him it was Leon Zawadzki, while casually mentioning that the Duke of Edinburgh called me Fred. He was a bit shocked by this but after he had gathered his composure, he replied, "Well, if the Duke of Edinburgh (who was ranked as a Marshal of The Royal Air Force) deemed it fit to call you Fred, it's good enough for me." This led to the conversation going into my military connections and the facts that I was at present, a serving member of the TAVR with the rank of warrant officer. Throughout the conversation, I never felt any superiority being shown to me which was completely unusual giving to whom I was talking to. When I dropped him off at his new residence where a welcoming committee was waiting to greet him, he shook my hand and thanked me for his car ride, saying, "I will catch up with you later, Fred."

The following day was the Air Officer Commanding (AOC) Inspection Day, which is when the Commandant visits all the locations and departments within the college grounds and meets all the personnel assigned to the college while carrying out an inspection of the complete camp. Before this day, the staff of the College spent many hours cleaning, repairing and painting to make sure that everything within the college was ready for the inspection. All service personnel used to wear best military dress. Civilians were not involved in these reviews although in my case I knew exactly what was going on, having experienced it at first hand in the army. When the Commandant was seen walking towards the MT Section with the station commander and the station WO along with a gaggle of other followers, it was evident to see that the RAF MT staff including the F/Sgt were a bit on edge. They had nothing to worry about. As I stood up I placed the book I was reading on the table and waited for the Commandant to enter our restroom. The majority of the other civilian drivers remained seated and carried on reading their morning newspaper.

As he came into the restroom, the Commandant spied my book, 'The Impossible Victory', on the table. He picked it up and turned round to me and said, "Fred, I bet this is your book." I replied, "Yes Sir." He then spent a few minutes talking to me about the Battle of the River Po before apologising and rushing off to his next port of inspection. All the RAF members were a bit dumbfounded as he had not said a word to anyone apart from me. They were also a bit startled when they heard him call me Fred. Ok, so just what is in a name?

I recall the day that I was late in turning up for work when I had been detailed to take an officer to some destination, and as he could not wait, one of the Met office drivers was asked to take him. It was not such a big deal, and believe it or not; it was the first time that I had ever been late as a civilian. The F/Sgt got himself worked up into a rage and told me to go home and to report in as being sick. I told him that I was not sick, but he insisted that I go home and report in sick.

This was something I had never done as a civilian and to report sick was a bit confusing. I knew that some of the Met Office drivers frequently reported sick and always put in a doctor's certificate to cover their days of sickness. Thinking about this, I decided to go and see the doctor at the local doctor's surgery. I should mention that I had never seen a civilian doctor since I was twelve years old. It was the first time that I had visited the local surgery and at the time they had no knowledge of who I was, which meant that I had to register myself with the surgery before they would allow me to see a doctor.

On seeing my first civilian doctor, I explained that there was nothing wrong me and told him why I had been sent home from work. He found my story and explanation a bit strange while at the same time having a good laugh. In fact, he had such a good laugh that he gave me a sick note covering four days off work and told me to go home and enjoy myself. I was so confused, but I now understand why so many people take sick leave from work. It's so easy.

I returned to work three days later and was asked by the F/Sgt as to where had I been. I gave him the doctor's sick certificate and told him that he had sent me home as being sick, so I had it confirmed with the doctor. Having taken the four days off sick was well worth the look on his face. To date that was the first and last sick note I ever had while in England.

On the evening of 1 April 1982, I was on night duty and got a phone call from a Group Captain (Gp Capt) asking me if I could pick him up from his married quarters and take him to Brookham House. As it was raining, I put on an old army camouflaged combat jacket before proceeding to collect the Gp Capt. As he came out of his door he spotted what I was wearing and said, "Are you expecting to go to war, Fred?" I just laughed and saw him into the car. Arriving at Brookham House, I opened the car door to allow the Gp Capt out and was spotted by the Commandant who quickly came over to me and invited me into his house to meet his guests. As you entered his house, there was a big drinks bar on the right; I was stopped by the Commandant and offered a drink. As I was on duty and not wanting to offend, I accepted a tomato juice before being ushered into his main reception room which was occupied by 25 to 30 men. He then called for silence and introduced me as Fred before explaining that I was also a CSM in the TAVR. He then personally took me around and introduced all his guests to me one at a time. It felt like going around the

War Cabinet – they were nearly all Generals, Admirals, and Air Marshals. They all shook hands with me, and there was a genuine feeling of appreciation and comfort in their handshakes, apart from one who must have been the lowest ranked officer there. He was a Squadron Leader (Sqn Ldr) and his handshake felt like a wet towel. At the same time you could read the expression on his face which blared out, "What the hell am I doing, shaking the hand of a civilian driver?" There is always one that spoils the occasion.

After a short while, I excused myself and said goodnight to all the guests and to the Commandant who, as we passed the bar, leant over and grabbed a half bottle of Brandy and slipped it into my pocket, telling me to have a drink on him when I was off duty.

That was one-night duty that I will never forget as the following day on 2 April 1982, it was announced on the radio that the United Kingdom was at war with Argentina and that the Falklands War had started.

Many years later, I was told that Prime Minister Margaret Thatcher and the War Cabinet had met and signed the required paperwork to 'Call Up the Reserved Armed Forces'. Although this was never enforced, many members of the TA&VR did serve in the Falklands. This had led me to believe that when I turned up at Brookham House wearing that combat jacket, all those senior officers were well aware of what was about to happen the following day and that I could be called up for regular service, in the not too distant future.

During the Falklands War which started on 2 April 1982 and lasted until 14 June 1982, as a civilian, I played my part along with others and helped in the conclusion of a successful outcome. One of the tasks entrusted to the Staff College MT drivers was to go to RAE Farnborough each evening and collect the meteorological photos taken by an American satellite over the Falklands. These were then rushed over to the Met Office in Bracknell for onwards transmission to our armed forces in the Falklands and planning committees. On a number of occasions, I was the second person in the world to see these photos, the first being the chap who downloaded the images from the satellite.

Apart from taking senior RAF Officers who were involved with the Falklands situation to various locations around the country, I also got involved in what I can only describe as one of the stupidest and most expensive screw ups imaginable. Well, that's my view on the following.

I had to go to RAF Honington to collect a package and take it to RAF Brize Norton where it was to be placed on a plane destined for the Falklands. In all, it took me about ten hours to complete the return journey in which I covered over 350 miles. The package, which was urgently required in the Falklands, consisted of a pair of standard 8" pliers which could have been bought from any ironmongery stores for a few pounds.

I was in London chauffeuring a Group Captain and a Member of Parliament, when the Gp Capt said to me, "Have you heard the good news that Lt Col H Jones has been awarded the posthumous VC (Victoria Cross)?" I replied, "'Yes Sir." He then asked me what I thought of it.

I replied that it had to be a VC or a Court Marshal. Both my passengers were completely dumbfounded by my response, and I was asked to explain myself. I indicated that if he had survived, he should have been Court Marshaled. This for the simple reason that, as a Commander, he should have been in a position to command his forces as he was the only person who knew exactly what was going on. By putting himself in danger, he was also putting his complete command in jeopardy. I also mentioned that if this was to come out in the public domain, not only would the British Armed Forces become demoralised, but also questions would start to be asked in the House of Commons. By awarding the VC not only did Margaret Thatcher boost the morale of the armed forces but she also boosted the general public's support for the war. For her, this was a win-win situation although it was wrong.

After a period of silence, both my passengers agreed with me. Today, you can go online and read many comments by members of the top brass who are now in total agreement with what I had stated in my conversation at that time.

Over thirty years later I met up with a good friend of mine who had transferred over to the Parachute Regiment while we were serving together in Malta. He told me the real facts of the situation at the time. Apparently, the CO of the 2nd Bn, The Parachute Regiment (2 Para) at the time had no faith in his A Company Commander to carry out the task he was given. He then took it upon himself to take charge of the forthcoming attack, which resulted in his death.

Working at the RAF Staff College was like working in history books as some of the people I met were living legends. One of the Gp Capt's that I became quite attached to, was responsible for collecting and recording the memoirs of persons involved in some of the greatest military incidents in modern times, going back as far as WW II and organising lectures at the college by prominent and distinguished speakers.

One of the speakers that I had to collect was a Senior RAF Officer who was responsible for overseeing the transportation of a German V2 Rocket that was captured by the Polish Resistance on 30 May 1944 and transported to the UK as part of Operation Most III, on 25/26 July 1944 in a Dakota of 267 Sqn RAF. I knew quite a bit about the incident due to the Polish connection, but as I was driving along, he told me how the airlift was close to becoming a disaster.

On another occasion, I had to collect General Sir John Hackett, a name that was familiar to me as he was the General Officer Commanding (GOC) BAOR while my unit was serving in Minden in the 1960s. I recall being on a parade when he was the inspecting officer, and if I were to say that he was treated like a God, I would not be exaggerating. On this occasion, however, I was driving him to the college and chatting to him as an equal. I had a lot to chat about with him, as he was the author of a book called 'The Third World War' which I had recently read. The book also covers a scenario that I was fairly well acquainted with. At times when I reflect on driving this General, I often wonder what my old COs and RSMs would say if they had seen me in this position.

During the Falklands War on 27 May 1982, Sqn Ldr Bob Iveson who was flying with No1 Sqn RAF took off from HMS Hermes and flew twice over Argentine positions. On his third flyover at an altitude of approximately 100ft; his Harrier was hit by two 35mm shells. He immediately ejected while his plane was travelling at a speed of around 450 knots and which exploded shortly after in mid-air. He hit the ground seconds after and suffered some injuries but managed to get away from the Argentinians and to go into hiding for two days.

He was rescued on the third day by an RAF Helicopter and airlifted to safety. I had the pleasure of picking him up and taking him to the college where he was to give a lecture on his experiences. He was a really nice bloke to talk to, but I could see that his nerves had been severely traumatised. Throughout his journey in the car which lasted less than an hour, he gave me the impression that he was a cigarette chain smoker.

Apart from the many distinguished people that I had the honour of driving, the RAF Staff College was regularly visited by world famous guests. Members of the Royal Family, film stars, foreign dignitaries, you name them, and they came. One of the chaps that visited the college was the American astronaut Buzz Aldrin who, on 21 July 1969, became the second person to set step on the moon. I wanted the opportunity to drive him but that chance fell to my mate who chauffeured him to Bracknell Railway Station where he caught a train back to London. I do not believe anyone at the train station recognised him and I'm sure that to this very day they do not know that the great American astronaut Buzz Aldrin stepped onto their platform.

The RAF Staff College was also the venue on a number of occasions for what was known as RAF Flag Officers Day. On this day all the senior officers of the RAF would gather, including all the Marshals of the Royal Air Force that were fit and well enough to travel and which, on one occasion, included the great 'Bomber Harris' or as members of the RAF would call him, 'Butcher Harris'. On the occasion that I saw him, he was accompanied by an additional five or six Air Marshal out of a possible nine living members of this rank. HRH the Duke of Edinburgh, who also holds this rank, did not attend.

Cars displaying four and three stars were very common on this day. As for two or one stars, you never even looked at them. Normally on this day, our driver's workload would be very limited, and we would remain in our restroom, but with the invasion of RAF and Women Royal Air Force (WRAF) drivers bringing in their Staff Officers, we were always swamped. During the course of the day, you would have a hundred plus drivers coming into our restroom trying to find a place to sit or scrounging cups of tea and coffee, never mind the slices of toast. This started to become too much for our drivers as we typically paid for all the tea, milk, sugar, coffee and other bits and pieces from our drivers' kitty which used to lead to arguments between us, in particular among the older drivers. To try to alleviate this problem I came up with a plan and got a dozen paper clips and stuck a card on each one with all the driver's names, to which I also attached an old used tea bag. I then suspended a long piece of string along a wall and clipped each paperclip to it with the tea bags dangling below. It looked hilarious and all the drivers had a good laugh when they first saw it. When the service drivers came in they never bothered to ask if we had a spare cup of tea, all they ask for was the directions to the NAAFI.

Later in the afternoon, it was normal to have a fly pass made by the 'Battle of Britain Memorial Flight' which brought the day to a close. In the evening, an Officers' Mess Function would be held which was attended by quite a few officers and special guests.

On one of these particular occasions, I was on duty as the coach driver which meant an early start at 6:30 am and finishing at 6:30 pm in the evening. The MT Flight Sergeant asked me if I could do some extra hours work, and to pick up two AVM from a local hotel at 8:00 pm and deliver them to the Officers' Mess. I was also asked if I could collect them again at 11:00 pm and take them back to their hotel. An extra five hours overtime for sitting around doing practically nothing was fine by me.

Everything went well until 11:00 pm when I drove the staff car with the displayed two stars and stopped in front of the Officers' Mess main door. As the door opened, I could see the Station Commander who was only a Sqn Ldr in rank, with the Station Warrant Officer and one of the Mess Stewards all looking tired and worn out. I mentioned the names of the two AVM that I was collecting and was told to wait while the steward went to check and call them.

The steward soon returned and told me that both AVM were standing at the bar and asked if I could come back in an hour's time, which I agreed to do. At midnight I returned only to be told that they were still at the bar and could I give them an extra half hour. Again I agreed as once 00:30 am came I knew I was entitled to be paid until 6:00 am.

At 00:30 am I again returned to the Officers' Mess only to be told that they were still drinking, to which I replied, "Tell them to phone for a taxi when they are ready, as I'm going home to my bed." The shock on the faces of the Sqn Ldr and the WO was a look to die for. How many times had I wished to do something like that while in uniform? It was like a dream coming true. I covered up the stars on the staff car and returned it to the garage before locking up the MT section and handing the keys into the guard room, as the night driver was out on an extended detail. It was a long day, but worth it.

As our civilian MT charge hand was fast approaching retirement, he asked me if I would be interested in taking over his role as the staff college's Union Representative of the General Workers Union (GWU). I was never a union man although I was a member, which came along with the job. My beliefs in unions had gone out of the window many years ago as I tended to see them more as a political party than an organisation looking after their workers. In the end,

I accepted the position and my name was put forward and accepted. All the civilian employees within the college were members of the GWU, and there were quite a few of them. I was quite surprised one day when I received a cheque made out to me from the GWU with a payment for my services. I honestly had thought it was a non-paying volunteer position.

My position as the GWU representative only came into play on one occasion, and that was the day when the driver of the Met Office's Director General was killed in a head-on car collision with another vehicle while driving in adverse weather conditions early one morning. All the drivers at the college were completely devastated at the news of their comrade's death and none so much as the chap who was on night duty; the last man to see him alive a few hours earlier.

As the union representative, it was my obligation to go to the GWU Branch's Headquarters in Reading and pass all the relevant details over to them and to put procedures into motion for his widow. I was also involved in his funeral arrangements alongside other members of the GWU HQ. The actual funeral was very well attended by his family and friends from the college and the Met Office where he was known and respected by everyone. After the funeral, his widow came up to me and said that without my help she would have never coped with the situation. For me, it was the only time I ever felt proud of being a member of the GWU.

That was the second driver from our small group to have died during my time at the college, but it was not restricted to civilians only as one day I was tasked with taking a SAC (Senior Aircraftsman) to a hospital appointment where he was being treated for cancer. Before picking him up, all the RAF personnel within the MT section were going around in a hushed sort of way telling the other drivers and me not to mention his cancer condition in his presence while at the same time telling us that they believed it to be terminal. Initially, for me, it would seem that I was going to be spending the rest of the day in a very sombre climate.

When I collected the chap from his married quarters just outside the college gates, I recognised him although I can't claim to have been one of his mates. As we set off his wife and children waved him off, and from the look on his face which was very pensive, I could see that this was going to be a long journey to the Charing Cross Hospital in London.

After a few minutes of driving I turned around to the chap who was sitting in the front passenger's seat and said, "John, you might not like what I am going to say, but it has to be said. I know that you have cancer and by skipping around and not mentioning it, it only makes thing worse. You know that I know, so can we just talk as normal without trying to hide it?"

From the moment I had finished the sentence, his face lit up and a smile spread slowly. I think we both sighed with relief before he said, "Thanks, Fred. That's what I needed, someone talking straight." The remainder of the journey, including the return, was just like any other journey where people who got on well together talked about everything and nothing.

I took John on a second appointment to the same hospital a short while later and saw that he had deteriorated and lost a lot of weight since I last saw him although when he saw me, he was relatively cheerful. As I was driving and talking, the subject came up as to what he was doing to try to stop the cancer, and he told me everything possible from various food diets to all sorts of medical treatments. From somewhere out of the blue, I came up with Spiritualism and asked him what he thought of it. He told me that he had heard about it but never done anything about it. I asked him if he would be interested in giving it a shot, to which he replied that he would try anything. I then suggested that after his appointment at the hospital, I would take him to a place that might be able to help him if he agreed but with no promises. He readily agreed to my proposal and even more so when his hospital appointment proved rather negative.

When I collected him from the hospital after his appointment, he was looking extremely glum, but I cheered him up when I told him that I was taking him to the HQ Building of the Spiritualist Association of Great Britain in Belgrave Road not too far from where we were. Ongoing into the building, we were directed up quite a few stairs to a waiting area which was occupied by a few people. I noticed a chap who appeared to be part of the establishment and explained John's situation. He told me to leave everything in his hands and that he would talk to me later.

A short while later a very apprehensive John was called into a room while I waited outside. As time passed waiting, I got into a conversation with a very attractive young lady, probably in her mid-twenties who told me she was being haunted by dead spirits. It was evident to me that she genuinely believed in her haunting, but at the same time it was hard for me to believe, even with my past experiences.

After a few hours of waiting, John came out of the room that he was in and from all appearances it was an entirely different John. He appeared to be so jubilant and alive and radiant that had I not seen how he was before he went into that room, I would not have believed it. The change was amazing and very hard to explain.

The chap that I had spoken to earlier called me over and gave me the harrowing news that there was nothing that could be done for John's condition as it had gone too far. He also told me that John would not suffer anymore. I thanked him for all that he had done and shook hands with him before we departed. John was a different person – that much was evident – as we went down the stairs with all the chatter coming out of him nonstop.

When we both got back to where I had parked the car, I got down and inspected the underbody and the wheel arches before getting in. All this was done under the glaring look of a Police Constable who walked over to me and asked me what I was doing. I explained that I was looking for any strange packaging as military vehicles were being targeted by the IRA and that it was standard procedure when leaving the car parked in an unfamiliar area over a period of time. He smiled and said, "Well done, I never thought of that."

I returned John to his home after a journey of constant chatter, and it was the last time I saw him alive. I learned the following morning that his wife had come downstairs in the morning to find him dead, sitting in his chair with a great big smile on his face.

After John's funeral, his wife came up to thank me and to find out exactly what had happened on our last trip to London together. John apparently could not stop mentioning my name while at the same time never telling her that I had taken him to see the spiritualists in London. She told me that from the minute he had got home, he was a changed man. He had also taken his first full meal in ages and was constantly smiling and cracking jokes.

She also mentions that during the evening while sitting in his chair; he told her that he could see his father and a few other friends who had passed away. She believed what he was saying, as she also heard him having a conversation with other people in an empty room. She also told me that he wanted to remain downstairs in his chair when she went to bed and about the big smile he had when she went over to him in the morning.

Although John's wife was very emotional at the time, she could not thank me enough for what I had done for John and when I left her I felt quite pleased with myself. As for spiritualism, do I believe in it? The answer is a resounding yes.

Over the years that I worked as a chauffeur/driver at the staff college, I was privileged to meet many exceptional and distinguished persons including the pilots of the Red Arrows in their mess at RAF Kemble just after they took delivery of their new planes, the BAE Hawk. I also got the opportunity to visit many army and navy bases where my MOD F90 or my military ID card as issued by the TA which was the same as the regular army's ID card that showed my rank as a WO II, got me into places that were restricted to civilians. I always carried my military ID along with my civilian RAF identity card. At times when driving into an army base and showing my MOD F90 to the gate sentry, you could see their surprise at seeing an Army Warrant Officer in civvies' driving an RAF Staff Car, even more so if you had stars showing at the front and back of the car.

On a wet, cold, overcast day, I reported for work with no driving details for the day to be informed that I was to go to the Officers' Mess to pick up a Flt Lt and deliver him to RAF Coningsby, a journey of over 160 miles. I was also told to get him there in the fastest time possible. This 'get him there in the fastest time possible' intrigued me as I did have a reputation of being a fast driver. So I asked the MT WO who had replaced the MT F/Sgt, "What do you mean by as fast as possible?" I finished by asking him if I was being given permission to break the speed limit of 70 MPH. He said yes and, in the event that I am stopped by a police car, I was to direct the police officer to escort me to RAF Coningsby as a direct order from Prime Minister Margaret Thatcher.

All the drivers in the MT at the time were now showing an interest in this detail, and it was not long before the MT WO was asked why it was so important for this Flt Lt to be rushed to the RAF Base so urgently. It was then that we found out that a delegation of dignitaries from Saudi Arabia were at RAF Coningsby where a deal was being drawn out between the British and Saudi Arabian governments in the procurement of a multi-billion pound deal in military hardware. We were also told that the Flt Lt who was responsible for some particular spare parts was the only person who could answer various questions that were being asked at the time. I asked why a helicopter could not have been dispatched to pick him up if his presence was required so urgently. I was told they had tried that route, but due to the present weather conditions, all helicopters were grounded.

I picked up the Flt Lt, and I was off. The weather and road condition were getting worse and it became entirely understandable why all the helicopters were grounded. I was making good progress with only one great scare that occurred when a TIR plate was blown off a large container lorry and smashed into my windscreen. Lucky for both my passenger and me, I saw it coming and managed to brake, although not stopping when it hit the front windshield, flat on. Again we were very lucky that it was flat on, as any other angle would have seen it smash through the screen and possibly have decapitated either of us, which would have resulted in a tragic accident.

I was not put off by the incident and continued on my journey. Although I talked with my passenger, it was quite apparent that he was not very happy and he must have sighed with relief when we arrived at RAF Coningsby just under two hours after leaving the Staff College. I left him there and made my way home at a very comfortable reduced rate of miles per hour while thinking to myself, where are the motorway police cars when you need them? And the TIR plate incident. It is only after some distance is created that the peril we were in started to sink in.

The trade deal went through some time later, but no mention was ever made in my regard by Margaret Thatcher or anyone else for the part that I played in making this possible.

The Royal Air Force is not only about the RAF; it's also about the parts that the combined three services take an interest in, such as the occasion that the Commandant specifically asked for me to drive him to the Royal Engineers (RE) Officers' Mess at Minley Manor in Hampshire. Here he was to meet up with many heads of government and service departments including Generals, Admirals and other senior ranks of our armed forces, along with guests from foreign military organisations, to see a demonstration laid down by the Royal Engineers. As he was about to move to the demonstration area, he turned around to me and said, "Fred, you're army. Why don't you come and watch this presentation?" The event was conducted by an RE Major who painted a scenario of a limited war using nuclear rocket warheads with the main part being the construction of a Nuclear Command Post / Shelter.

The demonstration started with a relatively flat area of ground in a field with fairly common soil. With the use of DB Diggers, members of the RE dug out a large hole that was big enough to house a 40 foot corrugated container, which was lowered into the hole and covered with soil and that was it. This was then passed off as a temporary nuclear shelter. I admit it did not take long to build but how effective was it as a nuclear shelter?

The Major then summed up the end of the demonstration and asked all those present if they had any questions only to be greeted with complete silence.

I could not leave it there and asked the Major what would happen if in the event of a close call from a nuclear rocket. Would the blast not blow away all the top layers of soil on the container and leave it completely unprotected from nuclear radiation? The Major was completely dumbfounded, and no answer was forthcoming. A few seconds later a mighty cheer went up from the spectators, and they all turned around and started clapping me.

To me, it was common knowledge, but I did feel sorry for the Major as it was never my intention to belittle him the way I did.

I spent eight years working at the RAF Staff College, and it was by far the most exciting job that I have ever had. During that time I drove many thousands of miles and suffered no accidents which resulted in me being awarded an ROSPA (The Royal Society for the Prevention of Accidents)

Diploma for every year of service. These Diplomas were always presented by the Commandant of the College with a degree of pomp and ceremony.

I was also given the privilege of being allowed to use the vast college library without hindrance from any staff, although a few officers were not very pleased with the arrangements that I had with the Commandant. I used to spend a lot of time in there especially when I was on a weekend shift with no or minimal driving duties. I used to lock up the MT Section and inform the guardroom of where I would be just in case I was required.

Apart from the miles I drove and the many locations that I visited, I spent a lot of time waiting at a place to return my passengers home with the result that I also had a lot of free time to myself. Most of my day would be spent in museums if any were close by. I also got the opportunity to visit places like the Mary Rose Museum before its opening to the general public in 1984. I also took the opportunity to go on board Concorde 002 at the RN Station in Yeovilton. As for air and military displays, I was regularly taking senior officers to these places along with events which again allowed me plenty of time to explore.

I would have been quite happy to remain at the college until I retired even though there was talk that the college was possibly going to move to and become a part of the RN Staff College at Greenwich.

This was not to happen due to family commitments that were to turn my world upside down.

Chapter 16
1 WESSEX &
2 WESSEX

Having enlisted into 1 Wessex and serving as a Platoon Sergeant in 1976 was only to be for a short time as the British Armed forces were going through a phase of reorganisations. This resulted in D Company 1 Wessex being transferred as D Company to 2 Wessex on 1 August 1977. It was not such a bad thing as we were now co-hosted with the Battalion Headquarters of 2 Wessex (V) and their Headquarter Company which were based in the Brock Barracks complex.

Our role forming part of a NATO-rolled battalion changed to being a strategic rolled battalion which meant that we were on standby for anywhere in the world. There was also a difference in dress regulation with minor changes such as the colour of our lanyard and staple belts. All in all, nothing really changed for D Company apart from the name change and the drill nights of both D and HQ Companies being held on the same evenings. All our training was the same, so we carried on as normal. The only real noticeable change was that the CO and the RSM now made unexpected visits to the Company lines.

Initially, a certain amount of suspicions were felt by the men of the Company, but this was soon dispelled when they noticed that there was a WRAC platoon attached to our Headquarters Company in Brock Barracks. Annual Camps were to become a new experience for many members of the company. Over the following year, changes were being made which resulted in me being promoted to Warrant Officer on 1 August 1978 and being appointed as the CSM of D Company.

With my promotion and appointment, I was given a clear mandate to make and carry out improvements within my company which enabled me to turn up at my office at any time during the week. I spent most of my time carrying out administration tasks and writing up training programs and exercises, including reconnoitring of training areas in conjunction with my company commander. Apart from the work that I used to carry out, I was also entitled to a full daily rate of pay which was equivalent to the daily rate of remuneration of a regular warrant officer. This was a very handy additional income. It was also backed up with fuel and overnight allowances.

Over the next nine years of service within the Territorial Army, I experienced many situations and adventures, meeting many wonderful and dedicated men and women who gave their all in making the TA what it is today. Many stories can be told, but I will only go into the ones that really left their mark in my mind.

On 30 June 1979, the Second Battalion of the Wessex Regiment (Volunteers) were to be presented with their

Colours for the very first time. This resulted in me attending a Regimental Drill Course at Pirbright in April/May of that year, which I passed on 4 May 1979. As the Pirbright Army Camp was only 12 miles from my house in Bracknell, I opted to travel back and forth on a daily basis; I also attended my regular drill nights at Brock Barracks during the period of the drill course. This did not exempt me from the routine room inspection which I had to attend as I was also allocated a room in the Warrant Officers Accommodation within the Pirbright Camp complex.

There were around 30 WOs and SNCOs on the course, including a few from overseas Commonwealth countries. All in all, we all got on well together, especially in the Sgts' Mess. The drill instruction was a waste of time for me, as over the past years with both my regular and TA drill experience, I did not actually learn anything. I did, however, discover why members of the Guard's regiments were always referred to as 'Wooden Tops'.

Shortly after having completed my Drill Course, it was a case of putting all that I had learned into regular practice on the drill nights and weekends. My company was about to feel the wrath of their Company Sergeant Major.

The Battalion Annual Camp was held in June 1979 with the highlight being the presentation of Colours on 30 June. Having taken part in the 'Presentation of Colours' to 1 Wessex (RV). I was looking forward to my part in the forthcoming ceremony, but I felt very disappointed when I found out that the Commanding Officer, in collaboration with the RSM, had sought out the services of the same drill instructors who had taught me on my drill course at Pirbright.

My main reasons for the disappointment was in the RSM not having any trust in the WOs and SNCOs of the Regiment to carry out the task before us. I had known the RSM since the day we both attended the first Junior NCOs Cadre in Malta and I could only conclude that he was looking after himself, in the event that anything went wrong on the day.

The following is the text from the front page of the ceremony programme:

Presentation of Colours

To the

Second Battalion the Wessex Regiment (Volunteers)

By

Brigadier the Duke of Wellington, MVO, OBE, MC, DL

Honorary Colonel of the Battalion

To be followed by

A Parade of the Colours

In Guildhall Square Portsmouth

In the presence of

The Lord Mayor and Members of the City Council

Portsmouth
30th June 1979

My Company (D Company) formed number 4 Guard and on the day of the event, and everything went perfectly. After the event, the Regiment went into celebration and party mood and also allowed me to add yet another distinguished person to my list: the Duke of Wellington who chatted with me, while at the same time enjoying a couple of pints of beer between us.

Over the years, D Company attended and practised many different military scenarios which involved travelling great distances to locations and training areas all over the UK. The main battalion training was done at the annual camps which were held each year at Main Military Training areas such as Knook Camp in Wiltshire, Stanford Training area in Norfolk and the Warcop training area in Cumbria.

On some occasions, we were sent abroad like the time that my company was selected to be part of a composite TA company deployed to Belize in Central America in August 1981. D Company was to supply two platoons and the command element of the company with a third platoon being provided by 6th Bn the Light Infantry (6 LI). As part of the command element, I was designated as the Chalk Commander with the responsibility of making sure that all persons were present for the flight. This proved a bit of a problem as apart from our composite company, quite a few officers from various units and HQ were also flying out with us as umpires and Ministry of Defence (MOD) representatives. Most of them were not keen on waiting for me to call out their names. Once everyone was accounted for, they were allowed to embark onto a civilian leased plane for the journey to Belize. I would like to stress that at this time we were all travelling in military clothing which proved to be a bit of a problem when we arrived at the J. F. Kennedy International Airport in New York to refuel.

When we landed, we were parked next to a Russian aircraft for refuelling and for some unknown reason, as we were all wearing military uniforms; it was deemed that we would remain on our aircraft while it was being refuelled. I was not too worried about staying on the plane as it was both comfortable and quite relaxing with music being played over the speakers. It was a far cry from my first experience when I flew in the RAF Hercules to British Honduras, renamed Belize in 1969.

Having landed at the airport near Airport Camp, the company was dispatched to their accommodation and given time to settle in while I went around exploring the camp. The camp had expanded and the military personnel along with it. My old room was still there and that had not changed one bit. But I was now in the WOs & Sgts' Mess that had grown to a large size with both male and female members, along with quite a few RAF personnel. I also noticed that the family of green iguanas still inhabited the same location as on my previous tour.

When I was here in Airport Camp in the late sixties, there was only one company of men plus the supporting staff that numbered around two hundred maxima. Now there was a full battalion of Gordon Highlanders with all the supporting staff, along with an RAF Fighter Squadron, a helicopter squadron, plus supporting staff and members of the SAS. It was now a very busy place with lots of activity going on all around us.

On my first night, I entered the bar of the WOs & Sgts' Mess to be greeted by quite a few derogatory remarks, mainly by members who had no idea on what the Territorial Army & Volunteer Reserves (TA & VR) was all about. All they knew was that we were going to test the security of the RAF base and their Harrier Jets-Pens along with an exercise acting as the enemy against the Gordon Highlanders who had only just taken up their posting to Belize. To be fair it was the RAF members that were the worst, and they mentioned to me that the RAF defences had been tested out by members of the SAS and that they had failed to penetrate their defences, so just what did I expect 'Dad's Army' to do?

Over the next few days, the company spent time getting acclimatised to the local weather conditions and being issued with olive green uniforms and green canvas jungle boots. They were also introduced to the American Armalite M15 rifle. It was then straight into training, first with the RAF and their Puma helicopters where they practised all the drills on embarking and disembarking and then into the jungle to learn how to make up a Sanger and the art of sleeping in the jungle with all the creepy crawlies. It was also a time where they learned about the dangerous and poisonous insects and snakes. I had the pleasure of handling one of the biggest tarantula spiders that I had ever seen. I knew that it was an extremely poisonous spider, but I also knew that it only struck when threatened and I was not perceived as a threat. Most of the lads were in awe as they watched me playing with it, but nobody had the guts to get near it.

As Exercise Montezuma's Revenge fast approached, details of the exercise started to come forward where we found out that one of the primary objectives was to get into the RAF Harrier pens and place dummy plastic explosives on each of the jets. Not an easy task as they were protected by RAF armed patrols including police dogs.

One of the RAF Flt Sgts' who was responsible for the security of the Harriers took lots of pleasure in trying to wind me up in the Mess, knowing that my company was being tasked with trying to get into his Harrier compound. I could understand his confidence especially as members of the SAS failed to get in. In fact, he was so confident that we would fail, that he challenged me to a wager of a bottle of whisky to whoever won the bet. I took up the challenge, but only after I had upped the stakes to a case of whisky, which he duly accepted with a look of glee in his eyes.

I had every faith in my men to carry out the task before them, for the simple reason that they made up for their lack of military knowledge by a determination to succeed regardless of the odds.

At the start of the exercise, two patrols were given the task to plant dummy explosives on the four Harriers, and I took it in hand to explain the best ways to carry out the mission, which meant a lot of crawling along river streams and waterlogged ditches. I must admit at the time I never mentioned the crocodiles that inhabited the area, but I knew that they seldom attacked human beings and kept in the background. I also mentioned the bet I had with the RAF Flt Sgt and how much faith I had in them to complete the mission.

The exercise was to last three days and started off with the company being airlifted to a point some distance from the camp from where we would make our way back to the camp area and the Harrier Jet Pens. To get to our final destination, we had to overcome the jungle terrain and the Gordon Highlanders along with the RAF who were also out looking for us. The company split up into three platoons, and each were given routes to follow. It was not long before encounters with the opposing forces were being made, and detours had to be taken. In fact, on one occasion I, along with my company commander, were walking along a dry river bed in the open, when we were attacked by a Harrier Jet fighter that came swooping out of the sun to a height of no more than fifty feet above our heads with all guns blazing. Luckily for us they were blanks being fired. As the jet passed us we were both almost thrown to the ground with the blast from its engine.

On the final day of the exercise and as we were nearing Airport Camp, a signal came over the radio with the code words for 'Exercise Ends'. This meant that the company that was still wildly dispersed had to make their way back to camp under their own steam. I well remember as we marched through the camp gates, receiving great cheers from all within the camp area. As we were waiting for other members of the company to return and before a debriefing of the exercise could be had, rumours started to circulate that a patrol had been captured by the RAF while attempting to plant their dummy explosives. I was soon to be greeted by the RAF Flt Sgt who could not wait to tell me his good news of the captured patrol. He was showing signs of laughter all over his face, with the thoughts of getting a case of whisky out of me, but that soon changed when I mentioned that he had only caught one of the patrols.

The mood in the Sgts' Mess was quite jovial when I entered it, and many members of the RAF started to commiserate with me while at the same time praising the TA even if they had failed in their objective of getting into their Harrier Pens. Again they stressed that if the SAS could not do it, what chance did the TA have of doing it? Yes, I started to feel slightly stressed with the thought of paying out for a case of whisky, when a member of the RAF burst into the Mess and announced that two Harriers were found to have dummy explosives attached to their bodies. As a great cheer went up from all within the Mess, I was grabbed and hoisted above the heads of all as the cheers reverberated around the mess for what seemed like ages.

True to his word, the RAF Flt Sgt brought me a case of whisky and after taking one bottle out, I took the remainder and shared it out between the company. I was later told by the Sgt who had led the patrol and succeeded in laying his dummy explosive that at one stage, while lying in one of the ditches, his face had come within two feet of one of the guard dogs. I asked him if he had seen any crocodiles while he was out on patrol. He replied that he had not seen any and then asked me if I was joking about the crocodiles. I told him I was deadly serious. The look on his face was quite amazing, and he might have said something to me about not having told him that there were crocodiles in the area.

During the debriefing of the exercise, the Brigadier who commanded the Belize Garrison highlighted the success of the exercise and heaped much praise on the TA elements that took part. The TA was seen in an entirely new light by many, and a lot of respect was shown towards us.

Just before returning to the UK, the company was stood down for a couple of days of Rest and Recuperation (R & R) which allowed all members of the company to go on leave and spend time on sightseeing trips to various location, which included trips to see many of the Mayan temples. Both my mate from 6 LI and I decided to go to Gales Point which I had visited on my last trip in 1970. Unlike my previous trip that took hours in the back of a 4-tonne truck, it was now possible to ask the RAF to provide a helicopter to take us on a trip that lasted no more than twenty odd minutes. Arriving at Gales Point was a bit of an eye-opener; it had transformed from a quaint fishing village to a hub for tourists.

It now had a small airfield littered by small single and twinned engine planes. The one bar that I had known from my earlier days had now been converted into a hotel, and the bay had many luxury cruisers moored up on the jetties.

We spent the following days visiting places and relaxing but this was to come to a sudden end as on the day that we were to return to Airport Camp, we were informed that the RAF could not send a helicopter to collect us. This caused a significant problem as not only did we have to return to camp in the morning, we were also due to depart from the main airport for our trip back to the UK later that afternoon. We both spent the next couple of hours trying to get a lift back in one of the small planes even if we had to pay, but no luck was forthcoming. As noon was fast approaching, to our relief, we were informed that a helicopter had been dispatched to collect us. We managed to get back to Airport Camp with just minutes to spare to collect our luggage and parade for the flight back home. I was extremely lucky that my SNCOs took all the administration tasks in hand by checking all the equipment, including weapons that were returning with us and also handing in all stores in my absence. All I was required to do was to load my personal luggage and make myself comfortable for the long trip home via Gander in Newfoundland for a short stopover for refuelling.

Throughout the seventies and eighties, the Territorial Army when through many changes and it came as no surprise when the D Company elements of 2 Wessex in Brock Barrack was transferred to HQ Company 2 Wessex. I took over the Company as their CSM; it also involved me taking over a platoon of WRAC plus all the supporting elements of RAPC, ACC plus many others. Although all the various detachments had their own officers, WOs and SNCOs, discipline within the company was my responsibility, and that's where my problems began.

After spending a few weeks getting to know the new men and women in the Company, it soon became very clear that the disciplinary side was not actually working and very few had any clear understanding of the rank structure, especially in the WRAC platoon. To put this right, I found that I had no option but to take this task in hand. So on the final parade on a Tuesday Drill Night, when all members of the Company were lined up in front of the Company Commander, I shouted out at the top of my voice the following order after having brought them all up to Standing to Attention.

"WRAC Platoon Stand Still, Remainder, Officer on Parade, Fall Out." On receiving the command, all apart from the WRAC, turned sharply to their right, paused, saluted, paused and then stepped off. As I shouted at the men to get away, my Company Commander looked at me and wondered what was going on; I respectfully asked him to go as I would like to have a word with the WRAC Platoon in private. He saluted and at the same time told me to carry on before turning around and disappearing into the building behind him.

I then turned around and got stuck into "my girls" as only a good Company Sergeant Major can and spent a good five minute shouting out the rank structures and expectations of members of the military service when in uniform. I was later reliably informed that a few of the girls broke down in tears while a few actually wet themselves. Others also informed me later, and it could be clearly seen, that my dressing down of the girls had the desirable effects.

There are many stories that I could tell of my experiences in the TA both of a serious nature or event of a comedy nature of which one always comes to mind. I was always a fairly heavy smoker, smoking 20 to 30 cigarettes a day. One day, one of "my girls" mentioned my smoking habit, which resulted in her asking me to "pack it up". As I was coughing more and more and with Josephine always complaining about the smell of my breath, I decided to give it a go.

I had no real problem giving up smoking as I have always considered myself as being strong-willed and stopped smoking quite quickly. It lasted for a few years, until the day I left to attend an Annual Camp in Warcop in Cumbria.

The day before the Battalion leaving for Annual Camp, I was on night duty at the RAF Staff College which meant I would not be able to leave with them, so it was arranged that they would leave a driver and a land rover for me. The only problem was that the WRAC driver they left me was one of the shortest drivers available. Don't get me wrong; she was a lovely Welsh Lance-Corporal and an excellent driver. The only problem was she was only 4'11" tall, and the vehicle she was driving was a lightweight Land Rover with a big spare wheel mounted on the front bonnet. She had a very hard time to see over it.

Initially, there were no problems until we reached the motorway. As we settled down for the long trip, she turned round to me and said, "Sir, is it ok if I smoke a cigarette?" I told her to carry on and that was when I started to get worried. First, she put her left hand into her left pocket and pulled out a packet of cigarettes while steering the vehicle with her right hand. At the same time, she was trying to see over the wheel on the front bonnet. She then grabbed the steering wheel with her left hand while holding the cigarette packet, at the same time as releasing her right hand to open the packet and to grab a cigarette, before putting it between her lips and closing the packet. She then grabbed the wheel with her right hand before proceeding to put the cigarette packet back into her pocket. Now the real problem was about to be realised as she reached into her pocket to produce a box of matches. I then watched as she juggled with the matches, the striking of a match and lighting her cigarette. It was a bit scary, but finally, she had lit her cigarette and took full control of the steering of the vehicle.

Sometime later she asked if she could have another cigarette which I agreed to providing she allowed me to light it for her. No problems, or so I thought.

As the time and miles were passing, yet again she asked for another cigarette, which again I lit for her and on handing it to her I asked if I could have one. She looked at me knowing that I had stopped smoking a few years ago but allowed me one of her cigarettes. After some time, we pulled into a service station for a break and yes, you guessed it; I bought myself a packet of cigarettes.

Sometime later that day, having arrived at the camp, a few of "my girls" noticed that I was smoking and quite a few comments were directed in my direction. Later I was asked why I had taken up the smoking habit again; I told them to ask the L CPL. She had to take quite a bit of stick for getting the CSM into the smoking habit again.

Over the years I attended many Annual Camps and participated in training all over the country in places like Salisbury Plains, on the Stanford training area in Norfolk to the Otterburn training area in Northumberland, along with Stretford and Warcop. We also took trips to places like London to visit the War Museum or Bovington to visit the Tank Museum. I, along with members of the Company, also took part in events such as the RMP Chichester Marches.

I was also involved in an exercise which involved taking over the security of the RAF Staff College in Bracknell where I worked. This was an eye-opener for those who knew me only as an RAF Staff Car Driver and not as a Warrant Officer.

My last major TA Army Camp took part in a NATO Exercise called 'Exercise Lion Heart' in Germany in September 1984. Being the CSM of HQ Company, I had very little to do with the majority of the Company being deployed to the various Rifle Companies. It was normal for me to take over the role of acting RSM within the barracks area where we were stationed.

At the end of a very strenuous exercise for some, I was detailed as the vehicle detachment commander responsible for overseeing the return to the UK of all our military vehicles by sea ferry. I put this occasion to full use to my advantage, by buying twenty odd cases of duty-free beer from the WOs & Sgts' Mess and transporting the cases in my 4-tonne Bedford which I was also a co-driver of. I was stopped at Harwich by the customs officer and asked about the beer, but he accepted my explanation that it was for a Company Do when we returned to Barracks and no customs duty payments were asked for.

On 26 November 1985, I was discharged from the TA at my request having served nine years and 192 days. My life was about to take over a new turning, and I honestly thought my days with the army were over. There are times that you should not predict an ending, as nobody can see what events are going to unfold in the future.

Chapter 17

APPLEDORE
1975–1995

Over the best part of twenty years living in Appledore, my life went through many challenging times. First came, the acceptance that I was no longer in the military and becoming an ordinary civilian with a regular type job. Secondly, I started to appreciate all that I had learned from my father in my younger days, especially those days when I was more or less forced by my father to help him in the gardening, whether I liked it or not. The same applied to all the carpentry skills that he had taught me, along with the art of decorating. At the time of learning all these skills, I never imagined that I would be putting many of these skills into practical use many years later.

Initially while working at Waitrose on shift work, I had plenty of time to carry out work within the house mainly on paper hanging and painting. I was restricted in many aspects within the house due to money constraints and was never a believer in getting things on tick although this was inevitable at times. If I was not working at work, it was a case of working in the house or my chief delight, working in the garden.

When we first moved into the house, the relatively large back garden was laid to lawn. My first job was to buy a lawnmower and cut the overgrown grass, and when it was done, it looked quite good and provided quite a nice play area for my daughters. This was not to last too long as I started to get a hankering to grow some vegetables for the kitchen, so I dug up half the garden and converted it into a vegetable plot. One year after moving into our house I was in a position to say that my vegetable plot was producing cabbages, onions, brussels sprouts, carrots and runner beans. My father's teaching was paying off, and I must say he was quite proud seeing the results of my endeavours.

The first two years at Appledore were quite hard although we had a lot of support from my family and it was not so long before we had Josephine's mother, aunts and uncles popping over for visits from Malta. I should say it was hard but also very enjoyable as both Josephine and I, along with Michelle and Alison, grew closer together to become a real family. No longer were they left alone while I was serving overseas or on a military course. For the first time, both Michelle and Alison had settled down knowing that they were not going to move at any stage during the next few years and apart from doing very well at school, they were also making some good friends. They were also delighted in being the owners of our first dog, General, a medium-sized black mongrel.

During the first two years, we were kept so busy that we never really got to know our next-door neighbours or even the neighbours within the surrounding area, although we would recognise them and pass the customary good morning or good evening remarks. Our next door neighbours were an elderly couple who very much kept to themselves and only spoke to us when General barked, and that was to complain.

As progress was nearing completion within the house and the gardening was well up to scratch, I found that I had more spare time on my hands and took up my old hobby of reading and making model planes, along with my stamp collection. I also found time to help my daughters with their homework. As I settled into the routines of everyday life, I began thinking about what my future might have in store for me. It was a godsend when my old mate and best man knocked on the door which led to me joining up with the Territorial Army and although it resulted in a change in my lifestyle and commitments, this must still be considered as a hobby.

I knew that working at Waitrose was basically a dead end job with no real prospects of improving my working status. So I took it upon myself to start looking for a better job and decided to start working for the Met Office as a driver which came under the control of the RAF Staff College in Bracknell.

With my commitments to my new job at the RAF Staff College, weekends away with the TA and Josephine also in a full-time job, the time spent at home with the family became a bit of a premium although we were now making good headway in civilian life. Money was starting to come in, and we were now in a position to spend out on sociable events and holidays. Life was looking quite good and comfortable even if we were all kept pretty busy.

I was now in a position to spend on the house which included installing a gas central heating system. This was a new experience for me, as I installed it by myself without any outside help. I also removed some walls to enlarge the living room and removed a wall to make a combined kitchen/dining room. Home DIY became a big thing which I really enjoyed when I had the time.

In 1980, Margaret Thatcher who at the time was Prime Minister, came out with the 'Right to Buy' Housing Act which allowed council tenants the right to buy their council homes at a reduced rate and with no initial deposit, providing a set criteria were met. As I met the stated criteria, I applied to buy my council house and was accepted, and it was soon after that I became the owner of my first home. As the proprietor, this spurred me on in carrying out further DIY to my home by installing double glazed windows throughout the house and two separate double glazed sliding patio doors, one in the dining room and the other in the living room.

As I now had patio doors, I had no option but to remove the lawn area in the back garden and to lay a patio with surrounding raised flower beds. This also led to the raising of the vegetable patch which now had a large greenhouse on it and the building of a relatively big fish pond with a small waterfall included in the design. As my car garage backed onto my back garden, I took the rear wall which was built with pre-concrete slabs out and replaced it with a slatted wooden structured wall with a door and two windows giving the impression of a small Wendy House. All told I put a lot of hours of work into the garden, but the end result was well worth it.

As time went by, I suppose the rest of the family and I went through the ups and downs of family life. As my daughters were getting older, their interest in boys started to get stronger which led me to a falling out with them on some occasions as they became more and more independent. I had always considered both my daughters to be very intelligent, and they are, but although I always saw both of them attending university and taking up a profession, they had other ideas. Much as I tried to persuade them, the more they turned against me and if I had carried on they would have both left the house. To some degree, I know that they both now regret not taking up the opportunity in going to university.

On 30 May 1982, my first brother-in-law Fred, who was married to my elder sister Sandra, died at the young age of 42. This was devastating news to all the family members as it was very sudden and unexpected. It brought the whole family together and brought home the real meaning of family.

Over the years both Josephine and I had a close relationship with her brothers, and we often went and paid them visits. Her youngest brother, Frankie, lived in Portsmouth, and we both attended their wedding before he moved to the London area. Both he and his wife Della often used to visit and spend time with us, to such an extent that they started to get ideas about moving to Bracknell. To me, it was a good idea as we all shared a good relationship with each other. It also meant that when I was away with the TA, there was always someone close by in case of an emergency.

He moved onto the same estate as us with his wife and two children a short while after, only to be followed by his brother Vincent who had been discharged from the RAF, with his wife Linda and their two children. All three families including mine were all within a few minutes walking distance from each other. Both Vincent and Frankie were excellent professional chefs which made visiting them very sought after as the food was always exceptional. Mind you nothing comes cheap, and my skills in DIY were always in demand. To some degree, Josephine felt as if she was right back at home in Malta with the Maltese language being spoken as normal.

All in all, as the ten-year mark approached of being in Appledore, I can honestly say that family life was going well. I had branched out even more into my hobby of gardening by building a large shed on the side of my house to accommodate my ever increasing passion for growing Fuchsias. I had over a hundred varieties, and when they were in full bloom and dotted around the patio and pond, they looked absolutely stunning. There was nothing I liked better than sitting in the garden on a warm summers evening in the company of family friends while sipping some homemade wine. Yes, all in all, life was good apart from the small hiccups of my daughters' choices in boyfriends, but life was to start turning from good to bad in a very short time.

Rumours began circulating around the RAF Staff College that the College was going to close down in Bracknell for incorporation into a Joint Service College. Initially, the rumours mentioned the college moving to the Army Staff College at Sandhurst and then it was moving to join the Royal Naval College at Greenwich. The majority of civilian jobs would be safeguarded as we were all considered as being part of the Civil Service, but it would mean either moving to new locations or being employed in other civil service establishments around the immediate area but not necessarily within the same job capacity. With this outlook on my mind, I started thinking of my future prospects.

It was always clearly stated that the closure of the RAF Staff College was not imminent but it would definitely happen in the not too distant future. Taking this into consideration, I was informed that my TA&VR Unit was trying to recruit an ex-army officer or warrant officer to take up the post as a member of the Non-Regular Permanent Staff (NRPS) in the rank of Captain in the Quartermasters Department. This appointment appealed to me and as I would still be classified as a civil servant, my civil servant pension contributions would continue. I applied for the job and was told that with my service record and the time I had spent with 1 and 2 Wessex, that I stood a good chance of getting the appointment. Unfortunately for me, significant changes were to unfold which would create a complete change in my present day lifestyle.

The first was the death of my father in May 1985 and the second was the breakup of the relationship between my brother-in-law Frankie and his wife, Della.

It's only right that I should mention my father for although he had fallen out with my mother and moved into a house in Slough where he lived alone, he was always a father to all my brothers and sisters. He treated us all as equals and was always there to offer any help where possible. To him, we were all his favourites, and he always used to stress "my favourite" when none of my brothers or sisters were around. The only animosity that was shown towards him was by my mother which was quite understandable, but that did not stop both of them from enjoying each other's company. I used to meet up with him on many occasions in my mother's house although he never spent the night there.

His favourite past time was going down to the local British Legion Club or the men's club to have a few beers. He also used to charm all the women, regardless of age and looks. He also enjoyed dancing and playing cards. I have never known my father as a great drinker, and if by chance he did get drunk, he never caused any trouble; he just found a place to sit and used to fall asleep. Unfortunately, his drinking habit was to be his downfall as over the years he developed kidney problems which ultimately led him to his death. During his last days which he spent in Wrexham Park Hospital, all my brothers and I would go and visit him in the evening after work and it always resulted in us all sitting around a table playing cards for money. We always had a seat set aside for dad and always dealt him a hand of cards. We were never dull; in fact, we were quite the opposite, cheerful and quite boisterous especially when he won. We used to be stared at by the nurses who often walked by, and they could never understand why we were so cheerful as opposed to being sad.

Our answer to that was, nothing was going to change, and our dad had always encouraged us all to be cheerful. I'm sure he was looking over us while we were playing cards and enjoying every minute of it.

As for my brother-in-law Frankie, well that's a story and a half. I first met Josephine's brother Frankie while stationed in Malta. I had just returned Josephine home to her aunties' house when we bumped into Frankie and a couple of his friends. I was parking up a hired Triumph Herald Convertible car at the time, and he asked me if he could take it for a spin around the block. He told me he had a driving license, so I let him, on the promise that it was around the block and back again. Josephine called me an idiot and told me that I should not have trusted him, and she was right. He returned the car over an hour later. He apologised for the late return, and it was here that I learned that he had the gift of the gab. He was always smiling, and he could tell you anything that you wanted to hear while at the same time putting a knife in your back.

When Frankie and Della moved to Bracknell, it was good. We all got on well together and spent quite a bit of time with both of them and their three children. In fact, the daughter and two sons were like our own kids and were always being spoiled by both me and Josephine. I have already mentioned that he was a great chef and he had no problems getting work in prestigious restaurants within the Ascot area. On occasions when he was short-handed at work, he used to get Josephine and sometimes me to help him out in the kitchen. We both enjoyed it, and at the same time, we were being paid for the extra work. It was also noticed that he was light-fingered in taking bits and pieces from the kitchen to his home. Initially, it did not really concern me as I knew that he was not to be trusted in that particular field.

Frankie was also a womaniser and could not see a pretty girl walk pass without some sort of comment being made. His wife was well aware of it, and from all accounts, she had a similar reputation with the men. It was not uncommon for Della to disappear for a few days and I suppose this is what led to a great bust-up with Della moving to a Battered Wives Home in Reading, although she still met up with Frankie at the house. Over the years, I was often called round to their house to try and sort out family arguments, but thing started to get worse and worse between the two of them, and I believe drugs started coming into the equation. Frankie started going downhill in a big way, and both Josephine and I were getting anxious especially for the children.

While all this was going on between Frankie and Della, I noticed in the local papers that the new Bracknell Town Center, Princess Square Complex which was opened by Princess Anne in 1984, was going to incorporate an American Styled Food Court within the building. I found this kind of interesting and thinking of Frankie, I made tentative inquiries into the complex to find out what it involved.

From initial inquiries, I learned that a first-floor area was being converted into a seating area catering for up to 400 people which would be served by nine outlets serving different types of refreshments and meals. All nine outlets would be hired out on a rental agreement with the central seating area being controlled by staff employed by the Princess Square Complex. I was quite interested in pursuing this and went to talk to Frankie and asked him if he would be interested in joining me in this venture as a partner. I believe that initially it was just an excuse to get Frankie interested and away from his drug habit. It worked after a bit of persuasion, and I took it upon myself to go into greater detail and to find out all I could about the project.

As I started delving into the prospects of going into the catering business with Frankie, I started pondering just what my prospects were. With the rumours of the RAF Staff College closing down, I knew that sooner or later I would be looking for new employment and at the time I also knew that my time with the TA was coming to an end unless I could be guaranteed the NRPS post within the QM Department. At times I felt that I was walking on a ticking time bomb as I had just passed my 41st birthday.

The thought of going into the catering business was completely new to me as I can truly say I had no experience whatsoever in this line and that I would be relying on Frankie's expertise as a chef in making this work for the both of us. I would also like to mention that at the time all this was going on in my head, I was receiving very little support from my family and friends. In fact, most of them thought I had gone off my head. The more that family and friends were against this project, the more resolved I became to make this endeavour a success.

'THE TOMATO'

The first problem that we encountered was what type of catering establishment we were looking at and also just how the food court would work. From my initial inquiries and talking to the manager of the Princess Square Shopping Center, it was explained to me that the Food Court located on the first floor of the complex would operate during regular shopping hours and would be closed an hour after the last shop closed. The complex was quite large with the usual type of shops that you would envisage within a shopping centre including a large Sainsbury's Stores as well as a large John Lewis Department Stores. The only catering establishment within the complex was a relatively large burger joint at the entrance to the complex.

The idea of the food court was based on the conception of an American Food Court where customers could go to a full range of catering establishments that catered to their particular choice of meals while allowing family and friends to sit together. This was to be the second of such a food court in the UK and initial reports from the first one appeared to be quite favourable. The biggest setback that was to be encountered was that wines, beers and spirits would not be served in any of the outlets.

With the information that we had in hand, both Frankie and I decided to embark on the Italian route and came to the conclusion that pizza and pasta would be a good choice. Pizza was becoming very popular, but there were no pizza outlets in Bracknell at that time. As for a pasta dish such as spaghetti bolognese, you either had to make it yourself or go to an Italian restaurant.

We now knew the type of catering that we were going into but now came the hard part. What were we going to call the establishment? Again we went into a bit of a dilemma as the name means everything and with that returned my perpetual questioning of what's in a name. It had to refer to pizza and pasta in some way or another, something catchy that people would find easy to say and remember. After a lot of dillying and dallying over names, I came up with 'The Tomato'. It was short, easy to pronounce and tomatoes were the main ingredient in both pizza and pasta dishes.

Now it was a case of working out all the details and putting plans to paper. Frankie was tasked with drawing up a menu, and it was at this time that I learned that Frankie had never cooked or made a pizza before in his life. While he was doing this, it was quite easy to see that he was picking up on life and getting out of his bad habits and ways. In the meantime, I was tasked with getting a business plan together which I would have to put forward to the complex managers for approval prior to applying for a bank loan.

The catering units were located in an L-shaped configuration on two sides of an oblong square that was designated as the seating area with a further side which overlooked the main entrance square on the ground floor. All the units were complete shells consisting of three brick walls in a square box formation with the back wall having a door leading to a back passage. All the catering units were being left to the occupiers to design and furnish as appropriate. The remaining surrounding area was occupied by various retail outlets which were already open and running.

Before making all the plans and going into greater detail, I approached the management and told them of our interest in taking over one of the units and establishing a Pizza and Pasta unit. This was initially agreed which meant no other person could take up this option. A short while later I was informed that a chap had taken three units with the intentions of setting up a Fish and Chip unit, a Burger unit and a Chicken unit. Another had taken two units to set up a Bakery serving sandwiches, rolls, and cakes. A seventh unit was taken as a Salad Bar while another was taken as a Malaysian unit. The last one was a bar dedicated to Kebabs. All in all, there was quite a choice of both snacks and main meals. All units were also allowed to serve tea, coffee and soft drinks, as well as chocolates and sweets.

When it came to the design of the unit, I had to take into consideration all the equipment that was required and the type of pizza oven that we were going to use. We were also required to install sink units along with all the modern equipment as determined by law to use, including a trap for grease under the main kitchen sink along with a further sink for use by the unit's staff.

As we were taking on the role of an Italian outlet, we had no option but to look into a Barista coffee machine for our cappuccino and espresso coffees. Again, this was not a common item in Bracknell at that time. Next came the problem of fitting an air extractor over the cooker and pizza oven. We needed the front service counter, fridges and freezers and the list went on and on.

Once we knew what equipment was required and the rough layout of the unit, it was time to get builders in to quote costs for tiling and building. At the end of the day, the price was quite high, but the outlook was good.

The menu was coming along quite well with over thirty pasta dishes and twenty-four pizzas. Apart from the typically named pizzas such as the Margherita and the Napoletana, we came up with our own ideas of toppings and names. Twenty of the pizzas were named after street names in the Bracknell area. The 23rd pizza was named 'Leon' after me, and consisted of salami, pepperoni, mortadella, chicken and Parma ham topped with asparagus plus the usual tomato sauce and mozzarella cheese. Frankie had the 'Franco' named after him which consisted of prawns, mussels, tuna, clams, crab and smoked salmon, topped with artichokes, tomato sauce and mozzarella cheese.

Staffing levels also had to be worked out, and it was agreed that apart from myself and Frankie we would require an additional four female staff members to cover the twelve-hour day six days a week. It should be remembered that while all this planning was going ahead, I was still working my full-time job and still committed to my service with the TA and to top it all, it was also the time when my father died.

Finally, I completed all the working and was in a position to make an appointment to see my bank manager as without a loan, all my work would have been for nothing. I will not say that I was nervous seeing my bank manager, as I always looked at it as either a yes or a no after I submitted my proposition to him. I can't say the same for Frankie who was really shaking with nerves big time. The manager was very impressed with our business plan and saw no reason for it not to go through and informed us that we would know the answers within a few days.

True to his word, a few days later we were informed that the plan had gone through and all we had to do was to sign some paperwork and the loan that we had asked for would be set up in the company account.

A few days later with the money set up into a new business account, there was nothing left for me to do apart from handing in my notice at the RAF Staff College. On my last day at the college on 30 August 1985, all my colleagues organised a farewell leaving party for me and also presented me with an RAF Staff College plaque. It was a sad day as over the years I had become a close friend with all my work colleagues and I knew that I was going to miss them.

I did not remain sad for long as I now had a deadline to keep to for the opening of our unit in Princess Square.

A time limit was set for the end of October, which only gave me two months to put into motion the plans from paper to reality.

Over the past few months many ideas were passed back and forth on just how we wanted to present the unit to the general public and how to make the unit stand out from the other units that were also being constructed within the seating area. As the company was going to be called 'The Tomato' we had no real choice but to use red and white for the majority of the tiling for the unit, with signage also incorporating the colour green.

Apart from the name signage over the unit we also had some logos designed with a large tomato with a knife and fork attached on both the left and right side of the tomato. It was a great design and really sent a message out to the general public.

The shopfitters who I employed to carry out the work were very professional, and within a few weeks, the unit was ready to receive all the various items of cooking equipment. My big main concern at the time was the pizza oven that I had on order which was being shipped in from Canada. At that particular time, the UK market did not have a lot of choices in pizza ovens and none that we considered as viable options for our unit and business at that time. The oven that we had ordered was a single level front opening oven that could take over 40 single 9" pizzas at one go with a cooking time of around eight minutes. Thankfully it arrived just in time for our opening.

As the opening date was looming my attention started turning towards the staffing of the unit. Frankie was definitely the Head Chef and Cook while I would see to the ordering of stock and accounts and help out where required. We also needed staff to take and serve orders at our front counter along with an assistant to help in the food preparation. It was decided that we would employ three full-time and one part-time female staff initially.

After a bit of persuasion, I managed to persuade Josephine to give up her full-time job and to come and work for us as we both knew that Josephine was an excellent cook and that her cooking skills would be a great asset. The other female staff were not a problem to find and all in all it looked like we were all going to make a good team.

My next task was to find a good looking staff outfit for the girls to wear and with Josephine's help, and a lot of shopping around we settled for the girls to all wear red skirts with a white and faint red striped shirt along with a red necktie. This was topped off with a white straw blotter with a red headband. The result was four members of staff that all looked really stunning in their uniforms and there was no mistaking where they worked as they blended in so well with the unit.

Both Frankie and I wore the same straw blotters and the red neckties along with white shirts and red and white aprons. Yes, we all looked professional and ready for business.

The day before we were due to open, I had arranged with the local press and some guests to attend an official opening ceremony. Apart from the local media representative, among the guests were all the owners of the other units with some of their staff members, the Princess Square management teams, family members and friends that included many of my RAF Staff College and TA mates. The event went off very well with many items of food that were on our menu being handed around as tasters. Frankie also got the opportunity to cook his first pizzas.

Many comments were passed around, along with lots and lots of congratulations, not only on the food but also on the staff turnout and the unit design. The local newspapers were to publish an article and photos in their local papers a few days later.

The opening event lasted until early evening with my staff and a few family members remaining behind to help clear up and get thing ready for the opening the following day. As a final gesture of thanking all that had made the event a success, I invited them all to my home for the last drink, something that I later regretted.

At home, as we settled down with a drink, we started to discuss the points that arose at the opening. Frankie also began to pay too much attention to one of our female staff. His wife, who was not living with him at the time but was still invited to the opening, became extremely jealous. This led to the onset of an argument, with the result that Frankie stormed out of the house and went home. Not being content with him going home, his wife continued to cause arguments in front of my mother and family guests, which left me no alternative but to throw her out of my house and almost resulting in her coming to blows with my wife.

As things calmed down, we continued chatting with our guests until around an hour later the telephone rang. I recognised the caller as being Frankie's daughter, who yelled out, "Come quickly, Dad's going to kill Mum!"

I rushed around as quickly as I could to find Frankie's three children huddled in the corner of the living room, crying and screaming with looks of sheer terror on their faces. I also heard Frankie and his wife screaming from upstairs where I rushed to find Frankie confronting his naked wife with a long kitchen knife. The look on his face was not good, so I stepped in between them and grabbed his wife and forced her down the stairs and out the front door. I knew that she was naked, but it came to my mind, "better naked than dead." I also knew that her friends who lived next door but one would look after her and would recognise what was not an unfamiliar situation.

I went back to Frankie and calmed him and the children down which took a few hours, with me mainly stressing that we were to open 'The Tomato' the following day and that if we could not sort this problem out we would both lose everything that we had worked so hard for. I also knew that by right I should have informed the Police, but the results would have been a disaster.

Once I had deemed it was safe to leave, I went around to the neighbour's house to see if Frankie's wife was all right and to check if they required any help. They confirmed that they had everything in hand, so I made my way home.

On reaching home, my mother and a few family members were still there waiting to find out what had happened and it was only when I was explaining the situation that my mother told me that my shirt was covered in blood. I checked myself over and found a small knife cut in my side which was superficial and only needed a large plaster. I knew that if I mentioned that I had been stabbed, all hell would break out, so I told all who were present that I must have scratched myself at some time and everything was all right. Everyone accepted my explanation, and I kept the knife wound a secret for many years including not telling Josephine.

The next day both Josephine and I made our way to Princess Square with much anticipation and a bit of trepidation to our first day in business trading as 'The Tomato'. Frankie had turned up and looked 100 per cent better than the last time I had seen him along with the other members of staff. It was now time for preparation and getting ready to open the shutters to our first customer.

We opened our shutters at 10:00 am on our first day of trading to be greeted by a small group of customers waiting to place their orders, and as many of them ordered cappuccino and espresso coffees, a great smell of fresh ground coffee beans filled the seating area. It was not long before customers started to tell us that they had no intentions of coming to the terrace area but as the smell of the coffee wafted all over downstairs, the temptation was too great to miss.

It was not long before we had queues of customers lining up and waiting to be served. If they ordered any food, they would be given a numbered ticket and asked to take a seat at a table and that we would call them when their order was ready. To say that both the staff and I were not panicking would be an understatement but all the orders were going out in a relatively short time and from what I could see, the customers were enjoying their meals. As the day progressed, I noted quite a few areas that we needed to improve on, including some sort of display to inform the customers, when their order was ready. I could not have the girls shouting out numbers all day long, although, from the remarks that I used to hear from the male customers, they obviously used to enjoy it especially when they called out the number 69.

One of, if not the biggest order, we had on that day was when a chauffeur arrived and gave us an order for half a dozen nine-inch pizzas and a dozen or so pasta dishes ranging from lasagne, tortellini, ravioli to spaghetti and tagliatelle dishes, not to mention the portions of garlic bread. It was a large order, and it took over half an hour to prepare, bearing in mind that we were also preparing other orders at the same time.

It was only when he was paying for the order and while I was apologising for the time that it had taken that he mentioned that he had driven down from Ruislip in West London especially for the order on my opening day. I was to find out later that it was my brother Richard who had ordered and treated all his staff to a free meal from 'The Tomato'. Although I did appreciate the order, I just wish he had allowed a few more days to pass before placing his order.

On our opening day, we were one of five units that were open for business with the remaining four units still boarded up and awaiting fittings. We were informed that all the units had been let but would not be ready until the early months of 1986. This would allow all the open establishments time to build up a local clientele and to get acclimatised to the opening hours of no later than 10:00 am until 7:00 p.m. Monday to Saturday. The shopping centre remained closed on Sundays.

As the days grew into weeks, with problems being sorted out, the concept of the food court started taking on its true meaning. It became a great meeting point for family and friends that were being catered for by the various units. It was also the location for the many office workers who took their lunchtimes breaks which accounted for our rush hours when we became very busy. As I had mentioned, pizzas were a relatively new food concept in Bracknell. Our customers liked to experiment with the various toppings and we did create some really unusual pizzas.

In the year 1986, the local Yellow Pages Telephone Directory took out an advert on television showing a chap going out in the rain to buy a tuna and banana pizza and to later indicate that his wife was pregnant. So it was not too long before we had our first order for a tuna and banana pizza. I can see the chap to this very day laughing his head off when he was asked if he was pregnant. It was not to finish there. To stop my staff from shouting out numbers, I had brought an electronic sign to display order number on. When they were ready, it could also post any messages that I wanted to show to all potential customers in the food hall. As the chap turned to walk away to sit at a table, I quickly grabbed the keyboard and typed in, "I HAVE JUST SOLD MY FIRST TUNA AND BANANA PIZZA." I pressed the display button which was greeted by a great roar of laughter from all those seated in the food court. I think the chap that had brought it was a little bit embarrassed, but he rose to the occasion and had a good laugh. I have tried this pizza and take it from a pizza expert; it tastes very good.

As the reputation of 'The Tomato' grew, I also got to know my customers as they did me. I recall on one occasion that one of our regular customers came up to me and said she did not know what to have as she was pregnant. I asked her what she usually had, and she said either a Napoletana pizza or a spaghetti bolognese, so I suggested, "Why not try a spaghetti bolognese pizza?" She really looked puzzled by my suggestion, but decided to give it a try. It was an easy pizza to make, just a base with tomato sauce, followed by spaghetti and Bolognese sauce mixed together spread on top and a topping of mozzarella cheese, then into the oven and lightly cooked and toasted. I gave it to my customer, and after she had consumed it, she came back and told me how good it tasted and that it had now become her favourite pizza.

All my staff had become intrigued when they had seen this pizza, and as was customary at the end of the day all my staff were given a free meal of their choice. On this particular occasion, they all settled for a spaghetti bolognese pizza which they thoroughly enjoyed, with the result that it was often recommended to other customers and became a best seller.

With the opening of the remaining food units in early 1986, a drop was registered in the client count although I believe my unit was the most successful of the nine that were operating. This resulted in cash flow problems which led to both Frankie and myself taking a drop in wages. It was not as bad for me as Josephine still had her full wages. For Frankie, who was living with and supporting his children, it became a bit of a struggle although Josephine helped out quite a bit in looking after them during her free time. To help alleviate this problem, we both decided that we would try to establish a phone in-home delivery service. The first service of its kind in Bracknell.

It was not the easiest of tasks to get this service running as I had to get the approval of the management team of the Princess Square Complex who controlled the security of the building after it closed, meaning that the security guards had to let us in and out of the building as required. Thankfully this was not a big problem and permission was given in allowing us to carry out this service. It was then a case of buying a new Peugeot Boxer van and employing a part-time delivery driver, while at the same time advertising the delivery service. It was also agreed between Frankie and me that I would start work at 'The Tomato' at 4:00 pm in the afternoon until closing time at 11:00 pm in the evening which also allowed me time to go to the local Cash & Carry as well as doing the office work and accounts. This would also enable him to take up a part-time evening job to help supplement his wages.

The home delivery service was not a great success but it did contribute to us managing to keep our heads just above water. Bigger problems started to arise, however, as Frankie started a relationship with one of our female members of staff, whom he moved into his house as a live-in partner. Problems began to grow between Frankie and me as till taking did not tally with recorded taking, and I knew that Frankie was spending all his monies he got on his new girlfriend.

Josephine was now spending a large chunk of her wages on feeding and supporting her brother's children and even feeding her mother who came over from Malta to stay at Frankie's house for a period.

As the friction escalated between Frankie and me, we both came to the same conclusion that one of us would leave the business which resulted in Frankie leaving after having worked in 'The Tomato' for the past six months, to take up full-time employment in a restaurant in the Ascot area. For me, it was a case of starting a 12 hour shift, six days a week. Lucky for me, I had the support of my wife and both my daughters along with other family members who were always with me in whatever support they could give.

My problems were soon to start to escalate when a large group of a dozen or more customers turned up early one evening and placed an order for a variety of pizzas and a selection of pasta dishes. When these were ready, they were taken to some tables that had been set together along with chairs for all to be seated together and that's when the fun started. I soon noticed that all the individual dishes that they had ordered were being passed from one person to another, with each person tasting each dish. I had seen this happen in the past where a person would allow another person to taste their meal but not a dozen or so individuals just taking a mouthful of each dish.

I was informed a few days later by the General Manager of Princess Square that 'Pizza Hut' had taken the lease on the unit at the entrance to the complex that used to be the Burger Bar. This led to an argument as according to my lease agreement, "No other pizza operator was allowed in the complex while I was still operating." His argument against me was that the unit was actually outside of the complex even though it was addressed as No1 Princess Square. I was in no position to contest this in court and knew that I would just have to accept more competition. I also found out that the large group of customers I had a few evenings ago were the senior staff of Pizza Hut checking out my operation and tasting items of food from my menu.

When Pizza Hut opened in Bracknell, both Josephine and I were invited as guests to their Champagne Opening Ceremony, which we both attended. One of the directors of the company took me to one side and stated that his company could not compete with my pizzas and pasta dishes and that there was no comparison in quality, so I should not see their business as competition. I must say that I did agree with him and I am sure that they took the idea of placing a few pasta dishes on their menu after having seen my business profile.

Initially, when Pizza Hut opened for business, a lot of my regular clients did try them out which saw quite a substantial reduction in clientele, but this was only to last a few weeks. Most of my returning customers informed me why they had returned with the most obvious reason that my food was not only better and cheaper but also that our service was faster.

On all the occasions that I passed by Pizza Hut while at Princess Square, I never saw more than half a dozen customers in their restaurant. In fact, on most occasions it was empty. Deep down inside, I knew that it would not be too long before I suffered some serious repercussions.

The name of 'The Tomato' was growing in name which resulted in quite a few TV celebrities and some popular musical pop groups becoming regular visitors. In fact, some of our customers travelled vast distances to visit us. One such customer was a gentleman who lived in Reading. He would often make a return home journey of over 40 miles, twice a week just for our coffee, but the biggest distance that our food was to travel was when a chap came and ordered a few pizzas and a dozen or more pasta dishes. He informed me that he had to take them to Heathrow Airport where they would be repacked and placed on a plane bound for Barbados that very day. It was a surprise when I had got the initial order, but when I learned about the Barbados connection, I knew that my brother who had moved out there a few months previously to set up a business, and who also had my mother staying with him, had placed the order. I never mentioned my brother, not even when I put a message on my electronic sign stating that I had just sent my first food delivery order to Barbados. This soon raised a lot of comment, and it was not too long before the local newspaper picked up on the story and sent a reporter around to interview me on the delivery to Barbados.

But, what's in a name? Regardless of your name and reputation, if business is bad it will not help. I was the most successful trader in the food court, but even I could not keep up. I was falling behind in my rent – a problem which, I believe, affected other food court operators. This was borne out one evening after the complex had closed and I was with a few members of my staff doing our regular late home deliveries when we were interrupted by the owner of three of the units, who was also accompanied by quite a few men. I asked him what he was doing and was told that he was making some changes to his units and replacing a lot of the equipment. They started removing not some but all of their equipment including all the food stock from all three units, and it was easy for me to conclude that they were clearing out. In order to keep me quiet and not to inform the security guards, I was passed quite a bit of consumable items that I could use within my unit. I was not going to say anything just then, but I would be saying plenty the following morning as I knew that none of the company employees knew anything about what was going on.

I arrived early the next morning to find all the staff of the three units waiting for their manager to arrive to open up shop. They could not see into their units due to the shutters and did not know that they had been more or less stripped bare. I told them what had happened the previous night while also informing them that it looked like they were out of a job as nobody had heard from the owner or his manager. I then told the General Manager of the Centre, who had no idea of what had happened, before phoning up the local newspapers. It was not long before local newspaper reporters arrived along with an ITV Southern News camera team and the Police. Everyone was being interviewed, and for my sins, I was also interviewed by the ITV News team which showed the new clips later on TV that day.

The Terrace was a hive of activity all day and I know that all the units made a killing in trade while at the same time the owners could see the death of the food court vastly looming. A short while later I was informed that a further two units were closing down. At the time I had no intentions of closing, but I had fallen behind in my rent, and I knew that Pizza Hut was putting pressure on the Management of Princess Square to close me down, which was quite understandable as without me they would gain my customers.

It was not long before I was given a few weeks to come up with my rent arrears or to vacate my unit. I had no real option, so I told my staff of the situation and told them that I would be laying them off in a few weeks' time after my last day of trading in Princess Square.

It was a sad time for all and I had informed my brother-in-law of the situation although he had not shown much interest and to some degree, he appeared to be happy with my situation. But I still had a card up my sleeve as the home delivery business had been picking up.

I had made an arrangement with my brothers and a few friends on the last day of trading which was a Saturday, to help me to move all my kitchen units, equipment, and stores to my house after I had closed. We managed to move most of the equipment with no real problems apart from the front counter and the air-filter unit which were left behind.

Before proceeding, I had taken it upon myself to clean out the shed that I had used to grow my Fuchsias, at the same time extending it and transforming it into a large area that I could convert into a kitchen. I knew that it would hold all my equipment including my pizza oven. After many hours of work laying out the kitchen including the connections of gas pipes, electricity, water, and telephone lines, I was ready for business by midday on the following Monday.

Initially, I had menus place in all the letterboxes of the immediate surrounding area advertising our delivery service, and it was not long before we had a good response and telephone orders started to be phoned through. The work experience was entirely different from working in Princess Square where everything you did was open to scrutiny from the general public. You were now working behind closed doors although the standard of food preparation and hygiene standards still applied. I knew that it was going to be an uphill struggle as I had accumulated large debts while I was at Princess Square including unpaid rent, while also being behind in VAT payments which resulted in the VAT Office reprocessing our Boxer Van and Coffee machine.

Our Home Delivery service was initially run by Josephine, myself and one other who was mainly responsible for doing the deliveries. These were done in my own private car to start with. As the business began to grow, both my daughters became involved along with their boyfriends and members of my family. Running a business from home is not the easiest of business ventures as you are required to get permission from your local council and a license for the change of use for the property. This was a big problem as we were located in a residential area and had to prove to the council that the local residents were happy with me being located and operating from my home. After some time we were granted a license to function as a Bakery, but again it did not stop there as we also had to get clearance from the local Health and Safety Committee who sent health officials around to inspect the place. After a few minor hygiene issues were cleared up, a certificate was issued, and from then onwards it was a case of all steam ahead.

We were open for business from midday to eleven in the evening seven days a week, and as the business grew over the following years, I had to take on additional staff especially delivery drivers. I also had to buy three delivery vans.

Initially, we stuck to our Italian theme with around 30 set pizzas and 30 set pasta dishes plus the standard sundries, but even with the create your own pizza which ran into the millions of different creations possible and the additions to set pasta dishes, our customers wanted more. This led to the creation of our own brand of curry dishes which had nothing in common with the Indian curries but more or less based of the curries that I used to enjoy while serving in the army.

We also included some risotto dishes, a sweet and sour pork/chicken dishes, a Chilli Con Carne and a very special dish of Calamari Di Crème, all of which proved very popular.

The name of 'The Tomato' was spreading, and as it became more and more popular, we were often asked to do deliveries way out of our initial delivery area. It was not too long before we were making regular trips of over 20 miles return. Mind you, they had to quantify the delivery by size and costs or an additional delivery charge.

One of my strangest delivery orders was placed by over 20 residents of Broadmoor Hospital and by residents I do not mean the staff or the security watchmen. All orders were required to be individually wrapped with the recipient's name on each package which was very time consuming but the order was dispatched and reached the destination at the time it was ordered for. The only complaint I had was from my driver with all the searches he had to undergo with his vehicle and his own personal body.

Many stories can be told about many of the escapades that both my staff and I found ourselves in; some which were hilarious, to others which were quite bad, such as the evening when one of my female delivery drivers was involved in a vehicle accident. She was quite traumatised when she returned to us and told me in between all her crying, that she was not going to drive, ever again.

It was an accident that she was in no way blamed for, and very little damage had been done to my vehicle, which resulted in my giving her the keys to my personal car along with her next delivery as I told her to get on with it. When she returned from the delivery, she thanked me for being so understanding and for putting her back behind the wheel so quickly as she did not have time to contemplate her accident and that she now felt a lot better. She remained with me as a delivery driver for quite some time.

One morning while watching an early morning breakfast show on BBC Television with the subjects being diets, a relatively chubby woman was explaining how over the years she had tried many different types of diets to lose weight, all to no avail which ended with her having her jaws wired together. Asked by the presenter how she managed to eat, she replied that she could only eat through a straw. I left it at that and went to my workplace only to be greeted by one of my delivery drivers later on in the day who asked me if I had seen the woman on TV with the wired up jaws. I said yes, and then he asked me if I knew who she was. My reply was no. His response was, "That's the woman who orders a large portion of Tortellini di Crema every other day, and now we know why she always asked for it to be nice and soft, so she can suck it up through her straw." I am not sure if she ever lost any weight, but I do know that she was a regular customer until the day I closed the business down.

At the time I was running the business from home, I also had two dogs, an Alsatian called Rebel and a Border Collie named Trooper. Both got on well with the drivers and often went out with them on their deliveries, sitting in the front seat in separate vehicles. All my drivers felt safe with them as they used to bark if anyone went anywhere near the vehicles when the driver was doing a delivery. On one occasion while carrying some deliveries in the back of his vehicle one of my drivers had to stop and was immediately surrounded by half a dozen youths. They demanded that the driver hand over all his pizzas. Initially they did not see Rebel, but when the driver asked the youths if they wanted to stroke the dog, who by now had shown his teeth, they declined and wished the driver a pleasant evening before rushing away.

At the end of the day, one of the things I used to enjoy was sitting in my back garden with my family and staff, as they ate their late-night meal, especially on a beautiful clear warm, starlight evening with all my coloured garden lights switched on and the fountain bubbling away in the pond. Such evenings were typically accompanied by a glass of my homemade wine, while listening to some classical or country and western music. Now that was sheer bliss.

Over the next three year business went from strength to strength and both Josephine and I were feeling the pressures. My staff was now able to cope without our presence. Michelle and Alison were also capable of running all aspects of the business. We booked for a two-week holiday in Malta, to be followed the next year with a three

411

week holiday in Barbados and the Carribean. The only problem I had was when I received a telephone call from one of my daughters asking me how to relight the pizza oven which had gone out.

I returned from a third holiday in Malta in August of 1990 where I had spent a lot of time thinking about the future of my business. Frankie had never been involved in our so-called partnership; in fact, we had not talked since he left Princess Square. He had also banned his children from speaking to both Josephine and me, but they kept coming around our house for pizza and other items plus a lot of mothering from Josephine.

The business had grown to such an extent that we were doing over a hundred deliveries a day, and I knew that we could not keep it up. I started to look for new premises, but Bracknell was going through a revolution in factories and office blocks which left no suitable premises available for setting up a large kitchen with attached car parking facilities.

I could see a big future for 'The Tomato' especially in franchises such as the takeaway, and home deliveries were still in their infancies. To proceed along this course, you needed the backing of your family, which in all honesty I never had. This used to lead to many arguments between both Josephine and myself, which at times made me feel like giving everything up, but I persevered and finally found a shop in Binfield which, although off the beaten course was on the market to rent and could be ideal.

'THE TOMATO AND GRAPE'

Binfield was a small old village with a relatively newly built housing estate adjacent to it and situated a few miles from the Bracknell Town Centre. The corner shop that I was interested in renting used to be the local post office and newsagent with its own car park set on the corner of the main crossroads in the centre of the village. A public bar again with its own car park was located on the opposite corner.

I was offered the place on a three-year lease with an option to buy the place, and although the rent on the building was very high, I found that I had no real choice but to take it. I moved into the premises in early May 1991 and made quite a few improvements to the building and accommodation. Everything was going well until I applied for a change of use with the local planning officers for the granting of a permit for a takeaway, which they tried to withhold on the excuse that I would create traffic problems including parking problems. As I already had a license for the use of the premises as a bakery, I could still operate but not as a takeaway. Lucky for me I knew a few councillors who were great fans of The Tomato, with the result that I received my permit. I still had to contend with the local Health Inspectors, but they were not a real problem. I spent many thousands of pounds fixing the place up to a good standard including bringing a new coffee machine to our counter for customers who were awaiting their orders. I also took the opportunity to change the name from The Tomato to the 'Tomato and Grape' which was more appropriate as apart from the wine used in many of our recipes, it also highlighted that we would be selling a limited selection of wines to accompany items on our menu.

From the day we opened our front doors to the general public we became inundated with customers, so many in fact that our home delivery service started to suffer. I had no option but to employ additional cooks and kitchen staff along with my counter staff and additional drivers. I was lucky with part-time staff as many young international students were attending a college just down the road from us.

Again we used to get quite a few strange orders like the customer that came into the shop and ordered a 12" pizza with everything on top. When I told him that we had over forty different toppings and that the pizza would cost over £20, he changed his mind and asked if he could only have twenty toppings. I told him yes but it would be very thick and would take a bit of time to cook as I had to do it in layers. It was roughly 2" thick by the time I had finished it, but he was delighted and shot away to eat it in the comforts of his home. A few weeks later he came back and ordered another one, but this time with all the toppings. Apparently, the previous one had lasted him three days and tasted great, but he expected this one to last all week. It was over four inches thick and took over an hour to cook.

Another strange order I used to receive quite regularly was from a film director who always used to order a 'Kingsride' – a pizza that was made up of the pizza base, tomato sauce, spicy ground beef, onions, mixed peppers topped with mozzarella cheese and sprinkled with fresh hot chilli peppers. A fantastic tasting, straightforward pizza that used to take approximately five minutes to prepare and cook but here is the difference. He always wanted it burnt. Not crispy, but cooked until it was turned into charcoal. It's very easy to burn something by accident but when you mean to do it on purpose, it's very difficult. I spoke to him about why he always enjoyed it burnt to a cinder. He explained that he suffered from stomach ulcers and that he found that this particular pizza was the best medicine that he could take to relieve the pain.

One day I thought I would have a change and do some deliveries myself just to get out of the kitchen and was given two or three portions of tortellini to deliver to one of our regular customers. When I had reached her house with her delivery, she asked me if I was a new driver as she had never seen me before. I replied that I was not a delivery driver but the owner taking a break from the kitchen. At that, she flew into a rage and started yelling and swearing at me. She called me all the names under the sun while blaming me for all the weight she had put on over the years. I had to run just to get away from her.

When I returned back to my kitchen, I mentioned it to all my staff, and that's when one of my drivers told me that she was the one that was on TV with her jaw wired up. We all had a good laugh, but I did feel sorry for her.

I believe all the drivers had their own funny stories to tell and even I had plenty when doing deliveries just to relieve a bit of kitchen boredom. Like when I knocked on a door to deliver some pizzas and a young female poked her head around the door and apologised for not opening the door fully as she had just jumped out of the bath and was soaking wet. Somehow she forgot that the door contained a full-size pane of glass which you could see through with no difficulty whatsoever. Or the time when I had to cross a small stream leading up to a farmhouse. It looked shallow enough for my vehicle and had been used many times. Unfortunately, my van got stuck, and I could not get it out which meant I had to deliver the order to the farmhouse on foot and ask them if they had a tractor that could be used to pull my vehicle out. Dare I say it that I did not make any money on that order?

In the early nineties, British Telecom came out with a new phone system that displayed the number of the caller on your telephone which became known as the Caller ID. I had this system installed next to my computer on which I had established a customer base. By entering a customer's phone number into the computer, it would display the customer's name, address and previous orders. It was a foolproof way of dealing with any false delivery orders, as when the customer gave his address on the phone; it had to correspond to the phone number on our system.

This system also led to quite a few laughs. For instance, we had a customer who always placed the same order which consisted of three nine-inch Moordale pizzas, which was a straightforward cheese and tomato pizza with anchovies, capers, and olives. It was the only pizza that they had ever tried, and it was only chosen because they lived in Moordale and they just loved it. On one particular occasion, they called and before they had said anything on the phone, the number had been put into the computer. I recognised the customer and I knew what their order was without being told, so, I spoke into my phone and said, "Good evening, this is The Tomato and Grape, and you would like three nine inch Moordale pizzas delivered to your premises." You could feel the tension at the other end as the women stuttered, "How do you know what I want and how do you know who I am?" I would have loved to have seen her face as I told her I was physic. I did explain later, and we both had a good laugh after that and I could sense her relief.

As with most businesses, we went through our ups and downs, one day you were busy and the next it was quiet. On many evenings when fully staffed and the evening would appear to be quiet, I would send some of the staff home early. Not generally a good thing to do as the moment they left, the telephone would start ringing or an unexpected coach load of customers would turn up out of nowhere. And when I say a coach load, I do mean a coach load of 30 or 40 customers. Somehow or other we had been put on a return coach route for day trippers.

At the peak of my business, I was employing 18 full and part-time staff including a full-time manager who I could rely on which allowed me to take breaks away from the business with Josephine. This was being noted by my landlord who started to mention that he was going to raise my rents when my lease came up for renewal. I was not very happy about this as he intended to double my present rent and I knew the business would not be viable as a number of home delivery outlets had also opened up in the area. I felt that I had no option and the thought came to my mind, that I could put the business up for sale. My manager was a good contender for buying me out, but I was looking at some other potential buyers.

In September of 1993, I had booked a holiday in Malta with Josephine to get away for a few weeks' break. While relaxing on vacation, we both started talking about selling the business and moving to Malta which resulted in us looking at some houses on the market.

We soon found a house that we both fell in love with and on the spur of the moment, decided to go for it. This led me to phoning up my manager back in the UK and asking him if he was serious about buying my business. When he affirmed that he definitely wanted it, both Josephine and I were really over the moon, so I went and placed a deposit down on the house.

On returning back from holiday, everything was going well until my manager backtracked on buying the business which caused a bit of turmoil between us as I now had a house in Malta that needed paying. It was also the time that the UK went into yet another recession resulting in a fall in trade. I was now running on borrowed time as my lease had expired and I had no intention of renewing it.

It was around this time that Josephine bumped into her brother Frankie who she had not spoken to for many years. From the conversation she had with him, it transpired that he was also returning to Malta to live with his family. It was also the time that we met up again to try and rekindle our friendship. As I have mentioned, Frankie always had the gift of the gab. So it was not long before I found myself helping him in his move back to Malta. First by moving all his furniture etc. into my garage and outbuilding and then by organising a 20ft container to take it all by sea to join him in his new apartment in Malta. His daughter who did not go to Malta with him was living with her mother and she soon started working for me.

I had a few potential buyers for my business, but my landlord kept ruining any chances of my selling as he was now more interested in selling his property. Without an established location to run my business, I had nothing. Again this led to many arguments at home which resulted in both Josephine and me selling our home in Bracknell to both my daughters.

Josephine then went over to Malta to take over our new house and to take delivery of all our furniture which had been dispatched by ships container while I sorted out the business end here in the UK.

I thought I had sorted out my problems when speaking to my local greengrocer who was also going through hard times, who told me that he was thinking of selling his greengrocers. After some initial talking, he agreed to rent out a part of his shop to me until he made a firm decision on whether to sell or not. The shop was in an ideal place for my business and would be an excellent investment that was too good to lose. I agreed to rent part of his shop, although I knew I would have to give up the pizza side of the business to start with, as I had no room for the oven and just concentrate on the other dishes.

The move to the new premises was not such a problem although I did have to take a lot of slack from many of my customers who were great fans of our pizzas. I also had to cut down on most of my staff. The move had great potential, and we managed to keep many of our customers, but after a few months the owner of the shop decided that as he was getting a decent rent coming in, to go out and buy himself a new house, meaning that he no longer wanted to sell his shop. I was now starting to get additional problems that I did not want, which led me to ask my manager if he was interested in taking over the business and running it in his name and paying me a monthly premium. Initially, he said yes and then decided not to, so I told him that his services were no longer required.

I then went home and had a meeting with my daughters to tell them that I was packing in the business and that I had been offered a job as a chef in Malta with Frankie starting the following week. I knew what I was doing; I was walking out on my business and all that it involved including all my equipment. I was walking out on everything apart from my daughter and the two dogs. I knew they could both cope and would be better off without me being around.

The following morning I grabbed a suitcase and my passport, went to Heathrow Airport and booked the first flight to Malta. It was 30 May 1995. I was fifty-one years old, and Josephine was in for a big surprise.

Chapter 18
MALTA

O ver the past twenty odd years of living in Malta, I often reflect on whether I had made the right decision on walking out on my business and moving to Malta, but I always come up with the same answer. Yes, it was a good decision even if at times it was hard. I have also come to understand and to appreciate the problems that my father had to endure as an immigrant in the United Kingdom.

Moving to a different country with the intentions of settling in and calling it home is nothing like the experience of going to the same country on holiday. I consider myself very lucky in that I had my wife's family who offered me a lot of support when needed. Although upon my arrival in Malta I had the knowledge of having a secured job as a chef, I was unaware of the lengthy legal procedure required in getting a work permit.

This included my wife having to give up her British citizenship and taking up Maltese citizenship which allowed her to legally work in Malta. She then had to give up this right to work so that I could legally work in Malta. Over the years, I took up many varied work practices from chef to general manager of a popular bar/restaurant/nightclub to working on a building site. Then I went back to being the general manager of the same bar/restaurant/nightclub, to managing a new bar and restaurant. I then moved on to an import and export company that I stayed with until I retired at the age of 65 years. This job started off with me being a salesman, followed by delivery driver, then onto storekeeper and finally the company accountant.

The Maltese pay scales at the time were very low and to make ends meet, I also took up quite a few part-time jobs that included pizza operator, hotel manager, salesman in petfoods plus for a short period of time, my own business of running the Nationalist Party Club in St Lucia.

Life was not as easy as it may appear as you can very well imagine from the number of jobs that I went through, but the experiences that I gained and the people, I met from Presidents and prime ministers to members of the Maltese Parliament, businessmen and many other influential individuals, to what I would call the 'salts of the earth' – the Maltese people, who I love to bits.

It was not all work, as after a period of time, I found out that many of my old army buddies who had also married Maltese ladies when my regiment was stationed in Malta, had also returned and settled in Malta. This led to my organising Regimental reunions in Malta on three separate occasions, with individuals attending from all over the world.

I believe that I have many stories to tell of my Maltese experiences but the most significant one that has given me my greatest pleasure is having influenced the Armed Forces of Malta to play my Regimental March 'The Farmer's Boy' on the occasion of their 50th Anniversary of Independence Day Celebrations. In fact they played it three times.

As I reflect on all that I have written in my autobiography, would I change anything if it was possible? Of course I would, but it is also impossible to do so and, despite all the ups and downs, life has been pretty good.

In 2018 the British television company, Independent Tele-Vision (ITV) brought out a storyline in one of there longest running TV Soaps called 'Coronation Street', the story of a young boy who was suffering deep pains in one of his legs, which was later amputated. This triggered my memories of having the exact same symptoms when I was a youngster as described in this book. The story was mainly about highlighting and raising awareness among the general public of the disease known as sepsis. I have never seen or read my own personal medical documents, but at least now, I am confident in saying that I had sepsis.

This autobiography has covered the first 50 years of my life with little snippets of the past 24 years. I could have written more but unfortunately, I have exceeded the maximum number of words as recommended by book publishers. This gives me the opportunity to start writing a follow-up book which will be published depending on the success of this book. What I will say at this point is that it will be interesting.

For those who can't wait? Join me for insights on my Facebook site by just googling **"Son of a Reluctant Immigrant"**.